Bangladesh's Graduation from the Least Developed Countries Group

Since the group of least developed countries (LDCs) was identified in 1971, only five countries have graduated from the group, all of which are characterised by small size or population. The projections are that the next decade will see a rapid increase in the pace of graduation, with Bangladesh in particular poised to be one of the largest countries, in terms of its economy and population, yet to leave the group. While previously many LDCs viewed the prospect of graduation with some apprehension, fearing significant erosion of international support, increasingly, the move is being seen as a more positive landmark. This book aims to articulate appropriate strategies and initiatives to help Bangladesh to maintain its developmental momentum and to prepare for a sustainable graduation in 2024. In doing so, the book explores themes such as key analytical issues of the LDC graduation paradigm, smooth transition and structural transformation, and post-graduation challenges and opportunities.

Further, against the backdrop of Gross National Income per capita, the Human Assets Index and Economic Vulnerability Index goals required for graduation, the Sustainable Development Goals (SDGs) set by the 2030 Agenda will also be in the process of implementation. Whilst some feel that the two agendas might be in conflict, the book teases out some of the important synergies which can be drawn when LDCs are undertaking the journey of graduation in the era of the SDGs. The book also takes into cognisance the uncertain external environment and the emerging global scenario within which Bangladesh's graduation is to take place. Conceptual discourse around LDC graduation and the particular narrative around Bangladesh's journey towards LDC graduation will be of interest not only to scholars of Bangladesh, but also to researchers and policymakers with an interest in LDC graduation for other countries facing similar challeng

Debapriya Bhattacharya is a Distinguished Fellow at the C   )ia-
logue (CPD), Dhaka, Bangladesh. He is a former Bangla   : to
WTO and UN Offices in Geneva and Vienna, Coordinat   ) in
the UN system and Special Advisor on LDCs to Secretary   AD.
He also chairs LDC IV Monitor – an international partne   ude-
pendent assessment of the delivery of the Istanbul Program   oA)
for the LDCs.

Routledge Research on Asian Development

Bangladesh's Graduation from the Least Developed Countries Group

Pitfalls and Promises

Edited by Debapriya Bhattacharya

Routledge
Taylor & Francis Group

LONDON AND NEW YORK

First published 2019 by Routledge

2 Park Square, Milton Park, Abingdon, Oxfordshire OX14 4RN
52 Vanderbilt Avenue, New York, NY 10017

Routledge is an imprint of the Taylor & Francis Group, an informa business

First issued in paperback 2020

British Library Cataloguing-in-Publication Data
A catalogue record for this book is available from the British Library

Library of Congress Cataloging-in-Publication Data
A catalog record for this book has been requested

ISBN: 978-1-138-58907-0 (hbk)
ISBN: 978-0-367-66532-6 (pbk)

Typeset in Goudy
by Wearset Ltd, Boldon, Tyne and Wear

Contents

Figures

Tables

Annexes

Contributors

Akashlina Arno is currently a PhD Candidate at the School of Economics of the University of New South Wales, Sydney, Australia. She is a former Research Associate at the Centre for Policy Dialogue (CPD), Dhaka, Bangladesh.

Estiaque Bari is a Lecturer at the Department of Economics at the East West University, Bangladesh and a former Senior Research Associate at CPD. His research interests span the broad spectrum of development challenges facing Bangladesh. His current works include the study of the dynamics of Bangladesh's macroeconomic performance, trade competitiveness, the labour market of Bangladesh, and agricultural economics. He completed his Master of Science in Economics from United International University, Dhaka, Bangladesh.

Debapriya Bhattacharya, PhD, is a macroeconomist and public policy analyst. Currently he is the chair of two global initiatives, namely, Southern Voice on Post-MDG International Development Goals and LDC IV Monitor. He is a Distinguished Fellow at CPD, where he had been earlier the Executive Director. He is a former Ambassador and Permanent Representative of Bangladesh to the WTO and UN Offices of Geneva and Vienna. He has published extensively on trade, investment and finance related issues of LDCs and Sustainable Development Goals (SDGs). He received his PhD in Economics from the Plekhanov Institute of National Economy, Moscow. His most recent edited book is *Southern Perspectives on the Post-2015 International Development Agenda*, Routledge (2017).

Muntaseer Kamal is an aspiring economist and currently working as a Research Associate at CPD. His primary research interests are in the areas of macroeconomics and development economics, with particular focus on Bangladesh's development. His other areas of interest include international economics, natural resources, energy economics and ICT issues. Prior to joining CPD, he received Bachelor and Master degrees in Economics from the University of Dhaka, Bangladesh.

Towfiqul Islam Khan is an economist and a Senior Research Fellow at CPD. He has published several articles on least developed countries (LDCs), SDGs and economic development. He has been member of a number of technical committees set up by Bangladesh government agencies including being part of the 'SDG Working Team' constituted under the Prime Minister's Office. He received the Australian Leadership Award in 2008 to undertake his post-graduation academic degree at University of Melbourne, Australia.

Sarah Sabin Khan is a Senior Research Associate at CPD. Prior to joining CPD, she had worked with a foreign aid supported market development project and at a consultancy firm specialising in power sector development. Her current research interests include international development cooperation, development economics and empirical microeconometrics. She has a Master of Arts degree in Economics from McGill University, Canada.

Fahmida Khatun is the Executive Director of CPD. She was a Visiting Fellow at the Christian Michelsen Institute, Norway; Korea Institute for Industrial Economics and Trade, South Korea; and Centre for Study of Science, Technology and Policy, India. She is a member of the Advisory Team of the *Connect to Learn* programme, a global education initiative run by the Earth Institute of Columbia University. She has a Masters and PhD in Economics from University College London and Post-Doctorate from Columbia University, USA.

Khondaker Golam Moazzem is the Research Director at CPD. As a specialist on industry and trade related issues, he extensively works on issues related to the LDCs. His major areas of interest include global value chain development, trade related issues in export diversification, entrepreneurship development and business environment analysis. He received his PhD from Kyoto University, Japan.

Shahida Pervin is a Senior Research Associate CPD. Currently she is pursuing an MSc in Economics at Queen Mary, University of London as a Chevening Scholar. She was a 'Young Global Changer' at the T20 summit awarded by the G20 German Presidency 2017. She has published research papers in reputed journals and book. She completed her BSS and MSS in Economics from Jagannath University, Bangladesh with Prime Minister Gold Medal.

Mustafizur Rahman is a Distinguished Fellow at CPD. He taught at the University of Dhaka where he is a member of the Senate. He was Senior Fulbright Fellow at Yale University, a Visiting Fellow at Oxford University and served as a member of the Panel of Economists for the Sixth and Seventh Five Year Plans of Bangladesh. His current research interests include issues of concern to LDCs, macroeconomic management, poverty and distribution, implementation challenges of the SDGs and regional integration.

Md. Masudur Rahman is an Assistant Director at Bangladesh Bank – the Central Bank of Bangladesh – and a former Research Associate at CPD. At CPD, he worked on issues such as green growth, interest of LDCs, Bangladesh's graduation from LDC status and SDGs. He completed his Master of Science in Economics from Jahangirnagar University, Dhaka, Bangladesh.

Foreword

This volume on *Bangladesh's Graduation from the Least Developed Countries Group: Pitfalls and Promises*, edited by Debapriya Bhattacharya and co-authored with his colleagues at the Centre for Policy Dialogue (CPD), provides a definitive interpretation of Bangladesh's transition out of the least developed country (LDC) ghetto and how we may better manage this transition to ensure the upward trajectory in our economic fortunes. The year 2018, when the UN Committee for Development Policy (CDP) formally recognises Bangladesh's graduation status, appears to be an age removed from the days when we struggled to be recognised as an LDC so we could avail of the variety of benefits available to countries which were deemed as being in need of special assistance from the global community.

Professor Nurul Islam, the first Deputy Chairman of the Bangladesh Planning Commission, in his memoir *Making of a Nation*, narrates the story of his investment in intense public reasoning in 1975, in his capacity as a member of the CDP, in securing recognition from his colleagues at the CDP for Bangladesh's status as an LDC. While Bangladesh decisively met the then three criteria set by the CDP for recognition as an LDC – per capita income, share of manufacturing in total output and literacy ratio – the members were uncomfortable about accepting a country with a population of 78 million as an LDC. Of the 25 countries then recognised as LDCs, 19 had populations below ten million and six had populations below 20 million. The prospect of a country with the population size of Bangladesh seeking acceptance as an LDC had not been envisaged by the UN when the idea of providing enabling assistance to a variety of disadvantaged countries was conceived and institutionalised in 1971. At that time the prospect of Bangladesh entering into the community of nations was also not conceivable.

In arguing the case for Bangladesh, Islam pointed out that the criteria already laid out by the UN system for classification as an LDC did not include population size as a criterion or cut off point. Islam therefore argued that the UN as a body would once again need to revisit the classification of LDCs. This was a challenge which his colleagues at the CDP, all globally recognised economists, were unwilling to face. Furthermore, Islam pointed out that not only was Bangladesh well below the threshold limit for all three qualifying criteria but it suffered from further unique disabilities, not yet recognised by the CDP, of an environmental nature which severely enhanced its economic vulnerability. Its severe population density was also accepted as yet another special disability for feeding its population.

These arguments were sufficient to persuade Islam's colleagues at the CDP to accept Bangladesh as an LDC. It may be pointed out that in contrast to Bangladesh's struggle to be recognised as an LDC, when Ghana was recognised by the CDP in the 1990s as eligible for inclusion its government declined to accept the 'privilege' deeming it to be an affront to national dignity to be officially categorised as an LDC.

During our 43 year tenure as an LDC, Bangladesh has benefited more than most other members from its inclusion in this category. For example, its status has been particularly advantageous in securing duty-free access to markets not available to most other developing countries. However, this privilege could only become meaningful once Bangladesh established itself as a highly successful exporter of readymade garments and other manufacturing products. Bangladesh's substantial growth in manufacturing exports served as a forerunner for structural change in its economy where the manufacturing sector eventually overtook its agricultural sector which also managed to significantly enhance and diversify its output.

Bangladesh's economy has come a long way from the difficult days of 1975 when significant dialectical skills were required to establish our LDC status. It could be argued that compared to other LDCs which have graduated out of the ghetto and those on the threshold of graduation, Bangladesh has a far stronger and more resilient economy. Island or resource rich microeconomies which have graduated out of the LDC category remain much more vulnerable in preserving their new status. Their economies remain essentially micro-product economies, dependent on single resources such as tourism, diamonds or oil, resources mostly developed through foreign direct investment and by foreign entrepreneurs.

In contrast, Bangladesh has developed across various fronts such as accelerated manufacturing growth and exports, quadrupling of food production and service exports. Most of these developments originate neither from nature nor from external support, but from indigenous sources: productive, innovative small farmers, a dynamic class of entrepreneurs, enterprising, risk taking workers willing to travel to the far corners of the world, rural women moving into the urban sector to work for low wages, micro-entrepreneurs, mostly women sustained by the microfinance revolution and a class of innovative, resourceful, dynamic non-government organisations (NGOs) which have underwritten the microfinance institution revolution, contributed to advances in human development and served to empower women. No incumbent or even graduated LDC can claim such a strong asset base.

If we are to look ahead at the post-LDC era it would be advantageous to move beyond the numbers which have so far provided the coordinates for Bangladesh's graduation to the human agents who have driven our economic growth and structural change. This will enable us to focus our future policies and invest our resources in further enhancing the capabilities as well as improving the productivity of our agents of change.

The contributors to this volume identify a range of critical interventions needed to prepare Bangladesh for formal graduation which progressively ends our special privileges and to then sustain our upward trajectory. These suggested interventions may be categorised under the following heads:

1   *Enhancing investible resources and ensuring their effective utilisation:*
    - significant enhancement in domestic resource mobilisation;
    - a conducive environment for private and foreign investment;
    - accelerating investment in infrastructure development;
    - enhanced investments in providing quality education and health care;
    - aligning official development assistance mobilisation and disbursement with national priorities.
2   *Policies and institutional measures to promote sustainable growth:*
    - prudent policies and economic management to ensure macroeconomic stability;
    - structural shifts to enable access to high value added markets;
    - strong governance.

These constructive suggestions by the authors for sustaining our upward trajectory may be strengthened through public actions which are targeted to invest in and incentivise the agents of change who have been the driving force behind Bangladesh's graduation. Such interventions may aspire to:

- incentivise small farmers, primary producers, small and medium enterprises to participate more equitably in value chains and share in value addition;
- incentivise workers by providing them with a stake in their place of work;
- graduate overseas migrant workers into service exporters through investment in skill development and through renegotiating the institutional arrangements and terms of migration;
- democratising governance to provide equitable access to public services, rule of law and political participation.

To carry forward the suggested interventions will require a politically strong, representative government which retains the capacity for creative policy design and capability to ensure its implementation. Such a government will need to reach out to the entrepreneurs, working people and NGOs who drive our growth and would need to transform them into active partners and stakeholders in Bangladesh's development journey in the years ahead.

Rehman Sobhan
Chairman, CPD

Preface

On 16 March 2018, the Committee for Development Policy (CDP), a subsidiary advisory body of the United Nations Economic and Social Council (UN ECOSOC), resolved to include Bangladesh in the list of countries poised to graduate out of the group of the least developed countries (LDCs). Thus, it is expected that the country will come out of the LDC group by 2024, provided the upcoming triennial reviews of the CDP (in 2021 and 2024) endorse its continuous performance as per the group's graduation criteria.

Bangladesh is one of the 47 countries currently labelled as LDCs based on low levels of per capita income and human assets, and high economic vulnerability. The number of LDCs has grown from 24, since the creation of this category in 1971, to a total of 52 inclusions over the 47 years. This disadvantaged group of countries accounts for 13 per cent of the global population as against 31 per cent of the global poor. These countries together command around 1 per cent of global GDP, 1 per cent of global foreign trade and around 2 per cent of global foreign direct investments. Moreover, about half of these LDCs are considered to be fragile and conflict-ridden.

To date, the incidence of graduation from the group has been pretty modest – only five (Botswana, Cape Verde, Maldives, Samoa and Equatorial Guinea). However, a host of LDCs is expected to depart from the group in the coming years. This encouraging process is partly inspired by the gradual change in the mindsets of these countries towards LDC graduation. The current decade is the time of implementation of the Istanbul Programme of Action (IPoA), which was adopted at the fourth United Nations Conference on the LDCs in Istanbul in 2011. One cannot but observe that these countries have embraced LDC graduation during the decade of the IPoA with a positive and proactive approach, notwithstanding the apprehension of losing substantial international support measures.

Bangladesh, however, stands out from the earlier graduates, particularly in terms of its significant size of population and economy. Indeed, Bangladesh might be one of the first countries in the group to fulfil all the three criteria at the time of its graduation.

The analysis and the conclusions contained in the present volume in connection with Bangladesh's pursuit to escape the LDC group are instructive for other countries pursuing similar objectives. For example, most of the LDCs are in the process of coming out of the low-income countries (LICs) group (a category deployed by the World Bank). Thus, it is useful to study the experience of Bangladesh which is also managing this 'double transition' – simultaneously moving out of the LDC group and the LIC category. Bangladesh's commendable performance in poverty alleviation and human development took place in the recent past within a state of weak governance. This particular development experience of Bangladesh may very well be of interest to other LDCs and beyond. The present volume also provides insightful cross-country comparisons to tease out the policy lessons learnt from the early graduations as well as the countries in the graduation pipeline.

Given the fact that moving out of the LDC group is not the end of the road, rather a milepost towards the structural transformation of the concerned economies, policy options for smooth and sustained graduation acquire special significance. Countries belonging to the peer group of Bangladesh would like to study how the interfaces between the policies for LDC graduation and inclusive development of productive capacities need to be addressed effectively. The other set of distinguishing features of the present volume also relates to its analytical attempt to seek policy synergy between the implementation of the Sustainable Development Goals (SDGs) of the global *2030 Agenda* and graduation with momentum from the LDC group. The volume also lays out the contours of the emerging, not so enabling, regional and global policy environment within which the LDCs currently have to undertake their graduation journey.

Curiously, the LDC graduation paradigm has been mostly approached from the vantage point of applied policy, rather than from theoretical perspectives. An attempt has been made in this volume to consolidate the implications of various economic theories for improved understanding of the rationale for LDC graduation.

Thus, it is a modest expectation that the present volume, from both analytical and empirical perspectives, will add to our stock of knowledge regarding the development challenges currently faced by the LDCs as well as other developing countries.

Dhaka
July 2018

Debapriya Bhattacharya
Chair, LDC IV Monitor
Chair, Southern Voice Network
and Distinguished Fellow, CPD

Acknowledgements

The present volume is an outcome of collective endeavour of the professional team of the Centre for Policy Dialogue (CPD). Sincere gratitude goes to the authors: *Fahmida Khatun*, Executive Director; *Mustafizur Rahman*, Distinguished Fellow; *Khondaker Golam Moazzem*, Research Director; *Towfiqul Islam Khan*, Senior Research Fellow; *Shahida Pervin* and *Sarah Sabin Khan*, Senior Research Associates; *Muntaseer Kamal* and *Sarah Sabin Khan*, Research Associate; *Estiaque Bari*, former Senior Research Associate; *Akashlina Arno* and *Md. Masudur Rahman*, former Research Associates. The authors have received valuable research support from *Mostafa Amir Sabbih*, Senior Research Associate; *Jishan Ara Mitu*, and *Nuzat Tasnim Dristy*, former Research Associates; and *Zareer Jowad Kazi*, former Programme Associate.

The draft chapters have greatly benefited from the insightful comments from external peer reviewers, who are leading global experts on the subject. They include *Mehmet Arda*, Member, Executive and Supervisory Board, Centre for Economics and Foreign Policy Studies (EDAM); *Ana Luiza Cortez*, former Chief, Committee for Development Policy (CDP) Secretariat at United Nations; *Lisa Borgatti*, Economic Affairs Officer, United Nations Conference on Trade and Development (UNCTAD); *Charles Gore*, Collaborating Researcher, United Nations Research Institute for Social Development (UNRISD); *Jodie Keane*, Economic Advisor with the Trade Division, Commonwealth Secretariat; *Sam Mealy*, Policy Analyst, Thematic Division, OECD Development Centre; *Mohammad A. Razzaque*, former Economic Adviser, Commonwealth Secretariat; *Dirk Willem te Velde*, Head of Programme, International Economic Development Group, Overseas Development Institute (ODI); *Susanna Wolf*, Senior Programme Officer, United Nations Office of the High Representative for the Least Developed Countries, Landlocked Developing Countries and the Small Island Developing States (UN-OHRLLS).

When approached with the request to write a foreword for this volume, *Rehman Sobhan*, Chairman, CPD readily responded. It is indeed gratifying to have words of appreciation from a person of his excellence and stature.

The key role played by *Anisatul Fatema Yousuf*, Director, Dialogue and Communication, CPD, in leading the preparation of the final typescript of the volume is thankfully recalled. The chapters have benefited from high quality professional editing by *Michael Olender*. *Asmaul Husna*, Publication Associate and *Maeesa Ayesha*, Publication Associate at CPD have played important roles in getting the chapters ready for publication. *Avra Bhattacharjee*, Joint Director, Dialogue and Outreach, CPD oversaw graphics and other technical issues concerning formatting of the text with assistance from *Md. Shaiful Hassan*, Programme Associate, Dialogue and Outreach, CPD. Valuable guidance was provided by *Nazmatun Noor*, former Deputy Director, Publication, CPD in the editing process.

The extraordinary contribution of Sarah Sabin Khan, Senior Research Associate, CPD deserves to be singled out as she managed the entire process in connection with the publication of this book – from preparation of the research design to coordinating the contributing authors and finalisation of the chapters.

Special thanks are due to *A. H. M. Ashrafuzzaman*, Deputy Director (System Analyst); *Tarannum Jinan*, Administrative Associate and *Teresa Gonsalves*, Executive Associate at CPD for their excellent support extended to the editor of the volume.

On behalf of the authors, appreciation is extended to a large number of policymakers, academics and business leaders who were consulted at various stages to tap into their experience and expertise. We would like particularly to mention the contribution of the participants of the public dialogue entitled 'Bangladesh's Graduation from the LDC Group: Pitfalls and Promises' which was held on 10 March 2018 in Dhaka. The key findings put forward in this volume were validated at the mentioned event.

We take this opportunity to thank DFID Bangladesh for its generous support extended towards preparation of the research papers based on which the volume has been prepared.

Finally, sincere thanks to the colleagues at Routledge for their keen interest in this work and providing the opportunity to share this intellectual contribution with a wider readership.

It had been a demanding dream project, and we can all celebrate the demonstrated commitment and hard work by all concerned towards its fruition.

Debapriya Bhattacharya
Distinguished Fellow, CPD

Abbreviations

7FYP	Seventh Five Year Plan
ADB	Asian Development Bank
ADF	Augmented Dickey–Fuller
BDT	Bangladeshi taka
CDP	Committee for Development Policy
CPD	Centre for Policy Dialogue
DAC	Development Assistance Committee
EBA	Everything But Arms
EPZ	Export processing zone
ERD	Economic Relations Division
EU	European Union
EUR	Euro
EVI	Economic Vulnerability Index
FDI	Foreign direct investment
FTA	Free Trade Agreement
FY	Fiscal year
GBP	British pound
GDP	Gross domestic product
GNI	Gross national income
GoB	Government of Bangladesh
GSP	Generalised System of Preferences
HAI	Human Assets Index
HDI	Human Development Index
HHI	Herfindahl-Hirschman Index
H-P filter	Hodrick-Prescott filter
IBRD	International Bank for Reconstruction and Development
ICT	Information and communication technology
IDA	International Development Association
IFF	Illicit financial flows
ILO	International Labour Organization
IMF	International Monetary Fund
IPoA	Istanbul Programme of Action
ISM	International support measure

LDC	Least developed country
LIC	Low-income country
LMIC	Lower middle-income country
MDG	Millennium Development Goal
MFN	Most favoured nation
MIC	Middle-income country
MMR	Maternal mortality ratio
NBR	National Board of Revenue
NGO	Non-government organisation
ODA	Official development assistance
OECD	Organisation for Economic Co-operation and Development
RMG	Readymade garment
RTA	Regional Trade Agreement
S&DT	Special and differential treatment
SDG	Sustainable Development Goal
SDR	Special Drawing Rights
SEZ	Special economic zone
SIDS	Small island developing state
SME	Small and medium enterprise
STI	Science, technology & innovation
TRIPS	Trade-Related Aspects of Intellectual Property Rights
UK	United Kingdom
UN	United Nations
UN DESA	United Nations Department of Economic and Social Affairs
UN ECOSOC	United Nations Economic and Social Council
UNCTAD	United Nations Conference on Trade and Development
UNDP	United Nations Development Programme
UNGA	United Nations General Assembly
US	United States of America
WDI	World Development Indicators
WTO	World Trade Organization
Yen	Japanese yen

1 Bangladesh moving out of the LDC group

Looking through the issues

Debapriya Bhattacharya and Sarah Sabin Khan

Context

Over the 47 years since the establishment of the least developed country (LDC) category in 1971, the performances of countries in the LDC group have been wanting. The option of graduation was introduced in 1991 and, to date, only five countries have graduated – Botswana (1994), Cape Verde (2007), the Maldives (2011), Samoa (2014) and Equatorial Guinea (2017). As graduation cases, however, these countries are not representative of the group, given their small sizes and populations. Currently, 12 LDCs, including Bangladesh, are expected to graduate between 2019 and 2024. After being an LDC for over four decades, Bangladesh has finally met the graduation criteria in 2018. In the absence of extraordinary circumstances, it will be one of the first LDCs to have met all three graduation criteria at the time of its graduation in 2024. Given its sizeable population and economic weight, Bangladesh is on track to be an exemplary success story in the history of LDCs.

The present volume aspires to inform Bangladesh's journey out of the LDC group through a smooth transition process and towards a sustainable development trajectory. Apart from this overview, the volume contains five stand-alone thematic chapters. The themes include analytical and conceptual issues of the LDC graduation paradigm and graduation experiences; structural transformation of LDC economies; the plurality of graduation pathways and challenges beyond graduation; the relationship between the graduation criteria and Sustainable Development Goal (SDG) targets and indicators; and the uncertain external environment within which graduations take place. In the following sections, the key messages found in these chapters are highlighted. While the messages largely relate to Bangladesh's experience, their relevance may be situated within the development pursuits of the LDC group as a whole.

Key analytical issues

Graduation from the LDC group has mostly been addressed in academic literature from an applied policy perspective with few or no theoretical constructs. Many issues demanding conceptual clarifications in country contexts have often remained unaddressed. Debapriya Bhattacharya and Sarah Sabin Khan, in Chapter 2, fill some of the gaps by elaborating relevant concepts and theoretical issues, which help in understanding the rest of the volume. Towards this end, they also present a narrative of Bangladesh's development experience that highlights governance issues in connection with the LDC graduation paradigm. Furthermore, they review LDC graduation cases and undertake cross-country comparisons to tease out lessons for Bangladesh.

The chapter starts by elaborating concepts including graduation, inclusion and graduation criteria, vulnerability and resilience, and smooth transition. Graduation connotes more than just meeting statistical thresholds – it signifies a stage of development where LDCs are able to escape vicious cycles of underdevelopment linked to structural handicaps. A set of three inclusion and graduation criteria – gross national income (GNI) per capita, the Human Assets Index (HAI) and the Economic Vulnerability Index (EVI) – evaluates LDCs' progress. These criteria have separate thresholds for inclusion and graduation that are subject to revision periodically. Vulnerability in the context of LDCs refers to their susceptibility to being affected by external events or shocks, the extent of which is captured by the EVI. This criterion includes more physical attributes and structural features as opposed to components embodying resilience. The latter is more informed by the internal policy choices of a country and less by persisting structural factors. Finally, smooth transition out of the LDC group is a process that involves a country's ability to withstand the pressures associated with LDC-specific benefits being phased out following graduation. The process, which entails both national efforts and international support, is crucial for LDCs to experience self-sustaining and irreversible graduations.

As part of the scrutiny of the LDC graduation paradigm, a number of pertinent theoretical issues are then reviewed in the chapter. Any discussion about the roots of underdevelopment in LDCs cannot overlook their colonial pasts, since most of them – 48 out of 52 – were colonised at some point in time. Exploitative colonial legacies contributed significantly to post-colonial structural stagnancy, institutional weaknesses and sub-optimal global linkages. External assistance in the form of international support measures (ISMs) has been thus imperative in attempts to pull these countries out of what many scholars have called 'underdevelopment traps' (Rosenstein-Rodan 1943; Nurkse 1953; Guillaumont 2009 all cited in Chapter 2). Whether or not ISMs have been truly helpful remains inconclusive, but it is widely acknowledged that effective utilisation of ISMs is contingent upon institutional strengths within LDCs.

Discussions about the growth experiences of LDCs, the majority of which are at early stages of development, may attach some relevance to early thinking like Rosenstein-Rodan's (1943 cited in Chapter 2) 'big push' theory or Rostow's (1960 cited in Chapter 2) five stages of growth, with particular pertinence to the take-off stage. More applicable to LDCs, however, are the structuralist views by the likes of Lewis (1954 cited in Chapter 2) and Kuznets (1955, 1973 cited in Chapter 2). While the former suggested that developing countries need to transform their economic structures to depend less on sectors with lower productivity of labour, the latter explicitly proposed a shift away from agriculture. Ranis and Fei's (1961 cited in Chapter 2) extension of Lewis to include the significance of agricultural productivity growth is also substantive. Further, literature on the importance of capital investment and human development appear relevant.

Recent literature on the subject of structural change is also comprehensive. Chang (2003 cited in Chapter 2) points out that developed countries adopted various industrial policies in their early stages of development to protect infant industries and catalyse structural transformation. The idea that quality of economic growth is important emerged in more recent literature. McMillan and Rodrik (2011 cited in Chapter 2) highlight the issue of 'positive structural change' characterised by a move towards more productive sectors that increase overall labour productivity of a country. If LDCs are to strive for smooth transition out of the LDC group induced by positive structural change, three things are pertinent – more diversified exports, competitive and undervalued currencies, and more flexible labour markets.

Lin (2012 cited in Chapter 2) proposes a new theory called 'new structural economics', which captures the dynamic nature of an economy's structure of factor endowments that evolves from one stage of development to another with different optimal industrial structures at each stage. As such, industrial upgrading and infrastructure improvement targets in developing countries should not necessarily draw from those that exist in high-income countries. Stiglitz (2016 cited in Chapter 2) recognises the role of government in instilling positive structural change in an economy. Evidently, theories of structural transformation are rather pertinent to LDCs and structural change can be used as a metric for LDCs' progress towards sustainable development.

Furthermore, the chapter clarifies the confusion between graduating from the LDC group and becoming a middle-income country (MIC). The two development milestones are very different in terms of motivation and technicalities. The purpose of the United Nations' (UN) classification of LDCs is to address a country's structural handicaps, while the purpose of the World Bank's income-based classification is to assess the credit worthiness of a country, not to oversee its development per se. The two classifications also differ in terms of identification criteria, thresholds, graduation process, benchmark years, strengths and weaknesses, and policy implications. LDCs can also belong to the different categories of the income-based classification. For instance, Bangladesh remains an LDC, despite recently transitioning from a low-income country (LIC) to lower middle-income country (LMIC). Like Bangladesh, many LDCs will be going through multiple transitions around the same time by graduating from the LDC group and moving on to a different income classification.

In setting the context for Bangladesh's upcoming graduation, Bhattacharya and Khan (Chapter 2) also address the issue of governance, which is usually missing in discussions about LDC graduation. They revisit Bangladesh's so-called 'paradoxical' development achievements in spite of apparently poor governance. Endowed with weak and unresponsive institutions following decades of foreign oppression, the country did not have a particularly strong start at the time of independence in 1971. It has consistently scored poorly on indicators that measure quality of governance and ranked high on indices that measure corruption. Yet, Bangladesh has demonstrated commendable resilience and significant progress across various socio-economic indicators, in particular remarkable growth of gross domestic product (GDP) and GNI per capita, stable exchange rates, steady influx of remittances, reduced fertility and maternal mortality rates, improved gender equity in primary and secondary schooling, improved performance in child immunisation and life expectancy at birth, and disaster management. In fact, Bangladesh has been an outlier in cross-country studies that investigate both the growth–governance nexus and human development–income nexus.

Notwithstanding, some amount of scepticism regarding the effects of governance on growth exists. For instance, democracy as practised in Bangladesh was found to have no significantly positive effect on economic growth. Despite governance limitations, successive governments have created an enabling environment for the private sector to thrive, export-oriented manufacturing sector to grow, agricultural productivity to increase, food security to be ensured, migrants to remit and effective partnerships to be maintained with non-government organisations (NGOs) to support social service delivery in the public sector. Incumbent governments were able to keep their differences with other political parties separate from their economic agendas.

Going forward, whether or not the issue of governance is relevant to LDC graduation, given its absence from the graduation criteria, remains arguable. On the surface, governance may appear irrelevant given that not only has Bangladesh progressed remarkably, but it has also met all the LDC graduation criteria. However, complacency is unwarranted if graduation is without momentum. The quality and inclusivity of growth are concerns. Also, space for growth may become exhausted. Institutional and policy reforms and consolidated efforts to improve governance in different sectors of the economy appear to be crucial in inducing positive structural change.

Bhattacharya and Khan undertake a cross-country assessment that compares Bangladesh with co-graduating countries. Only five LDCs have graduated since 1991 and 12, including Bangladesh, are in the pipeline to graduate between 2019 and 2024. Bangladesh is the only graduating LDC with an increase in average GDP growth rate between the periods 2005–10 and 2011–16. Dependence on official development assistance (ODA) has been low for the country compared to its Asian counterparts, the remarkable inflow of remittances aside. The country has been managing current account surpluses. Also, the share of value added and employment in the manufacturing sector has been comparatively larger in Bangladesh. Yet, the country's foreign direct investment (FDI) as a share of GDP has been comparatively low, domestic resource mobilisation has been extremely poor, exports remain largely undiversified and labour productivity remains an area of great concern.

Lessons from the experiences of graduated countries, especially post-graduation developments, were teased out for the benefit of graduating LDCs. Real GDP growth, ODA as a per cent of GNI and remittances as per cent of GDP fell in almost all former LDCs after graduation. On the other hand, FDI as a per cent of GDP invariably increased across all countries, indicating improvements in investors' confidence following graduation.

Good governance, which translated into macroeconomic stability, management and prudent policies, were key in the experiences of former LDCs. Countries focused on structural shifts towards productive and high value added sectors. Environments conducive for private and foreign investment as well as mobilisation of domestic resources prevailed. LDC-specific benefits and ODA were well aligned with national priorities. Sufficient efforts were dedicated towards developing infrastructure and improving public health and education. Finally, all graduated countries were proactive in negotiating their graduation related terms and conditions before their graduations became effective. Importantly, there were formidable challenges to manage, especially following graduation. Early negotiations with bilateral and multilateral trading partners on phasing out benefits were instrumental in facilitating transitions out of the LDC group. Identification of alternative sources of finance proved critical. Graduated countries seemed to have difficulties managing external debt, fiscal and current account deficits. Continued engagement with development partners was also found to be essential beyond graduation.

Smooth transition and structural transformation

Bangladesh's graduation from the LDC group is almost certain. It is thus imperative to conduct an *ex-ante* assessment of whether the country will experience a smooth transition. Khondaker Golam Moazzem and Akashlina Arno, in Chapter 3, empirically assess the prospect for Bangladesh's smooth transition with regard to historical trends in structural transformation and future outlook. The chapter also looks at the extent of structural transformation captured by LDC graduation criteria. In essence, it investigates whether graduation entails structural transformation or vice versa.

Moazzem and Arno (Chapter 3) find that Bangladesh has experienced slow progress as far as structural transformation is concerned. Between 1995–96 and 2015, the share of employment in agriculture decreased by 7.2 per cent, the share in industry increased by 6.9 per cent and the share in services increased only by 0.3 per cent. The agriculture sector in Bangladesh continues to have the largest share of employment (43.9 per cent in 2015) despite its low contribution to GDP (15.5 per cent in 2015), which indicates a slow movement of labour to sectors with higher productivity. On the other hand, notwithstanding the heavy reliance of Bangladesh's exports on the industry sector (especially manufacturing), the average rate of growth in the share of labour in this sector over the last two decades was very low, at only 0.4 per cent per year. Trends in overall labour productivity as a measure of structural transformation are also assessed.

At first glance, it appears that Bangladesh's total labour productivity rose significantly between 1985 and 2010. However, a large proportion of this rise can be attributed to growth in productivity within a sector rather than structural change as would be indicated by productivity changes between sectors.

A cross-country comparison between Bangladesh and selected Asian emerging economies – India, Indonesia, Pakistan and Vietnam – with substantial export-oriented manufacturing sectors, reveals that Bangladesh has had the lowest level of labour productivity among the five countries since 2000. The gaps in labour productivity between Bangladesh and particularly India and Indonesia have been widening over the years. Further investigation into labour productivity growth disaggregated by 'within sector and between sector' productivity growth for these five countries indicates that between 2011 and 2015, India and Vietnam had significantly higher proportions of growth, attributable to structural change, compared to Bangladesh. Labour productivity growth for Bangladesh during the same period was higher than that for Pakistan and Indonesia at an average of 4.39 per cent. While Pakistan suffered from a weak macroeconomic environment, Indonesia already experienced significant structural change and therefore faced a slowdown. Moreover, evidence suggests that Bangladesh is characterised by lack of export diversity and weak structural transformation. Given its macroeconomic environment, Bangladesh's economy is capable of higher level of structural change required for smooth transition.

Against this backdrop, Moazzem and Arno analyse Bangladesh's pathway towards structural transformation as the country moves towards graduation from the LDC group. The analysis, using International Labour Organization (ILO) estimates for labour force trends in Bangladesh until 2025, finds that the shift of labour towards the industrial sector, which includes the export-oriented ready-made garment (RMG) industry, is almost stagnant. Notwithstanding, labour movement away from the agriculture sector is on a downward trend and labour movement towards the services sector, albeit slow, is on an upward trend.

Since there is no set benchmark for the optimal level of structural change to ensure smooth transition, the outlook for Bangladesh is compared with that for other emerging economies to understand how Bangladesh may fare as graduation approaches. Moazzem and Arno deploy a linear forecasting tool to predict trends in 'between sector' productivity growth – an indicator of structural change – in Bangladesh, India, Indonesia, Pakistan and Vietnam beyond 2015. 'Between sector' productivity growth for Bangladesh has not decreased, but has not increased significantly either. Thus, the linear estimation for structural change until 2025 is illustrated as a flat line. In comparison, structural change prospects for India and Pakistan are stronger.

The chapter also analyses how the LDC graduation criteria affect the level of labour productivity caused by shifts between sectors. Following a model similar to that of McMillan and Rodrick (2011 cited in Chapters 2 and 3), a panel data analysis on selected Asian economies including Bangladesh, between 1992 and 2014, finds that none of the three graduation criteria had a significant effect on structural change. In other words, meeting the graduation criteria does not guarantee the structural transformation needed for smooth transition following graduation.

A key conclusion by Moazzem and Arno is that overcoming post-graduation challenges and integrating into global markets requires significant increases in labour and sectoral productivity. Bangladesh's Seventh Five Year Plan (7FYP) defines a number of policies for upgrading and transformation of the economy. These policies highlight three key areas – industry-related policy and strategy, infrastructure-related policy and strategy, and development of the information technology sector. If these policies and strategies are fully implemented, they could sufficiently boost the economy in its preparation for graduation and beyond. Concentration on developing the manufacturing and services sectors, continued infrastructural development, and investment in and timely completion of transformational projects are essential. Strategies to increase and direct FDI towards the export-oriented manufacturing sector, and facilitate the transfer of better technology and managerial skills to increase productivity, are also needed.

Post-graduation challenges and opportunities

The positive tone of the political discourse in Bangladesh, with regard to the country's expected graduation, suggests that the advantages of leaving the LDC group may be taken for granted. While pride and sense of achievement associated with graduation cannot be denied, the resultant fewer ISMs can have adverse implications. Mustafizur Rahman and Estiaque Bari, in Chapter 4, undertake an in-depth examination of the costs and benefits of LDC graduation for Bangladesh. They stress that there are formidable challenges the country will need to address alongside opportunities that will emerge.

Rahman and Bari's (Chapter 4) projections indicate that Bangladesh, which has met all three graduation criteria at the 2018 review by the Committee for Development Policy (CDP), a subsidiary advisory body of the United Nations Economic and Social Council (UN ECOSOC), will continue to meet all three graduation criteria at the subsequent triennial reviews of 2021 and 2024. This would mean that Bangladesh's graduation will be more broad based compared to many countries that have graduated and co-graduating countries. All graduates and co-graduating countries (except Bangladesh, Nepal and Myanmar) have not been able to meet the EVI criterion, which is indeed a key driver of sustainable graduation. As seen in three of the five graduation cases, continued vulnerability led to deferment of graduation. In contrast, vulnerability was the first structural handicap that Bangladesh was able to overcome since it crossed the threshold for EVI at the 2015 CDP review.

Bangladesh's graduation will open a number of opportunities for the country, not to mention the advantage emanating from branding as a non-LDC emerging economy. The newly gained status will improve the country's credit rating and consequently provide better access to commercial loans at preferred interest rates. This will be of benefit if the Bangladesh government decides to raise capital through sovereign bonds or when the private sector raises capital on the international financial market. Improved credit worthiness and an indication of higher economic potential that stems from non-LDC status are also likely to attract interest from potential foreign investors. Bangladesh's graduation will also attract attention from the international community because of its dominant shares in the correlates of the LDC group – population (17.3 per cent), GDP (18.3 per cent) and exports (13.6 per cent). Although Bangladesh's dependence on ODA has gradually declined over time, ODA still constitutes about one-third of the Annual Development Programme financing in Bangladesh and it remains important for social sectors and infrastructure development.

Since Bangladesh becoming eligible for LDC graduation coincides with its recent shift in status from LIC to LMIC, the country is already moving from International Development Association (IDA) only type (commercial) financing to blended financing. This shift will significantly increase borrowing costs arising from shorter maturity periods and higher lending rates. Rahman and Bari observe that, notwithstanding the country's outstanding record in terms of debt servicing of foreign loans (less than 2 per cent of its earnings from export and remittances), Bangladesh will have to adjust to the new realities of rising costs for development financing and recurring higher debt servicing liabilities following graduation.

However, what is going to affect Bangladesh most adversely following graduation is the loss of ISMs that favour LDCs. There are as many as 136 LDC-specific ISMs covering a range of diverse areas that include development finance, trade, technology and technical assistance (United Nations n.d. cited in Chapter 4). Utilisation of these ISMs varies significantly across LDCs depending on their needs and capacities as well as delivery on commitments by development partners. However, Bangladesh is among the few LDCs that have been able to take significant advantage of ISMs, which means that losing them is going to have consequences. The most important adverse impact will be the loss of LDC-specific tariff preferences enjoyed by the country's exports in over 40 countries. Currently, Bangladesh enjoys duty-free market access for all products in all developed countries (except apparels in the United States) and also in a number of developing countries including India (for all products) and China (for more than 1,000 tariff lines). The impact of preference erosion will be especially high in the European Union (EU), where the country enjoys duty-free, quota-free market access under the Everything But Arms (EBA) initiative, and also in Canada where the rules of origin provisions are highly favourable for LDCs. Following graduation and the end of any negotiated smooth transition period, Bangladesh will have to face tariffs on its exports in these markets, leading to loss of competitiveness due to most favoured nation (MFN) tariffs. The analysis in this chapter shows that, at the prevailing MFN rates, Bangladesh will lose an estimated US$2.7 billion in export earnings, which is equivalent to 8 per cent of total exports. However, these adverse effects could be reduced over time if MFN rates decrease, thanks to multilateral negotiations or if Bangladesh joins regional trade agreements (RTAs).

Rahman and Bari also highlight other special and differential provisions for the LDCs accorded by the World Trade Organization (WTO), for which Bangladesh will cease to be eligible following graduation, such as LDC-specific Aid for Trade measures to enhance supply-side capacities in trade-related areas, as well as technical and financial capacity development support through the Enhanced Integrated Framework. Another significant benefit that will be lost relates to flexible enforcement of the intellectual property rights regime. Bangladesh's pharmaceutical sector has been benefitting from special treatment under the WTO decision on Trade-Related Aspects of Intellectual Property Rights (TRIPS) and Public Health. The stringent trade rules that the country will have to face following graduation are likely to have adverse impacts on this promising sector. Other possible losses due to graduation may include foregone climate change-related technology transfer support targeted towards LDCs, non-applicability of budget caps for LDC contributions to the budgets of the UN, its agencies and other international organisations. As a non-LDC, Bangladesh will also lose international support to participate in various overseas meetings.

Rahman and Bari further emphasise that Bangladesh meeting the thresholds of the different sub-indices under the three graduation criteria reflects the underlying strengths of the economy, continuity of economic performance and resilience of the economy. However, to have smooth transition and graduation with momentum, Bangladesh should design a well-crafted graduation strategy, to be pursued during the run up to 2024. Towards this end, they suggest a number of ways forward. They stress the need to take advantage of the reporting requirements by the United Nations Department of Economic and Social Affairs (UN DESA) regarding graduation-related progress, to design a forward-looking transition strategy that will not only facilitate domestic preparedness, but also help mobilise global support. Emphasis should be on productivity enhancement and skill upgradation to boost competitiveness. The government should explore all opportunities and negotiate its possibility for continued eligibility for ISMs beyond graduation. The country should be proactive in pursuing the Generalised System of Preferences (GSP) plus status in the EU once eligibility for EBA ceases. Moreover, Bangladesh's bilateral relations with key development partners and institutions should receive high policy priority. Negotiation regarding softer credit terms (e.g. interest rate, repayment and grace period, procurement conditionalities) and untying of assistance should remain on top of countries' agendas.

SDGs and smooth transition

The adoption of the 2030 Agenda for Sustainable Development by the UN in September 2015 redefined the international development discourse. Bangladesh will likely graduate at a time when the SDGs should be at an advanced stage of implementation. Fahmida Khatun, Shahida Pervin and Masudur Rahman, in Chapter 5, examine whether pursuing the SDGs will complement or distract Bangladesh from experiencing a smooth transition. They review the linkages between the SDGs and LDC graduation criteria as well as the Istanbul Programme of Action (IPoA) for LDCs and national policies by conducting a mapping exercise, network analysis, and Granger causality and correlation analysis.

Khatun *et al.* (Chapter 5) map as many as 94 of the 169 SDG targets that might support the LDC graduation criteria. Strengths of the links were further studied with the help of network analyses between each graduation criterion at the indicator level and number of SDG targets to which each criterion is connected. The strongest link observed was between Partnerships for the goals (Goal 17) and GNI. Decent work and economic growth (Goal 8) and industry, innovation and infrastructure (Goal 9) are also strongly linked to GNI. Understandably, the objective of the HAI criteria are more in tandem with goals good health and well-being (Goal 3) and quality education (Goal 4). Zero hunger (Goal 2), climate action (Goal 13) and life below water (Goal 14) have strong connections with EVI.

There are 47 goals and targets, 126 actions for LDCs, 109 actions for development partners and 16 joint actions to implement the eight IPoA priority areas. The IPoA and SDGs have similarities in the cases of a number of goals and targets notwithstanding differences in terms of coverage, targets and indicators. A network analysis between IPoA priority areas and SDG targets suggests that as many as 83 SDG targets have potential linkages with goals, targets and selected actions of eight IPoA priority areas. The analysis confirms that pursuing the SDGs is in support of Bangladesh's efforts towards graduation, implementation of the IPoA and possibly smooth transition. To further elaborate on this finding, Khatun *et al.* also explore linkages between SDG targets and seven key areas for 'graduation-plus' strategies identified by the United Nations Conference on Trade and Development (UNCTAD) (UNCTAD 2016 cited in Chapter 5). A total of 50 unique SDG targets were found to be aligned with six broad areas, namely: rural transformation; industrial policy; science, technology and innovation policy; development finance; macroeconomic policies; and employment generation. Gender is a cross-cutting area.

The chapter further includes an alignment exercise between the SDGs and some of the national policies, especially the 7YFP of Bangladesh. The methodology of this exercise closely follows that of a similar exercise undertaken by Bhattacharya *et al.* (2016 cited in Chapter 5). The exercise finds that six SDG targets are 'fully overlapped', 40 SDG targets 'partially overlapped', 26 SDGs are aligned in essence and finally as many as 21 SDG targets have no alignment with national policy objectives stated in the 7FYP. To see if these 21 non-aligned SDG targets were reflected in some of the other key policy documents of the country, several sectoral policies were reviewed and 12 targets were found to have some sort of similarity in essence with some of those policies, if not directly aligned.

While the network analysis provides a holistic visual representation of SDGs' linkages with LDC graduation criteria, it neither indicates whether these two objectives are mutually reinforcing or hindering, nor does it depict the magnitude of such linkages. Addressing this concern, Khatun *et al.* also include an empirical analysis based on a few SDG indicators notwithstanding the limitations due to the dearth of available data. A Granger causality and pairwise correlation between selected SDG indicators and LDC graduation criterion of GNI in the context of Bangladesh, and for the 1990–2015 period, indicates that at least eight SDG indicators have significant causal relationships with GNI per capita. Furthermore, the direction of such causality can be one way or both ways. Not surprisingly, an increase in GNI per capita would positively affect SDG indicators like proportion of budget funded by domestic tax revenues, total revenue as a per cent of GDP and total number of air passenger movements. On the other hand, GNI per capita itself will be positively affected by SDG indicators like per employee real GDP growth, industry value added as a per cent of GDP and share of manufacturing employment. GNI per capita and disbursement of project aid to the agriculture sector were found to be mutually reinforcing. The only indicator found to be negatively affected by GNI per capita was personal remittances received. This finding may not be unusual as evidence from various countries indicate that remittance flow is not necessarily associated with higher GNI per capita. For Bangladesh, however, the role of remittances in the economy is significant. As suggested by Uddin and Sjö (2013 cited in Chapter 5), remittance inflow and the expansion of the financial sector drive GDP growth in Bangladesh over the long run (1976–2011), while remittances act as a shock absorber to income changes in the short-run.

Khatun *et al.* suggest that pursuing global development goals in the national context can be favourable for the purpose of graduation from the LDC group and smooth transition. There may be significant alignment of the SDG targets relevant to the GNI per capita criterion in the national plans, but there is also room for better integration of some of the other targets. Finally, the dearth of quality data at the SDG indicator level may have limited the empirical findings of the chapter, but the qualitative assessment reiterates the importance of flanking measures, that is to prioritise implementation of selected SDG targets in national policies that will assist in a smooth transition after graduation for Bangladesh. Moreover, attention needs to be paid to SDG targets that are not reflected in its national and sectoral policies for smooth transition, specifically to maintain genetic diversity (SDG 2.5), facilitate responsible migration and mobility of people (SDG 10.7), support positive links between urban, peri-urban and rural areas (SDG 11.a), increase the number of cities and settlements abiding to the Sendai Framework for Disaster Risk Reduction 2015–2030 (SDG 11.b), reduce violence (SDG 16.1), reduce illicit financial flow (SDG 16.4), increase efforts towards inclusive decision-making (SDG 16.7), strengthen national institutions (SDG 16.a) and promote non-discriminatory laws and policies (SDG 16.b). The country needs to encourage inflow of remittances by developing the skills of potential migrants, facilitating the migration process, having better arrangements with destination countries, ensuring better use of remittances and maintaining a favourable foreign exchange regime. Proper utilisation of project aid to the agriculture sector is important – aid should not only support employment generation but also productivity enhancement in the sector. The chapter also reinforces the importance of the industrial sector's value addition (SDG 9.2.1) and employment generation (SDG 9.2.2). Finally, the chapter calls for efforts geared towards revenue generation through increasing GNI coupled with increasing the tax base, curtailing tax evasion, strengthening institutions and ensuring good governance.

The global and regional environment

Bangladesh is setting out to graduate at a time when the international arena is confronted with multiple transitions and challenges. Towfiqul Islam Khan and Muntaseer Kamal, in Chapter 6, highlight this crucial issue and contextualise the relatively unconducive global and regional environment in view of the several upcoming LDC graduations. With Bangladesh becoming increasingly integrated with global and regional economies, its susceptibility to external adversities also increases. The chapter, in this regard, follows a derived analytical framework to assess the implications of global and regional challenges for Bangladesh. These challenges are categorised under four broad clusters, namely, economic, technological, environmental, and governance and security.

According to Khan and Kamal (Chapter 6), major economic pitfalls that threaten smooth and sustainable graduation from the LDC group include tepid global recovery, plateauing flow of ODA, protectionist measures by developed countries and the slowdown of trade liberalisation.

According to *World Economic Situation and Prospects 2017*, estimates for projected global economic growth for the years 2017 and 2018 are 2.7 and 2.9 per cent, respectively, which are lower than the average growth of 3.4 per cent observed in the decade prior to the global financial crisis (United Nations 2017 cited in Chapter 6). Projected growth for LDCs at an average of 5.2 per cent and 5.5 per cent for 2017 and 2018, respectively, also fall below the IPoA target of 7 per cent. Recovery from the global financial crisis has been slower in LDCs with declining income growth and rising inflation, compared to advanced economies where growth rates have improved, albeit slowly. This faltering recovery in LDCs is likely to threaten private financing as well as public expenditure on health care, education, social protection and climate change adaptation (United Nations 2017 cited in Chapter 6).

LDCs are also generally ill equipped in terms of resources to effectively tackle external shocks and often rely upon aid from developed countries. However, the availability of ODA from the international community is declining. Most members of the Organisation for Economic Co-operation and Development's (OECD) Development Assistance Committee (DAC) fell short of their annual ODA commitment of 0.15–0.2 per cent of GNI towards LDCs. Net ODA as a share of GDP has also declined for LDCs compared to 2001. Moreover, ODA distribution among LDCs remains highly skewed. The low disbursement of ODA is a key policy concern for Bangladesh notwithstanding actual aid disbursement will rely more on the country's absorptive capacity rather than the availability of aid itself (Rahman *et al.*, 2010 cited in Chapter 6). By calculating a specialisation index on allocation of ODA commitments across sectors in Bangladesh, Khan and Kamal find that social and economic infrastructure have been the major receivers of ODA since 2005. The index also depicts that Bangladesh receives more aid allocation for basic education compared to other developing countries, while it remains relatively underfunded in production sectors.

The slowing pace of international trade in recent years implies that the LDC economies' prospects to grow, relying on the global market, are also limited. Countries face a number of trade barriers, and graduating from the LDC group will further expose the LDCs to these barriers. The recent emergence of mega-regional trade agreements can also significantly reduce market access for LDCs' exports to countries participating in RTAs (Palit 2015 cited in Chapter 6). Bangladesh's absence in mega-RTA negotiations may impact its future trade potential. Furthermore, the changing dynamics of the global political economy and repurcussions – whether directly from Brexit and ensuing loss in preferential treatments to the United Kingdom, or indirectly through ripple effects of the increasing trade barriers in the US under the new Trump administration – can be of concern for Bangladesh.

The technological revolution that has been swaying the global economy is both a blessing and a curse, especially for countries still at the lower stages of development. Newer technologies enable supply-side alterations through creating novel ways of serving existing needs but also disrupting industrial value chain norms and labour markets. Jobs that might be adversely affected due to automation are mostly in developing countries. LDCs with vast unskilled labour forces are especially at risk in contrast to the skilled labour forces in developed countries. As automation becomes increasingly cheaper, LDCs are also losing their comparative advantage of lower labour costs, which seriously affects trade, remittances and FDI inflow.

Advancements in technology, despite replacing human labour, contribute to increasing skills and productivity as well as freeing up human and financial resources to be used in sectors with higher returns. In essence, such advancements go hand in hand with structural transformation. However, an alarming trend associated with such structural transformation is the incidence of 'premature deindustrialisation' – the fall in the share of manufacturing employment or an absolute decline in said employment at a much lower level of GNI per capita compared to the historical trend of today's advanced economies (Dasgupta and Singh 2007 cited in Chapter 6).

Climate change is undoubtedly a significant global threat to which LDCs are particularly vulnerable. LDCs in general lack economic, institutional, technical and scientific capabilities to manage and adapt to climate-related shocks. High incidence of poverty adds to their vulnerabilities. Climate change severely threatens agricultural production and food security as these countries lack effective adaptation and mitigation measures. Financing is a critical aspect in this regard. The sources of finance for the LDC Fund set up under the United Nations Framework Convention on Climate Change remain insufficient and insecure. Available data show that only 86 per cent of the pledged amounts by major donors was actually deposited.

Climate finance in the Bangladesh context mostly refers to flows from domestic and external sources geared for adaptation measures rather than mitigation efforts. Judging from the available data on external funds to Bangladesh, the multi-donor Bangladesh Climate Change Resilience Fund does not appear very encouraging. The same can be said about other sources such as the Climate Investment Fund, Green Climate Fund and Global Environment Facility. Moreover, LDC graduation will have a direct impact on climate financing, since graduates lose their access to the LDC Fund and have to compete against developing countries for other sources of finance, the application procedures for which are usually quite complex.

Amidst the intensifying global crisis with respect to conflicts and forced displacements, a noteworthy phenomenon is the increase in the share of refugees originating from LDCs since 2008, which reflects an increase in socio-economic and security concerns. Further adding to their already burdened resources for development and humanitarian needs of their own populations, LDCs are now susceptible to influxes of large numbers of refugees. The share of total refugees hosted by LDCs has been on the rise since 2010, which has put immense pressure on the economies of LDCs. Terrorism is also a key governance and security concern for LDCs. According to the *Global Terrorism Index 2016*, deaths from terrorist activities increased almost ninefold since 2000 (IEP 2016 cited in Chapter 6). In smaller economies, incidences of terrorism instigate a shifting of resources towards less productive but unaffected sectors, levying greater and protracted macroeconomic costs.

Finally, illicit financial flows (IFFs) have emerged as a pervasive phenomenon in developed and developing countries alike. Every year, LDCs lose a significant amount of money in IFFs that could have been used to provide numerous public services and alter development trajectories. IFFs are estimated to exceed FDI and ODA in LDCs (OECD 2014 cited in Chapter 6). In Bangladesh, such flows have consistently exceeded total ODA inflows to the country since 2004. Persistently increasing IFFs from Bangladesh have put the country in a deteriorating position compared to other countries. If 25 per cent (the highest income tax rate in Bangladesh) of these flows was received as revenue, the health budget could have been tripled or the education budget could have been doubled in 2013 (Khan 2016 cited in Chapter 6).

Undoubtedly, there is a need for Bangladesh to stay abreast of policy options in view of global and regional challenges. Khan and Kamal have extensively studied the existing policy framework of Bangladesh that is in place to mitigate some of these challenges, and call for effective implementation of these policies. Addressing the issue of inadequate infrastructure facilities is crucial, especially to boost private investments. There needs to be more investment in the information and communication technology sector to encourage diversification towards production of higher value goods and services. Skill development of human resources for higher productivity should also be given high priority. There may be potential for a substantial rise in productivity through channelling FDI in the RMG industry beyond export processing zones. This could potentially push RMG exports up the value chain and raise export earnings. The investment environment could be improved through reforms in the financial sector and tax laws, while strengthening governance and regulatory measures. Finally, it is important to mobilise as much global support as possible, given that combating external challenges demands global and united solutions.

Looking ahead

Bangladesh's pathway towards graduation and beyond is based on a number of remarkable economic achievements observed during the recent past. These include, *inter alia*, steady and decent growth of GDP and GNI per capita, robust growth of foreign exchange earnings through exports and overseas remittances, enhanced school enrolment at both the primary and secondary levels, discernible improvement of child and maternal mortality rates, and significant reduction of natural disaster-related risks. Indeed, the LDC graduation process has been boosted by the country's shift to lower middle-income status. Like Bangladesh, a number of other LDCs are also in the course of experiencing multiple transitions in their development trajectory.

Although there is no ready theory for the LDC graduation paradigm, a heterodox review points to the importance of structural transformation in sustaining the impetus of graduation. It should be recognised that Bangladesh will be leaving the LDC group with unfinished structural transformation of its economy. A large proportion of the labour force remains stuck in the low-productivity agriculture sector, the export basket remains too dependent on a single product, the level of domestic resource mobilisation is too low, and inequality is increasing in the economy and society in various forms. Weak governance characterises policy and programme delivery efforts. The country remains immensely vulnerable to the impact of climate change. It will also be facing a less-than-enabling global policy environment as it graduates from the LDC group. Evolving global economic, technological, environmental, and governance and security circumstances will pose new challenges to the country as well.

Thus, in celebrating Bangladesh's commendable performance in reaching the LDC graduation eligibility, the country needs to be mindful of the fact that its new situation will be coupled with new challenges. Addressing this new set of challenges entails designing and delivering a well-thought out and smooth transition strategy that will ensure both sustainability and graduation with momentum. Such a strategy will greatly benefit from being designed in line with a select set of SDGs. It is also necessary to properly articulate the measures to be undertaken to compensate for the loss of international preferences, and to cash in on the new economic opportunities usually associated with being a non-LDC emerging economy.

Bangladesh's graduation scenario is undoubtedly unique, albeit the journey has been nothing short of exemplary. The lessons emanating from the Bangladesh experience could very well be instructive for the remaining LDCs, as well as LICs, as they gear up to come out from these groups.

2 The LDC paradigm, graduation and Bangladesh

Concepts, comparison and policy

Debapriya Bhattacharya and Sarah Sabin Khan

Introduction

In the decades since the establishment of the least developed country (LDC) category by the United Nations (UN) in 1971 (United Nations 1971), a marked change in mindsets towards graduation from the LDC group has become apparent globally. A palpable 'fear' of and 'resistance' to graduation among LDCs had been evident ever since the provision for graduation was introduced in 1991 (Drabo and Guillaumont 2016). Instead of looking at graduation as an accomplishment in their development trajectories, most LDCs viewed it as the discontinuation of special international support measures (ISMs). This mindset is being replaced by a more proactive one – LDCs are increasingly open to the prospect of graduating. This ongoing change in mindsets is reflected in the Istanbul Programme of Action (IPoA) for LDCs adopted in 2011, which targeted half of the LDCs to meet graduation criteria by 2020 (United Nations 2011). To facilitate the attainment of this target, the UN General Assembly (UNGA) further adopted a resolution to strengthen the smooth transition provisions that promote the gradual phasing out of ISMs following exit from the LDC group (United Nations 2013).

After almost five decades of lacklustre performance characterised by a total of 52 inclusions on the UN list of LDCs and only five graduations (CDP and UN DESA 2015), the LDC group's outlook is finally becoming somewhat optimistic. The UN Conference on Trade and Development (UNCTAD) predicts that at least ten countries will graduate from the LDC category between 2017 and 2021 (UNCTAD 2016). Bangladesh, an LDC, remains on track to graduate. It met all three graduation criteria for the first time in the United Nations Committee for Development Policy's (CDP) 2018 triennial review of LDCs. Unless affected by major unanticipated setbacks in the near future, the country is highly likely to meet the graduation criteria for the second time in 2021 and graduate as early as 2024. Following its transition from low-income to lower middle-income country (LMIC) in 2015, Bangladesh is gearing up for a 'double transition' in view of the imminent LDC graduation.

Bangladesh's graduation is expected to be a landmark success in contemporary development experience. The five countries that graduated from the

LDC category – Botswana (graduated in 1994), Cape Verde (in 2007), the Maldives (in 2011), Samoa (in 2014) and Equatorial Guinea (in 2017), are all characterised by smallness in terms of size of the economy and population. Botswana is a landlocked developing country, Equatorial Guinea a small oil- exporting developing country, and the other countries are small island developing states (SIDS). Two additional countries with scheduled graduations, i.e. Angola (in 2020) and Vanuatu (in 2021) corroborate the trend of being either an island or an oil-exporting country. Bangladesh's graduation would be important since it is the first large developing country – in terms of population, size of the economy and volume of exports – poised to leave behind LDC status. The country has had remarkable achievements in socio-economic outcomes including poverty alleviation. Bangladesh is also likely to be one of the first LDCs to meet all three graduation criteria at the time of graduation, namely, the income criterion of gross national income (GNI) per capita, the Human Assets Index (HAI) and the Economic Vulnerability Index (EVI).

Besides Bangladesh's steady and positive performance in terms of EVI, the only criterion met at the CDP's 2015 review, the country's achievements recorded in the 2018 review in terms of GNI per capita and especially the indicators of the HAI have been significant in improving graduation prospects. This development trajectory may seem like a paradox. The country has consistently scored low or very low on key indicators of the quality of governance, while maintaining remarkable progress as regards health, education, gender equality and sustained economic growth (ESID 2017). Notwithstanding the absence of a governance component in the graduation criteria, Bangladesh's success is anything but ordinary and makes its case even more interesting. Whether the anticipated graduation will be smooth and sustainable will largely depend on, among other things, the country's ability to implement positive structural change entailing developing productive capacities, strengthening capacity of the concerned institutions and addressing the challenges emanating from the evolving regional and global environment.

Objectives and research questions

The present chapter has three core objectives. It seeks to deepen understanding of the LDC graduation paradigm through its analytical scrutiny. It strives to contextualise Bangladesh's graduation in a comparative perspective. It aims to identify policy challenges that are associated with the country's graduation. Towards this end the chapter attempts to answer five research questions.

First, does the graduation paradigm have theoretical underpinnings? The concepts of graduation, inclusion and graduation criteria, smooth transition, and vulnerability are discussed at length and theoretical approaches to economic growth and development are reviewed to construct an analytical framework for the case of LDC graduation. Second, why do misconceptions about the issue of LDC graduation and becoming a middle-income country (MIC) persist? Misconceptions are dispelled with a nuanced narrative that uses Bangladesh as an example. Third, how does Bangladesh's apparently paradoxical development trajectory against a track record of weak governance align with its efforts towards graduation? In this regard, the country's development model is assessed through the lens of LDC graduation. Fourth, how does Bangladesh's performance look from a cross-country perspective? Its trends across various socio-economic indicators are compared with those of LDCs expected to graduate or have graduated. Finally, which lessons can Bangladesh draw from previous graduation experiences? The pre- and post-graduation experiences of the countries that graduated from the LDC category are reviewed and common lessons and implications for Bangladesh are identified.

Methodological approach, sources and structure

The chapter undertakes both narrative elucidation and empirical analyses using a methodological approach that involves reviewing a combination of scholarly literature, comparative country analyses, trend analyses and analytical policy-oriented perspectives. A country-oriented analytical approach that draws on historical perspectives is used to review the state of the knowledge on Bangladesh's development model and political economy through the lens of LDC graduation, to identify key contemporary issues and to undertake cross-country comparisons.

The various sources that were consulted include, among others, publications by the UN CDP, UN Office of the High Representative for the Least Developed Countries, Landlocked Developing Countries and Small Island Developing States, UNCTAD, United Nations Economic and Social Council (UN ECOSOC) and LDC IV Monitor. Data for empirical analyses mainly came from international sources including the World Bank, UNCTAD and International Labour Organization (ILO).

Following this introduction, the rest of the chapter is organised into five sections. The next section discusses the conceptual and theoretical underpinnings of LDC graduation. The section that follows contributes to the conceptual understanding by clarifying confusion between graduation from the LDC group and becoming an MIC. The next section elaborates on Bangladesh's development model from a graduation perspective. The following section offers a comparative perspective by juxtaposing Bangladesh's development performance with that of other countries that are expected to graduate, or have graduated and then discusses the pre- and post-graduation experiences of former LDCs. The chapter concludes by reflecting on answers to the five research questions posed in the introduction.

An analytical framework for LDC graduation

Literature on the development challenges of LDC graduation rarely situates the process within a theoretical framework. For most scholars, graduation appears to be a matter of applied policy and less of an issue of development theory. Yet, without a proper understanding of the theoretical underpinnings of LDC graduation, the motivation for and implementation of policies may remain inadequate.

Clarifying concepts

In order to situate the LDC graduation process in a theoretical framework, relevant concepts need to be clarified.

Graduation

The concept of graduation from the LDC category and thus forgoing preferential treatments was suggested long before provisions for LDC graduation were introduced in 1991, when the CDP began reviewing LDCs' performances (United Nations 1991). Frank (1979) advocated the gradual elimination of ISMs for 'economically advanced' LDCs that may stand to benefit from orienting their domestic trade policies with the 'generally applicable rules of the international trading system'. Such economic advancement, characterised by a certain level of self-sufficiency, would entail an LDC embarking on a development path that goes beyond graduation.

Exiting from the group of LDCs would ideally indicate that countries have successfully escaped the underdevelopment traps linked to the structural handicaps that made them eligible for inclusion in the list of LDCs at the outset, and that they are no longer in need of ISMs. It may be worthwhile mentioning that when the concept of LDCs was being considered, ISMs were considered necessary to bridge the substantial gap that persisted between the poorest of the developing countries and the comparatively advanced ones. The former required additional measures to be able to take full advantage of the support already available for all developing countries (Alonso *et al.* 2014). The motivation for ISMs is to pull LDCs out of underdevelopment and help them integrate and sustain in competitive global markets.

An ideal graduation case for an LDC is overcoming entwined vicious cycles of development challenges and structural human and economic vulnerabilities to set out on a path towards sustainable development (UNCTAD 2016). The agreed terms of graduation thus entails that countries not only reach a certain level of income but also exceed a certain threshold of human development and gain a certain capacity to deal with exogenous shocks.

Inclusion and graduation criteria

The CDP, a subsidiary advisory body of the UN ECOSOC, has been responsible for the process of classifying LDCs since the inception of the concept. The CDP has been reviewing LDCs' performances at three-year intervals before making recommendations to the UN ECOSOC regarding inclusion and graduation decisions. It develops the criteria upon which countries are included in the list of LDCs and identified for graduation. The CDP has also revised and refined the

Table 2.1 Inclusion and graduation thresholds in the 2018 triennial review

Criteria	Inclusion threshold	Graduation threshold
GNI per capita	US$1,025 or below	US$1,230 or above
HAI	60 or below	66 or above
EVI	36 or above	32 or below

Sources: CDP (2018a, 2018b).

criteria on a number of occasions based on various circumstances (CDP and UN DESA 2015).

The CDP understands LDCs to be countries with low income who face acute structural handicaps, namely, 'high vulnerability to economic and environmental shocks' and 'low levels of human assets' (CDP and UNDESA 2015). The criteria used for inclusion and graduation decisions at the 2018 CDP review were GNI per capita, HAI and EVI. The income criterion looks at three-year averages of GNI per capita using the World Bank's Atlas method. The HAI and EVI are structural indices comprising several indicators each. The inclusion and graduation thresholds for each criterion according to the 2018 CDP review are given in Table 2.1.

According to the CDP review in 2018, indicators for HAI included under-five mortality rate, percentage of population undernourished, maternal mortality ratio, gross secondary school enrolment ratio and adult literacy rate. The EVI indicators included population; remoteness; merchandise export concentration; share of agriculture, forestry and fishing in gross domestic product (GDP); share of population in low elevated coastal zones; instability of exports of goods and services; victims of natural disasters; and instability of agricultural production.

To be included in the list of LDCs, all three inclusion thresholds need to be met, with a population limit of 75 million (since 1991). Graduation, on the other hand, entails meeting graduation thresholds for any two of the three criteria (e.g. GNI per capita and HAI, GNI per capita and EVI, or HAI and EVI) at two consecutive triennial reviews. In exceptional cases, an LDC with GNI per capita that is more than twice the graduation threshold level can be eligible for graduation. This is known as the income-only criterion. Equatorial Guinea and Angola are two cases in point, graduating based on the income-only criterion.

Smooth transition

A smooth transition is associated with the period after graduation when a country may no longer exclusively count on LDC-specific support measures. The transition process is, however, hoped to be made smoother by the UN mandated practice of gradually phasing out ISMs instead of withdrawing them abruptly following graduation. The international community recognises the need for some form of continued support to help former LDCs cope with the loss of ISMs and attainment of non-LDC developing country status. In most cases, countries do not lose all benefits immediately upon graduation. Most benefits are phased out over a number of years, as suggested by several UNGA resolutions (e.g. Resolutions 46/2006 (1991), 59/209 (2005) and 67/221 (2013) (United Nations 2005)), to facilitate the smooth transition. The transition period does not have a specified length and can vary depending on country circumstances, negotiations by governments and types of ISMs. However, the period for reporting and monitoring activities by the CDP to track development progress of former LDCs are limited to a maximum of nine years (CDP and UN DESA 2015).

The UNGA's resolutions explain that graduation should not disrupt or impede the development efforts and progress that have led countries to graduate in the first place. Resolution 67/221 calls for smooth transition strategies to be articulated under national leadership and in a consultative manner involving all stakeholders. A transition strategy should ideally include a comprehensive and coherent set of specific and predictable measures informed by national priorities. The process of developing a strategy should start as early as a country is likely to meet the graduation criteria for the first time (United Nations 2015).

Vulnerability and resilience

In smooth transitions, the issue of vulnerability is especially pertinent. LDCs are seemingly 'caught in a trap' since the structural obstacles that they face in development make them more vulnerable to exogenous economic and natural shocks (Guillaumont 2011). This vulnerability and associated instabilities in turn become major structural handicaps themselves, which indicates the need for special policy interventions. The EVI is a crucial criterion in the identification of LDCs because it is designed to capture an LDC's susceptibility to and frequency of being affected by events that are, to a large extent, beyond its control. An essential feature of the EVI is its focus on persisting factors rather than favouring countries with misguided policies (Guillaumont 2011). Most former LDCs, even after reasonable periods of time since their graduations, have been scoring poorly on the EVI, notwithstanding their continued growth in terms of GNI and progress in HAI.

An LDC, that meets the EVI criterion to become eligible for graduation, could improve prospects for a smooth transition through greater economic diversification and capacity to withstand natural shocks. When the EVI was conceived in 1999, the 'resilience' components underlying vulnerability, which had more to do with policy choices, were left out in favour of physical factors and 'structural' variables like size of and exposure to external shock (Guillaumont 2011). Even after meeting the thresholds of the EVI criterion, a country may remain vulnerable according to other indicators on climate change or social and political fragility (Guillaumont *et al.* 2015). For instance, Bangladesh has met the EVI criterion, but remained one of the top ten countries on the Global Climate Risk Index 2016 (Kreft *et al.* 2015). Resilience is thus relevant in the context of graduation in its capacity to ensure smooth transition and sustainability after graduation, especially by mitigating the consequences of structural vulnerabilities.

The key concepts pertaining to LDC graduation illustrate the reality that LDCs can be trapped by a set of structural factors. Some countries may remain so beyond graduation. The following sub-section constructs a theoretical framework that incorporates these concepts.

Reconstructing a theoretical framework

Graduation from the LDC group has rarely been linked with development theories or studied according to a theoretical framework in contemporary literature. It has been viewed rather from an applied policy perspective. How the evolution of development thinking has paralleled this process and where it stands in terms of new motivations is unclear. The literature review that follows surveys older as well as recent literature. In constructing a theoretical framework for LDC graduation, a number of development issues that require theorisation come up: colonial legacies as the roots of underdevelopment, effectiveness of ISMs, sources of economic growth, positive structural change, the relevance of structural transformation and the political reasoning of graduation.

Colonial legacies and associated structural handicaps

More often than not, many of the 'underdevelopment traps' (Rosenstein-Rodan 1943; Nurkse 1953; Guillaumont 2009) that still affect LDCs can be attributed to colonial legacies. At the time of its establishment, the LDC category mostly applied to countries that had been colonised or have geographical constraints. Of the 24 countries initially included in the list of LDCs, only three landlocked countries – Bhutan, Ethiopia and Nepal – had never been colonised. Of the 28 countries that were later included, only Liberia remained uncolonised.

The association between colonial legacies and post-colonial development has been discussed in the literature. Bertocchi and Canova (2002) found that the economic growth rates of several African countries can be explained by the identity of their metropolitan ruler when they were colonies and the degree of economic penetration to which they were exposed, while decolonisation is correlated with economic growth. They also attributed the exploitative nature of Africa's colonisation as a significant cause of the continent's post-colonial underdevelopment. The commodity dependence of many LDCs (especially in Africa) that persist to date can also be traced back to the practices of their colonial powers who forced production of certain primary commodities to cater to the demands of the concurrent industrialisation happening in their own home countries (Blanton *et al.* 2001).

The extractive policies of former colonisers also fostered the establishment of weak institutions of private property that persist and inhibit development processes (Acemoglu *et al.* 2001). Price (2003) estimated that the legacies of extractive colonisation strategies and associated growth-inhibiting institutions can explain approximately 30 per cent of the growth gap between former colonies in Sub-Saharan Africa, the majority of which are LDCs, and other non-industrial countries. To demonstrate linkages between colonial legacies and underdevelopment, Nunn (2007) used a model with multiple equilibria which showed that a society moves from an initial high production equilibrium to a stable though sub-optimal low production equilibrium, when external extraction is severe enough. The stability of the low production equilibrium causes the society to remain trapped even after external extraction ends. Escaping this situation requires external and domestic intervention.

Developed countries' recognition that developing countries in general and LDCs in particular deserve special assistance may be the result of guilty consciences or mounting evidence about the root causes of their persisting structural handicaps. Whatever the reason, a consensus among developed countries was formed that preferential treatment for the poorest developing countries is needed to break their vicious cycles and integrate them into competitive global markets. In this context, 'graduation' for most LDCs would entail leaving behind their colonial and post-colonial production structures and embarking on new development paths based on economic diversification and structural transformation.

Sources of economic growth

To understand how LDCs can embark on development paths towards full self-sufficiency, identifying sources of economic growth in these countries at early stages of development is important. Rosenstein-Rodan (1943) saw large-scale modernisation of production and large investments as prerequisites for economies to be self-sufficient and evade underdevelopment traps. Similarly, Nurkse (1953) suggested that the governments of underdeveloped countries should simultaneously invest in several industries to generate 'balanced' growth.

Rostow (1960) introduced an economic growth model with five stages that all countries go through – traditional society, preconditions for take-off, take-off, drive to maturity and age of high mass consumption. Especially relevant for LDCs in the run up to graduation may be the key underpinnings for take-off – high levels of social overhead capital investment, technological revolution in both agriculture and industry, presence of a leading manufacturing sector and institutions which internalise the promotion of national economic growth. The model assumes that all countries go through these stages irrespective of their heterogeneity and developing countries should invariably follow the development processes that were followed by currently developed countries. Such generalisations could constrain the model's applicability to developing countries in Africa, Asia and Latin America. Notably, Cornia and Scognamillo (2016) showed that most LDCs' structural change from 1993 to 2013 strayed from Rostow's stages of growth.

Many early works in modern development thinking considered the needs of the war-torn West and Eastern Europe's ambitions for industrialisation following the Second World War. More relevant to developing countries were development theories on economic growth and structural transformation. Lewis (1954) proposed the dual-sector model that focuses on structural transformation, specifically labour transition from the subsistence sector with lower productivity to the capitalist sector with higher productivity. This model, which considers economic development with surplus labour, is more relevant to developing countries than the economic growth models of Keynes, Harrod-Domar and Solow (Ranis 2004).

A similar view regarding economic development was held by Kuznets (1955), who pointed out that the shift away from agriculture was a common means of growth for developed countries at the time, though there were increases and subsequent decreases in inequality. Later, he identified structural transformation as one of the six characteristics of economic growth along with the increase in overall productivity and a structural shift towards urbanisation and modernisation (1973). Kuznets also argued that the conditions of underdeveloped countries at the time were different from those of developed countries at their early stages of development. He criticised the simplistic view that all countries go through the same 'linear stages' in their growth (1955).

What may have been missing in these development accounts is the role of the agriculture sector. Ranis and Fei (1961) extend Lewis's dual sector model to include the significance of this otherwise overlooked agriculture sector's productivity growth and its contribution to the growth of the industrial sector. In underdeveloped economies' transition from 'stagnation' to 'self-sustaining' growth, the authors propose the importance of simultaneous and balanced productivity growths in both agriculture and industry. The larger the agricultural surplus, the higher will be the rate of growth in the industry sector.

Robinson (1971) emphasised that capital investment is a more important source of growth for less developed countries than the United States and Western Europe. He also pointed out that due to the wider disparities in productivity across sectors and the ensuing structural disequilibrium in factor markets in less developed countries, the effects of factor transfers to non-agriculture sectors are significant for their economies. Barro (1991), on the other hand, found initial human capital to be the driving source of economic growth for a sample of 98 countries (19 of which were LDCs at the time) over the 1960–85 period.

Links between growth and development were the basis for the human development approach proponents (Haq and Kirdar 1987, Haq 1995, Anand and Sen 2000), which focused on improving people's lives through giving them opportunities and letting them make their own choices. The successive human development reports by the United Nations Development Programme (UNDP) embodied the human development approach by adopting the Human Development Index (HDI) in acknowledgement of the notion that monetary measures and economic growth are insufficient metrics of capturing development of a nation. Three dimensions of human development are captured by the HDI, namely, health, education and standard of living. Variation in HDI measures in countries with similar levels of income can be helpful in raising questions about national policy priorities (UNDP n.d.)

Lewis's dual-sector model and its many descendants continue to be relevant for policy guidance in countries from the global South including Bangladesh, China and India (Ranis 2004). Overall, the literature on sources of economic growth reiterates that LDCs should shift their economies towards manufacturing industries, increase capital investment, mitigate productivity disparities among sectors and improve human capital through skills development and technological advancement.

Positive structural change and recent theories of growth and development

Recent literature on structural change is also vast. According to McMillan *et al.* (2017), the quality of economic growth is important. They evaluated economic transformation as a continuous process of 'positive structural change' and increasing sectoral productivity. Highlighting *positive* is necessary because there have been instances where transformation proved to be growth inhibiting, as examined by McMillan and Rodrik (2011) in their empirical analysis of 38 (mainly developing) countries. They found that since the 1990s, labour transitions in Africa and Latin America have been away from the more productive sectors. Three factors were identified as probable determinants of the direction of structural change: the less diversified the export basket, the smaller the chance of productivity-enhancing structural change; competitive and undervalued currencies encourage growth-enhancing structural change; and more flexible labour markets translate into more positive structural change. They observed that it is better for overall labour productivity if workers move towards more productive sectors than if productivity increases within a sector. This is especially significant when increase in productivity within a sector is not accompanied by an increase in employment share.

The performances of developed and developing countries, especially LDCs, have been increasingly diverging in recent years, which seems to defy mainstream growth theories that envision convergence for all countries. Lin (2012) observed that growth researchers in the past did not adequately pay attention to heterogeneity among countries, such as the differences between LDCs and other developing countries. He proposed a new theory – 'new structural economics' – that looks at structural change from a neoclassical approach and captures the dynamic nature of an economy's structure of factor endowments that evolves during development, with different optimal industrial structures at each stage. The theory sees an economy's development stages as points along a continuum from being a low-income agrarian economy to a high-income industrialised economy, which implies that industrial upgrading and infrastructure improvement targets in LDCs should not necessarily draw from those in high-income countries.

Further, the role of the market as the basic mechanism for effective resource allocation aside, economic development as a dynamic process requires industrial upgrading at each stage, where government institutions and policies should play an active role. Stiglitz (2016) corroborated the idea that markets by themselves do not realise structural transformation that is necessary for successful development and endorsed governments playing a dominant role in creating enabling environments and minimising negative externalities. Chang (2003) demonstrated that although most developed countries like the US and United Kingdom preach the benefits of freer trade and competitive markets for developing countries, they protected their infant industries, primarily manufacturing industries, in their early stages of development through various industrial policies to catalyse structural transformation.

Overall, relatively recent theories of growth and development also highlight capital investment and productivity growth as pertinent issues for LDCs. Both can be increased by diversifying production, transitioning labour to more productive sectors and establishing an effective role for government in the protection and facilitation of these sectors.

LDC-specific literature on structural transformation

The significance of structural transformation in assessing progress has been highlighted in various literature that focus on LDCs (UNCTAD 2006, 2014, 2016). The IPoA could not stress more the importance of structural change as a driver of sustainable economic growth in LDCs. Since the IPoA was adopted, several studies have assessed LDCs' efforts towards structural change. Reviewing the implementation experience of the IPoA, Bhattacharya and Khan (2014) maintained that efforts towards LDC graduation entail structural change in favour of sectors with relatively higher labour productivity. Considering structural transformation in terms of economic growth, changes in sectoral composition and the development of productive capacities, they found that LDCs have been faltering in their recovery from the global financial crisis and are yet to meet any of the core objectives of the IPoA.

Notably, Basnett et al. (2014) addressed the implicit nature of the targets related to structural transformation in the IPoA and proposed specific indicators to enable monitoring and evaluation by LDCs. Using these indicators, Keane et al. (2016) tracked LDCs' progress and found that while some trade-related targets will be met by 2020, more limited progress across the selected indicators is likely to be based on current trends. They called for greater efforts to mobilise international support and confront LDCs' trade-related challenges with novel, timely solutions. Referring to smooth transitions, UNCTAD (2016) underscored graduating with 'momentum' through structural transformation, particularly the development of productive capacities. A shift towards higher value added goods and services through investment in technological upgrading of productive facilities is needed. The establishment of new sectors and activities will upgrade the export structure with a greater number of higher value-added products that can exploit forward linkages and positive externalities.

Lin and Monga (2012) proposed the growth identification and facilitation framework to enable policymakers to take effective measures towards structural transformation. The framework is relevant and applicable to LDCs. Applying it to the case of Uganda, Lin and Xu (2016) identified several sub-sectors where the LDC can excel given its labour-abundant, natural resource-rich, capital-poor endowment structure and recommended policies for improving institutions in view of the country's specific structural deficits. However, it is still too early to assess the framework's effectiveness in enabling LDCs to achieve structural transformation and smooth transitions after graduation.

Effectiveness of ISMs

LDCs' performance over the past few decades has been rather dull (Bhattacharya and Hossain 2011). The situation can be characterised by stagnant economic growth at low levels of per capita income, which according to the development theories of Young (1928), Rosenstein-Rodan (1943) and Nurkse (1953), can be compared to being stuck at the lower equilibrium in a multiple equilibria model with alternative stable and optimal solutions. Notably, Myrdal (1957) proposed the applicability of the theory of circular cumulative causation to underdeveloped regions and highlighted their tendency to become trapped in a 'vicious cycle'. These theories suggest that an underdeveloped country cannot escape the underdevelopment trap without external interventions aiming to change initial conditions. Berthélemy (2006) investigated the effectiveness of 'big push' policies and the idea that 'massive' external assistance is necessary to lift less developed countries out of poverty. He found that external transfers do not catalyse successful movement from an initial equilibrium unless accompanied by structural transformation and external assistance has not played a significant role in facilitating movement from initial to new equilibria in these countries. This finding is important for LDCs if they were to understand the significance of ISMs in their development.

ISMs have been found to be inefficient and insufficient. Cortez (2011) found that ISMs for LDCs, such as non-tariff special and differential treatment (S&DT), are inefficient in at least four ways: access to S&DT is contingent upon LDCs' institutional capacities, effectiveness may require complimentary policies, some types of S&DT may not respond to LDCs' needs, and many are too vaguely defined to provide real benefits. The role that certain ISMs, such as official development assistance (ODA) played in the graduation of former LDCs aside, UNCTAD (2010, 2016) indicates that current ISMs may be insufficient as far as LDCs' development needs are concerned, particularly in the context of the IPoA target of half the LDCs meeting the graduation criteria by 2020 and the achievement of the Sustainable Development Goals (SDGs) by 2030. Issues that hinder the realisation of ISMs' full potential include vague formulation, weak commitments, insufficient funding and slow implementation. Moreover, LDCs are constrained by weak institutions while strategically leveraging ISMs to pursue their national development and graduation agendas.

Addressing LDCs' diverse needs with broad ISMs is another area of concern. Klasen *et al.* (2016) found that conventional trade preferences have positive effects on LDCs' exports. However, Cornia and Scognamillo (2016) showed that standard LDC support measures are yet to trigger broad-based development and suggested a differentiated approach to identifying policy options that are sensitive to local contexts and patterns of underdevelopment.

Discerning from an eclectic mix

Reviewing the myriad literature on economic growth and development, what strikes is the absence of any one particular school of development thinking that can be explicitly applied to the LDC graduation paradigm. The development paths of LDCs may not match those of currently developed and emerging economies. Their endowment of weak institutions and sub-optimal production structures from colonial legacies led to further underdevelopment traps. What is, however, discernible from theory is that graduation by no account will be the means to an end of a successful development route for LDCs. There is a need for continued transformation of their economic structures. This structural transformation further can be positive or negative for economic growth depending upon its impact on overall productivity growth. Graduation from the LDC category with a smooth transition essentially entails facilitating structural transformation through productivity growth, export diversification, reduction of productivity gaps across sectors, capital formation, labour transition to more productive sectors and productivity-enhancing capacity development. The role of government is critical, specifically adopting effective industrial policies, facilitating domestic policy reforms, creating an enabling environment for capital investment, developing infrastructure, diversifying the economy and effectively utilising available LDC-specific external assistance.

Political reasoning of graduation

The political calculus behind LDC graduation is a significant tool in understanding policy approaches towards graduation. The prospect of graduating from the LDC group boosts a country's self-esteem. The incumbent government is likely to take credit for graduation and any progress that led to it, irrespective of how long the actual process may have taken. In LDCs, there is an opportunity to exploit the information gap among voters regarding the benefits and drawbacks of graduation. The possibility that governments will take advantage of this opportunity cannot be completely disregarded given relatively short terms in power and little time to prove themselves worthy of re-election. Many governments, such as Nepal, Bhutan and even Bangladesh, have developed national strategies that explicitly target graduation by a specified date and political considerations may have come into play (UNCTAD 2016). Indeed, there is nothing wrong with treating graduation as a policy objective, particularly if the process is conducive to structural transformation. Often, however, development efforts with specific targets have the potential to fall short of being sustainable and inclusive.

Notwithstanding pro-graduation stances from a political perspective, many of the structural deficits in developing countries can be attributed to their political economies (McMillan *et al.* 2017). Combining Sen's (2013) three channels through which politics influences economic growth – credible commitment by the state, provision of public goods and overcoming of coordination failures in investment decisions – with Rodrik's (2007) work on industrial policy, McMillan *et al.* (2017) identify four areas where political economy factors negatively affect economic transformation. These are, credibility of commitments to potential investors, limited political time horizons for adequate investment in public goods, insufficient empowerment and motivation of bureaucrats actively partaking in coordination of required policies and private investment and the inability to accommodate 'information externalities' and 'learning costs' as well as an absence of consultation and mutual performance monitoring recommended by industrial policy specialists. The political calculus of graduation has the potential to override economic considerations regarding the costs of graduation. The political economy perspective of an LDC approaching graduation is thus relevant and requires understanding in order to prepare for a smooth transition.

LDC graduation versus becoming an MIC

Confusion is prevalent regarding the concepts of graduating from the LDC group and becoming an MIC. These two different development milestones should be better understood going forward, especially in Bangladesh.

Manifestation of the problem

In Bangladesh, the national development discourse often mistakenly considers LDC graduation and becoming an MIC as interchangeable.[1] Senior level policymakers continue to express their aspiration for the country to join the MIC group by 2021, the fiftieth anniversary of its independence. However, this status was achieved when Bangladesh joined the LMIC category on 1 July 2015. Conversely, graduation from the LDC group is almost certain, but not until 2024, if the country meets all the technical requirements in the coming years. It is not obvious whether inadequate comprehension or just political rhetoric has led to the confusion.

The roots of the ambition to be an MIC can be traced to the publication of Bangladesh Vision 2021 by the Nagorik Committee 2006, convened by the Centre for Policy Dialogue (CPD), one of the leading think tanks in the country, in August 2007. One of the goals in this aspirational document, which emerged from a country-wide consultative process, reads, 'We believe that Bangladesh has the potential to join the ranks of the middle-income countries by 2021' (CPD 2007). The ruling Awami League party's path-breaking election manifesto of 2008 resonated with similar optimism. The Sixth Five Year Plan for the 2011–15 period explicitly targeted the attainment of MIC status by 2021 (Bangladesh Planning Commission 2011).

The issue of Bangladesh graduating from the LDC category did not gain momentum until IPoA in 2011. In fact, Bhattacharya and Borgatti (2012) pioneered the prediction of Bangladesh's graduation using an 'atypical' approach based on the HAI and EVI criteria rather than the income criterion. Since then, LDC graduation and MIC status have often been wrongly equated. While not totally mutually exclusive, the classifications are conceptually very different.

Distinguishing the two concepts

Authority for classification

LDC and income-based classifications differ in terms of the authority responsible for defining them. As mentioned, the CDP of the UN ECOSOC confers LDC status on countries based on the three inclusion and graduation criteria – GNI per capita, the HAI and the EVI – at triennial reviews. The LDC is thus an official UN country classification santioned by the General Assembly.

The World Bank, for its operational lending activities, categorises countries into four groups, namely, low-income country (LIC), LMIC, upper-MIC and high-income country, thresholds for which are updated every year. Such categorisation, which is based solely on income, does not capture countries' structural strengths and weaknesses. Even if a country has high income owing to, for instance, its natural resources, it may still be considered an LDC due to weak social progress or vulnerabilities to external shocks. Moving to a higher income category alone cannot guarantee leaving LDC status. A case in point is Equatorial Guinea which was once a high-income country retaining LDC status that later slid back to the upper-MIC group despite its graduation from the LDC category (World Bank 2017a). Table 2.2 shows how LDCs have undergone changes in their income-based classifications in recent years.

Unlike in the income-based classification where the graduation threshold from one category and inclusion threshold for the next category is continuous, in the LDC classification there is a lag between the graduation thresholds and the inclusion thresholds. This arrangement provides a safety net for countries so that they can avoid sliding back once they have graduated out of the LDC group. The thresholds for the income criterion are updated periodically, while

Table 2.2 Changes in LDCs' income-based classifications over last five CDP review years

Year	LDC	LIC	LMIC	Upper-MIC	High-income country
2006	50	41	8	1	0
2009	49	37	11	0	1
2012	49	30	18	1	1
2015	48	30	15	2	1
2018	47	29	16	2	0

Sources: CDP (2015a) and World Bank (2017a).

Table 2.3 Differences in graduation thresholds for income in the LDCs and income-based classifications over last five CDP review years

Classification	2006	2009	2012	2015	2018
LDC graduation threshold (GNI per capita in US$)	900	1,086	1,190	1,242	1,230
LIC graduation/LMIC inclusion threshold (GNI per capita in US$)	876	976	1,026	1,046	1,025

Source: World Bank (2017a).

the thresholds for the structural indicators that make up the two indices are fixed at the 2012 level.

Even if only the income criterion of the LDC classification and the income-based classification were considered, the thresholds would differ though both classifications use the World Bank's Atlas method to calculate GNI per capita. The graduation threshold of the LDC classification's income criterion is set 20 per cent above the inclusion threshold, which itself is calculated by taking the three-year average of the World Bank's low-income group's upper threshold for the reference years. Table 2.3 presents the LDC graduation income thresholds and the LIC graduation/LMIC inclusion thresholds at the times of the last five triennial reviews.

Benchmark years

As stated before, Bangladesh will likely graduate from the LDC category in 2024 and it achieved the LMIC status in 2015. There are three reasons why the planned objective was achieved before time. These are, revision of the base year to calculate GDP, sustained inflow of remittances and stable exchange rates. When the CPD initially highlighted Bangladesh's potential to join the ranks of MICs by 2021, its predictions were centred on GDP data that had a base year of 1995–96. The Awami League party's subsequent election manifesto was likely based on similar conjectures.

In 2013, however, the base year for GDP calculations in Bangladesh was revised to 2005–06 to better reflect the role of emerging sectors in real economic growth. As a result, GDP growth and GNI per capita estimates were increased by 0.15 per cent and 13 per cent, respectively. CPD's predictions also considered the positive contributions of steady economic growth and exchange rates. Notably, personal remittances grew exponentially between 2005 and 2014 and exchange rates remained stable defying historical trend. The substantial growth in GNI per capita that followed was unforeseen in initial predictions. Thus, Bangladesh crossed the LMIC inclusion threshold of US$1,046 six years earlier than expected. While greatly acknowledged as a milestone everywhere, the achievement did not make it into updated political statements.

Process of graduation

Another difference between LDC graduation and becoming an MIC is the plurality of pathways for the former. There are two ways a country can graduate from the LDC category – meet two out of the three graduation criteria or have GNI per capita that is twice the graduation threshold level (GNI per capita of US$2,460 at the 2018 CDP review).[2] These criteria must be met at two consecutive triennial reviews for CDP to even consider recommending a country for graduation. Decisions are not automatic as country considerations are duly assessed before recommendations are made. Recommendations are further endorsed by the UN ECOSOC and then by the UNGA who set an effective graduation date at least three years later. As such, it takes at least six years for an LDC to graduate after a country has met the criteria for the first time. On the other hand, as long as a country meets the income threshold in a particular year, it is considered an MIC. There is no endorsement process or lag involved, only a statistical exercise.

Finally, a country has the option to refute its LDC status at any point in time. Once identified an LDC, a country has the choice of accepting or rejecting the status (United Nations 1991). Even if it initially accepts LDC status, a country can opt out whenever it wants. Three countries have met the CDP's eligibility criteria for LDC status but refuted it – Ghana, Papua New Guinea and Zimbabwe (CDP and UN DESA 2015). Graduation decisions reside with the CDP, UN ECOSOC and UNGA. Once it is earmarked for graduation, a country does not have a choice but to graduate.[3] As far as income-based classification is concerned, decisions reside with the World Bank.

Strengths and weaknesses

Besides differences in authority for classification, categories, criteria and overall processes, the LDC and income-based classifications differ in their underlying strengths and weaknesses. The income-based classification is fairly easy to understand and simple to measure, notwithstanding the limitations of the Atlas method in determining thresholds (Alonso *et al.* 2014). It also uses the latest information available on a particular country. Nevertheless, it falls short of fully capturing a country's performance and the structural deficits that it faces.

The LDC classification, on the other hand, is grounded by a holistic approach to development that accounts for human assets and exposure to vulnerabilities in addition to income. The length of the process of LDC graduation is an opportunity for countries to adequately prepare for any loss of benefit. Having said that, there are many arguments against the effectiveness of the inclusion criteria for LDCs, specifically pertaining to whether they adequately capture all relevant development issues. For instance, the criteria do not include explicit indicators on structural transformation and vulnerability to climate change. However, they are subject to scrutiny and periodically updated by the CDP in accordance with expert opinion.

Implications of clarifying the confusion for Bangladesh

Arguably, while the purpose of the World Bank's income-based classification is to assess the creditworthiness of a country, the purpose of the UN's LDC classification is to eliminate a country's structural handicaps. Relatively higher costs of external borrowing are an immediate result of becoming an MIC and also there are various costs and benefits associated with LDC graduation that have implications beyond financing. Graduating with momentum and smooth transition after graduation is a major concern for the soon to graduate LDCs, whereas MICs are more likely to be concerned with avoiding what is known as the 'middle-income trap' – the difficulty in maintaining the high rate of growth necessary for convergence with high-income economies. Though, graduated LDCs are also showing tendencies to fall in to the middle-income trap (UNCTAD 2016).

Since Bangladesh cannot graduate from the LDC group before 2024, there is ample time to map and organise efforts to facilitate and support smooth transition in ways that address the country's socio-economic challenges. Forgoing ISMs would prove challenging since the country is among the few LDCs that could effectively utilise many of the ISMs, if not all (Cortez *et al.* 2014). If Bangladesh graduates from the LDC group and loses its many market access-based preferential treatments, the estimated loss of exports could be in the range of 5.5 to 7.5 per cent (UNCTAD 2016), which could amount to a loss of between US$1.8 billion and 2.4 billion.

As far as becoming an MIC is concerned, Bangladesh should be recognised as having achieved that milestone back in 2015, well ahead of the target of 2021. The next milestone along this path would be achieving the upper-MIC status. Towards that end, challenges of curbed concessional flows need to be managed and opportunities of new windows of financial flows that come with improved creditworthiness need to be harnessed.

Nevertheless what the implications of the differences between the two classifications mean for Bangladesh, will affect the policy options that the country should pursue in view of the forthcoming transitions and associated costs. A nuanced understanding of the differences between the two classifications among policymakers, government officials, development partners, civil society and all other stakeholders is imperative to inform policy design and strategic outcomes.

Revisiting the role of governance in the development experience of Bangladesh

Understanding the 'paradox'

To be fair to its development history, Bangladesh too has a colonial past where British rule from 1757 to 1947 was followed by decades of repression under the dominion of Pakistan. The country rebuilt itself as it strived to emerge from physical destruction, impaired institutions and severe destitution in the aftermath of the 1971 war of independence (Mahmud *et al.* 2010). These conditions were compounded by a large population, lack of resources, natural disasters, and enduring weak governance and political uncertainty (Riaz and Rahman 2016). This past endowed the country with weak institutions (Shehabuddin 2016) and a highly 'centralised', 'bureaucratised' and politicised administrative system (Zafarullah 2016), which have created a political culture of patronage and competitive clientelism (Ahmed *et al.* 2014). Faaland and Parkinson (1976) called post-independence Bangladesh a 'test case for development'.

Yet, on the verge of the fiftieth anniversary of its independence, Bangladesh has demonstrated commendable resilience and significant progress across various socio-economic indicators. Over the past 25 years, the average real GDP growth rate has improved and recently reached a peak of over 7 per cent (UNCTAD n.d.). GNI per capita more than quadrupled during this period from US$320 in 1992 to US$1,330 in 2016 (World Bank 2017b) largely due to the influx of private remittances from mostly low-skilled labour migrants (Rahman *et al.* 2014a). Exchange rates have largely remained stable against major currencies since Bangladesh entered the floating exchange rate regime in 2003 (Rahman *et al.* 2014a). The impressive economic performance was accompanied by remarkable achievements in human assets whereby Bangladesh had a higher average annual HDI growth rate between 1990 and 2015 than most of its South Asian counterparts (UNDP 2016). The country has outdone most of its neighbours, including India, with respect to lowering fertility and maternal mortality, maintaining gender equity in primary and secondary schooling, and improving performance in child immunisation (Mahmud *et al.* 2013, ESID 2017). It has the third highest life expectancy at birth of 72.2 years, in South Asia, which is not only higher than the LDC average of 64 years but also the global average of 71.9 years (World Bank 2017b).

Compared to countries with similar levels of income, Bangladesh has fared significantly better across most social indicators (see Asadullah *et al.* 2014). It also achieved many of the targets of the Millennium Development Goals (MDGs), especially in the areas of poverty reduction, gender parity in education and health (Bangladesh Planning Commission 2015), and was one of the top performers among LDCs (Bhattacharya *et al.* 2013). Notably, Bangladesh is recognised as a global leader in disaster management and risk reduction given its substantial reduction of the number of deaths due to natural disasters (UNDP 2011).

Bangladesh's development model has often been described as a 'paradox' or 'surprise' for its achievements given weak governance (World Bank 2007, 2010, Mahmud *et al.* 2010, Ahmed *et al.* 2014, ESID 2017). Indeed, the country has consistently scored poorly on the World Bank's Worldwide Governance Indicators, which measure the quality of governance, and ranked high on Transparency International's Corruption Perception Index – though traditional governance indicators have not been entirely free of criticism as regards their reliability and comparability. The apparent paradox is based on the assumption that good governance and institutions are prerequisites for sustained economic performance (Barro and Lee 1994, Olson *et al.* 2000, Rodrik *et al.* 2004).

Alternative views exist regarding the importance of governance in economic growth and human development. For instance, Khan (2012) points to the non-existent or, at best, weak relationship proven by empirical analyses between improvements in traditional indicators of good governance and augmented economic growth. He rather emphasises developmental governance that is capable of tackling specific problems and enhances growth. Sundaram (2015) also expressed scepticism about governance reforms inducing inclusive growth and development. While some have argued democracy leads to good governance (Stockemer 2009), Bhattacharya *et al.* (2013) found that democracy as practised in Bangladesh had no significant positive effect on economic growth.

Growth and governance interface

Bangladesh is an outlier in cross-country studies that investigate the growth–governance nexus (World Bank 2007 cited in Mahmud *et al.* 2010) and human development–income nexus (Asadullah *et al.* 2014). According to the World Bank (2007), governance in Bangladesh may not be unvaryingly weak in all areas, especially in terms of economic management in important sectors. For instance, successive governments have created an enabling environment for the private sector to thrive, migrants to remit and effective partnerships to be maintained with non-government organisations (NGOs) to support government social service delivery. Since independence, political divide among major political parties did not manifest in diverging economic policies and were more or less based on similar ideologies of promoting the private sector and developing an open market (Khatun 2016). Policies adopted under different governments have been consistent with regard to development of human assets, expansion of export-oriented industries, growth in the agriculture sector and expansion of physical infrastructure. In the late 1970s, deregulation in the agriculture sector promoted private sector involvement especially in distribution of agricultural inputs and outputs. During the same time, technological innovation in rice production and market oriented policy reforms that promoted adoption of high yielding varieties largely translated into agricultural productivity growth (Khatun 2016). The national development plans in Bangladesh even before the MDGs were adopted, had high policy priority areas that were later found to be relevant to the MDGs (Rahman *et al.* 2014b).

Ahmed *et al.* (2014) explained Bangladesh's so-called paradoxical development specifically in the context of export growth linked to its thriving ready-made garment (RMG) industry. The industry's growth can be attributed to 'non-interventionist' and 'decentralised' industrial policies combined with a preference for privatisation and export-led economic growth, which have remained more or less stable across changing political regimes that have mostly diverged on nationalist sentiments, rather than economic policies and ideologies. Corruption in Bangladesh, albeit high, has been predictable, which makes any associated costs manageable and, as such, less of a bottleneck for growth and investment (Kang 2002, Malesky and Samphantharak 2008). Collier (2007) believed that Bangladesh is 'a classic case of a resource-scarce, coastal, low-income country' that capitalised on labour-intensive manufacturing exports – such export growth may not require much governance so long as the external environment is favourable. Foreign direct investments (FDIs) from South Korea were instrumental in introducing Bangladesh's RMG industry to international markets, the first of which was an indirect result of a trade preference Bangladesh enjoyed as an LDC. Moreover, LDC-specific ISMs in the form of preferential market access has been significant in retaining the growth momentum in RMG exports (Cortez *et al.* 2014).

Export-oriented growth, predominantly led by the RMG industry, is also identified as one of the major sources of Bangladesh's development 'surprise' by Mahmud *et al.* (2010). The other sources identified are micro and small enterprises in manufacturing and services as well as remittances from migrant workers. Aside from a favourable external environment, low-cost female labour has played a role in steering the RMG industry to prosperity. Besides significant contributions to GDP, the RMG industry has been an avenue for female empowerment in Bangladesh. Not only has women's bargaining power at home increased as a result of their financial contributions to their households, but their newfound 'voice' (Kabeer and Mahmud 2004) has led to household expenditure decisions in favour of education (Ahmed *et al.* 2014). Notably, new jobs in garment factories were found to be positively associated with the schooling of girls in rural Bangladesh (Heath and Mobarak 2011). Increased female empowerment and gender equity also improve health outcomes. Indeed, the use of woman-mediated channels has been one of the key reasons for successful programme delivery by NGOs in the health and education sectors (Chowdhury *et al.* 2013).

From a comparative perspective, Asadullah *et al.* (2014) found that Bangladesh performed significantly worse historically in terms of quality of governance compared to countries with similar levels of income, though better in terms of social development outcomes. Not surprisingly, governance was found to have made limited contributions to progress in social indicators. If anything, weak governance has likely hindered the effectiveness of already low social expenditure. According to the authors, development has been the result of simultaneous efforts by governments, development partners and especially national and international NGOs. These organisations have been instrumental in bridging gaps in government social service delivery and raising awareness of the importance of health and education.

Governance and LDC graduation

None of the three criteria for LDC graduation includes indicators that directly gauge governance, though proponents of good governance may argue that the issue is embedded by default as a precondition for progress on indicators that are included. There is no straightforward answer as to why the CDP has refrained from accommodating specific indicators for governance in the identification of LDCs. Besides the challenges of measurement and the scepticism surrounding the World Bank's index, one possibility could be that governance is seen as an internal matter that either cannot be redeemed by external support or does not require external judgement. Guillaumont (2011) asserted that the purpose of LDC classification is to tackle structural issues rather than problems arising from misguided policies. Moreover, the income-only graduation criterion is based on the underlying assumption that a country can fund its own human development and protection against external shocks when its GNI per capita is high enough. Bhattacharya and Borgatti (2012) pointed out that this assumption, inadvertently or not, overlooks governance issues.

So, is governance relevant to LDC graduation? Bangladesh seems to have progressed remarkably and has met all three graduation criteria in spite of scoring low in 'good governance' indicators. However, a country cannot be complacent about graduation – it must be concerned about sustaining progress through structural transformation. The IPoA identified 'good governance at all levels' as one of the priority areas in its call for greater structural transformation in LDCs and emphasised development of productive capacities. If Bangladesh were a country characterised by good quality of governance, development outcomes to date may have been better (Collier 2007, Asadullah *et al.* 2014).

Another issue to consider is the inclusivity of Bangladesh's economic growth. Between 2010 and 2016, both income inequality and wealth inequality rose owing to the poor getting poorer and the rich getting richer (CPD 2018). Dahlman and Mealy (2016) demonstrated that the country's economic growth has not resulted in commensurate growth in employment. The unemployment rate among youth was 11.4 per cent in 2016 (ILO 2017). There is dearth of skills and productivity levels required for high value added activities. The quality of mainstream education is low and school attendance hardly contributes to the development of human assets. Sobhan (2010) identified access to quality education as probably the fastest growing source of inequity within and among countries, with particular reference to South Asia. A private–public divide in the education system has been increasingly granting quality education to the few 'elites' and leaving the poor perpetually undereducated and less skilled. Asadullah *et al.* (2014) attributed the gap in quality to governance problems in the education sector and argued that the inadequate quality of governance and education will be a hindrance to realising the country's potential to enter a virtuous cycle, as envisioned by Ranis (2009).

In theory, governance may not be a necessary condition for LDC graduation, but to sustain momentum beyond graduation, improvement is essential in the applied governance model. The general postulates of such a model include strong institutional oversight, rule of law, independent judiciary, open media and peoples' participation in decision-making processes. Rahman and Bari (2016) identified governance, strengthened institutions, rule of law, transparency and accountability, enhanced productivity and efficiency, structural transformation, and distributive justice among factors important for Bangladesh to maintain its growth momentum and avoid the middle-income trap. According to Collier (2007), as an economy becomes more sophisticated and aims to move up the global value chain, primitive institutional set-ups may prove to be serious obstacles. Improvement in productivity requires governance in the areas of information and communication technology (ICT) infrastructure and domestic resource mobilisation (UN-OHRLLS 2016). Bangladesh's export-led growth has thus far been reasonably successful in boosting social development outcomes. However, exports remain highly concentrated in a few low value added products and markets remain undiversified. A valid concern is whether Bangladesh would be exhausting all space for growth. Economic growth may not remain high and stable without institutional and policy reforms. Unless governance efforts are consolidated in the different sectors of Bangladesh's economy to enhance labour productivity and facilitate structural transformation, the issue of governance will remain relevant to the country as an LDC especially in the absence of ISMs following graduation.

A comparative perspective on Bangladesh's graduation outlook

Bangladesh was included in the LDC category back in 1975, four years after its independence, after much deliberation by the CDP. The country had to fight its way into the category despite meeting all the inclusion criteria, except the implicit criteria of being a small country (Bangladesh had a relatively large population of 78 million at the time). It was eventually included in the category considering its technical eligibility and additional development constraints imposed by natural disasters and overpopulation (Islam 2003). Decades later, it remains an LDC. The country met the graduation criteria for the first time in 2018 with a GNI per capita of US$1,274, HAI of 73.2 and EVI of 25.2 (the lowest among the LDCs, i.e. the least vulnerable to external shocks).

As mentioned earlier, Bangladesh's graduation is set in a backdrop of new found optimism surrounding the overall outlook for the group of LDCs. Currently, the number of LDCs stands at 47. Sixteen countries, including Bangladesh, were projected to graduate between 2017 and 2024 (UNCTAD 2016).[4] Of these: Equatorial Guinea graduated in 2017; Vanuatu and Angola have been earmarked for graduation in 2020 and 2021 respectively; Tuvalu, Nepal and Timor-Leste are still under review for recommendations despite having met graduation criteria in more than one triennial review; Bhutan, Kiribati, São Tomé and Príncipe, and the Solomon Islands have been recommended for graduation; and Bangladesh, Lao PDR and Myanmar met eligibility for the first time in 2018. The remaining countries – Afghanistan, Djibouti and Yemen – are yet to meet eligibility, contrary to UNCTAD's predictions.

A number of LDCs have made graduation from the LDC group an explicit target in their national development plans. Bhutan and Nepal established clear objectives and timelines for graduation criteria in their respective plans. Cambodia, Laos and Myanmar also included clear timelines for graduation in their national plans. Many of these countries have initiated exchange of views with former LDCs to assess the impacts of graduation in terms of loss of ODA and trade preferences. African LDCs such as Ethiopia, Rwanda, Tanzania and Uganda have expressed aspirations to attain MIC status in their national plans, which could translate into leaving the LDC group. These national plans commonly envision fostering economic growth, eradicating poverty, realising structural transformation and diversifying economies (United Nations 2015).

Comparison of Bangladesh with co-graduating countries

Comparing Bangladesh's performance on various economic indicators with those of countries that graduated or are likely to graduate between 2015 and 2024 can be insightful. Table 2.4 compares the performances of Bangladesh and co-graduating countries on graduation criteria at the 2018 CDP review. Considering the proximities to graduation thresholds, Bangladesh seems to have the most balanced accomplishments across all three criteria, followed by Myanmar. Graduating oil-exporting African LDCs and SIDS, despite having very high income, either lag behind in terms of their human development or vulnerability to shocks.

Bangladesh's real GDP has been growing favourably. The country is the only one among its graduating peers that has experienced an increase in average GDP growth rate between the periods 2005–10 and 2011–16 (see Table 2.5). Despite being one of the largest recipients of ODA among LDCs, Bangladesh's dependence on ODA has been rather low compared to its Asian counterparts and SIDS. Any loss in ODA as a result of graduation from the LDC group is thus likely to have minimal impact for the country. In terms of volume, Bangladesh has also been one of the largest beneficiaries of remittances regardless of a

Table 2.4 Performances of graduating LDCs at the 2018 CDP review

Graduating LDC	Graduation criteria (threshold)		
	GNI per capita (>US$1,230)	HAI (>66.0)	EVI (<32.0)
Bangladesh	US$1,274	73.2	25.2
Bhutan	US$2,401	72.9	36.3
Lao PDR	US$1,996	72.8	33.7
Myanmar	US$1,255	68.5	31.7
Nepal	US$745	68.7	26.8
Graduating oil-exporting African LDCs	US$7,071	55.9	32.3
Graduating SIDS	US$2,915	80	54.4

Source: CDP (n.d.).

Note
Angola and Equatorial Guinea are oil-exporting African LDCs. Kiribati, São Tomé and Príncipe, the Solomon Islands, Timor-Leste, Tuvalu and Vanuatu are SIDS.

Table 2.5 Trends in GDP growth, ODA, remittances and FDI of graduating LDCs

Graduating LDC	GDP growth (%)		ODA (% of GNI)		Remittance (% of GDP)		FDI (% of GDP)	
	Average (2005–10)	Average (2011–16)	Average (2005–10)	Average (2011–16)	Average (2006–10)	Average (2011–15)	Average (2005–10)	Average (2011–16)
Bangladesh	6.05	6.45	1.59	1.30	9.05	9.15	0.99	1.28
Bhutan	9.17	5.91	9.47	6.83	0.34	0.78	2.34	1.09
Lao PDR	7.92	7.64	9.22	3.79	0.37	0.66	4.61	5.49
Myanmar	11.60	7.00	1.09	2.51	0.35	0.89	2.47	4.25
Nepal	4.29	3.68	5.67	4.69	19.89	27.52	0.14	0.38
Graduating oil- exporting African LDCs	8.06	1.21	0.57	0.17	0.04	0.01	3.50	1.64
Graduating SIDS	6.70	2.93	24.55	25.30	6.55	6.15	8.01	3.81

Sources: authors' calculations based on data from UNCTAD (n.d.) and World Bank (2017b).

sharp decline in 2015. In terms of the contribution of remittances to GDP, the country lags behind Nepal but outperforms other co-graduating countries.

Further, Bangladesh is a small recipient of FDI with relatively little contributions to GDP over the years (see Table 2.5). The country is also a poor performer with respect to mobilising domestic resources. It has one of the lowest tax–GDP ratios in the world, let alone among LDCs. Between 2004 and 2014, average tax revenue as a per cent of GDP for Bangladesh was 8 per cent as opposed to 11 per cent, 13 per cent, 12 per cent, 15 per cent and 39 per cent for Bhutan, Lao PDR, Nepal, graduating oil-exporting African LDCs and graduating SIDS, respectively (World Bank 2017b). The average for the external resource gap has increased over time in Bangladesh, with the average for gross fixed capital formation increasing at a higher rate than increase in average gross domestic savings (Annex Table 2.a.1).

Balance of payments in LDCs are often seen as constraints to their growth (UNCTAD 2016, Thirlwall 1979). Bangladesh and Nepal are the only two graduating Asian LDCs with current account surpluses – averages of 1 per cent and 4.1 per cent of GDP, respectively, between 2011 and 2016. During the same period, graduating oil-exporting African LDCs' current account balance was an average deficit of 0.65 per cent of GDP. Deficits in Bhutan are alarming and amount to around 26 per cent of GDP (UNCTAD n.d.). In this context, even Bangladesh's small surplus may be an optimistic indicator of sustainability beyond graduation from the LDC group.

A look at trends in sectoral shares of total value added and employment in graduating LDCs indicates that the manufacturing sector has been more dominant in Bangladesh and Myanmar than other co-graduating countries (Annex Table 2.a.2). Bangladesh had the highest estimated average share of employment in the manufacturing sector in the period 2011–16. The shares of both manufacturing and services in total value added increased in Bangladesh over time, albeit marginally. In Nepal, the share of manufacturing in total value added and share of employment decreased between 2005–10 and 2011–16, while the share of agriculture increased. Productivity estimates for workers or output per worker have also been slightly higher in Bangladesh than Nepal. Nevertheless, Bangladesh is estimated to have one of the least productive labour forces among graduating LDCs (ILO 2017).

Bangladesh lags behind all of its Asian counterparts, especially Nepal, in terms of export diversification. Bangladesh has had an estimated average export concentration index of 0.41 between 2011 and 2016 compared to Nepal's average index of 0.14 for the same period (UNCTAD n.d.). Diversification is essential to protect against shocks. For Bangladesh, diversifying exports is a matter of concern in view of the loss of preferential market access that will follow graduation from the LDC category. Bangladesh's RMG industry, a major beneficiary of LDC-specific international support, comprises approximately 81 per cent of the country's exports (EPB 2017).

Although the analysis above depicts that Bangladesh is positively situated among its peers across major economic indicators like growth, remittances, current account balances, gross fixed capital formation and prominence of the manufacturing sector, there are certain areas that need attention. The country needs to attract more FDIs and mobilise more domestic resources in view of its increasing external resource gap. To be able to have a smooth transition towards a sustainable graduation ensued by positive structural transformation, exports need to be more diversified and productivity of the labour force needs to be significantly improved.

Learning from former LDCs

Out of the five former LDCs, Botswana, Cape Verde, the Maldives and Samoa graduated by meeting thresholds for GNI per capita and HAI (or the Augmented Physical Quality of life criteria used before 2002), while Equatorial Guinea met the income-only criterion. The four countries that graduated from the LDC category before 2015, besides being LDCs, were either landlocked or SIDS. All four countries graduated on the basis of the income and HAI criteria, albeit maintaining high scores on the EVI. To date, all former LDCs have avoided sliding back into the LDC category. Table 2.6 presents former LDCs' trends in graduation criteria since the 2009 CDP review. Improvements are apparent across the board.

Useful insights can also be gained from comparing where Bangladesh would stand in terms of key economic indicators a few years before its final graduation, with where former LDCs (except Equatorial Guinea) stood before their own[5] graduation (see Table 2.7). While Bangladesh's real GDP growth over the past five years is comparable with that of Cape Verde before its graduation, Bangladesh's growth is slower compared to what it had been for Botswana and the Maldives. Bangladesh is also relatively better off in terms of its current account and merchandise exports (as a share of world trade), though relatively worse off in terms of FDI (as a share of GDP) and tax–GDP ratio.

Post-graduation developments in former LDCs are quite instructive in drawing lessons for Bangladesh (Table 2.7). Curiously, following graduation, real GDP growth slowed down for almost all former LDCs (except Samoa) which reinforces the need for smooth transition efforts to avoid economic shocks and stagnation. ODA as a per cent of GNI and remittances as per cent of GDP also fell in all former LDCs after graduation. Changes in pre-graduation levels of current account balances, tax–GDP ratio and share of world merchandise exports varied across countries. However, FDI as a per cent of GDP invariably increased across countries, which may be as a result of improved investor confidence associated with leaving the LDC status behind.

Looking at sectoral compositions, it is apparent that the contribution of agriculture in total value added and in employment (except Botswana) declined in the LDCs after graduation (Annex Table 2.a.3). Bangladesh has a relatively higher, though declining, dependence on agriculture compared to what former LDCs had before their graduation. On the other hand, the country has a favourably higher share of manufacturing in total value added and employment

Table 2.6 Trends in graduation criteria since 2009 CDP reviews among former LDCs

Former LDC	EVI				HAI				GNI per capita (in US$)			
	2009	2012	2015	2018	2009	2012	2015	2018	2009	2012	2015	2018
Botswana	57.3	43	43.4	45.5	70.6	73.5	75.9	79.0	5,627	6,513	7,410	6,845
Cape Verde	48.1	35.2	38.8	35.9	81.9	86.8	88.6	89.5	2,180	3,110	3,595	3,161
Maldives	58.2	55.2	49.9	50.9	87.5	91.7	91.3	91.4	2,940	5,473	6,645	9,200
Samoa	64.7	51.1	44	39.7	92.2	92.8	94.4	94.1	2,240	2,880	3,319	4,124
Equatorial Guinea	60.5	43.7	39.3	27.8	49.5	43.0	54.8	58.4	8,957	15,090	16,089	9,665

Source: CDP (n.d.).

Table 2.7 Changes in key indicators of former LDCs and comparison with Bangladesh

Country	Reference year	Real GDP growth (%)	Current account (% of GDP)	FDI (% of GDP)	ODA (% of GNI)	Remittances (% of GDP)	Tax revenue (% of GDP)	Merchandise exports (% of world trade)
Botswana	Before graduation (5 years)	10.55	7.78	-0.66	3.67	2.01	26.15	0.0510
	After graduation (5 years)	5.05	7.93	1.32	2.06	1.16	17.21	0.0430
Cape Verde	Before graduation (5 years)	6.18	-8.50	6.66	15.92	13.14	21.91	0.0002
	After graduation (5 years)	3.89	-13.74	10.46	14.04	8.64	20.20	0.0003
Maldives	Before graduation (5 years)	9.09	-16.67	7.83	3.08	0.26	11.56	0.0020
	After graduation (4/5 years)	7.40	-8.14	12.14	1.70	0.12	18.47	0.0020
Samoa	Before graduation (5 years)	0.43	-4.70	1.73	16.44	21.05	20.68	0.0004
	After graduation (1/2 years)	1.53	-5.90	2.41	11.98	18.91	23.06	0.0003
Bangladesh	Average (2011–16)	6.45	0.93	1.28	1.30	9.15	8.76	0.1663

Sources: authors' calculations based on data from UNCTAD (n.d.) and World Bank (2017b).

compared to former LDCs. In terms of structural change, Bangladesh may thus be exhibiting better trends. The trends also indicate that graduation does not necessarily ensure structural transformation.

Pre- and post-graduation experiences

None of these former LDCs were typical LDCs. Compared to Bangladesh, they are structurally quite different in terms of their geographical constraints, sparse populations, dependence on ODA and other factors that make them vulnerable. As such, their graduation experiences may not necessarily be comparable to Bangladesh's trajectory. Nevertheless, understanding former LDCs' policy approaches towards graduation and strategies for smooth transition can be helpful for Bangladesh.

Samoa first met the LDC graduation criteria in 1991 and graduated from the LDC category almost 23 years later in 2014. This trajectory can be attributed to government policies that increased productive capacities in the labour-intensive agriculture sector and high value added services sector. A national strategy that promoted diversification in agriculture was formulated. Efforts were made to combine local production with commercial investment and improve food security (UNCTAD 2016). Recognising the potential of the tourism industry, the Samoan government also invested heavily in supporting infrastructure and promotion. FDI was channelled towards the development of hotels. The government was proactive in managing ODA through well-defined leadership and ownership of its development agenda. Donors were required to align ODA with policy interventions that already existed in national plans. During the three years preceding graduation, on average 54.8 per cent of ODA was allocated towards social infrastructure development and 35.6 per cent was directed towards economic infrastructure development (UNCTAD 2016). A conducive environment for private sector investment prevailed in the country due to prudent investment and fiscal policies. Utilities, infrastructure and access to ICT were improved and the costs of doing business were reduced, especially in rural areas. Like in other former LDCs, the government emphasised the development of education and health care. Disaster preparedness and climate change mitigation were mainstreamed in national plans.

Post-graduation lessons from Samoa are limited because only a short time has elapsed since the country graduated and the effects of graduation may not be fully apparent until after the smooth transition phase. Apart from duty-free access to the European Union (EU) for three years, the country's government negotiated a similar transition period for certain key products with other trading partners, such as zero-tariff access for noni juice and other agro-processing products with China until 2017. The International Monetary Fund (IMF) classified the country as being at high risk of debt distress in 2013 (2013 cited in CDP 2016). The country's high economic and environmental vulnerabilities make it prone to widening fiscal deficits. Implementation of the government's Medium Term Debt Management Strategy for the 2013–15 period to reverse trends in the debt–GDP ratio and fiscal deficits was successful, with the risk status being revised to moderate in 2015. Also, bilateral ODA flows to Samoa were maintained at 2014 levels or had increased in some cases, while remittances were stable and increasing (CDP 2016).

The Maldives was the third country to graduate from the LDC category following boosts to its tourism industry and an average real GDP growth rate of 10 per cent between 1977 and 2003. The country was initially earmarked for graduation in 2007, but the 2004 tsunami delayed graduation until 2011 (CDP 2012a). A structural shift towards the services sector, especially tourism, during the 1980s contributed largely to economic growth. The First Tourism Master Plan, which was formulated in 1983, laid the foundation for the sustainable development of the industry by emphasising environmental protection and the integration of tourism into the social and economic development of the country (Kundur 2012). Government incentives in the shape of low taxes and rents successfully attracted foreign private sector actors, which partially drove growth. Tourism stimulated infrastructure development, especially in terms of transportation and communication facilities. Employment opportunities were generated in many areas including tourism-related construction (Kundur 2012). The Maldivian government also focused on improving education and health care. The country allocated on average 36.4 per cent of ODA towards social infrastructure development and 37.4 per cent towards economic infrastructure development during the three years preceding graduation (UNCTAD 2016).

The Maldivian government was preemptive in its preparation for the post-graduation period. Besides retaining its European Everything But Arms (EBA) privilege and access to Enhanced Integrated Framework funds for three years, it benefited from an additional two years of partial funding from the Enhanced Integrated Framework on a project basis. The country's graduation was also 'instrumental' in the negotiation of the UNGA resolution that allowed extension of travel benefits to international meetings for three years beyond graduation (CDP 2014). Immediately after graduation, the Maldives encountered an economic slowdown prompted by the weak European economy and a subsequent decline in tourism revenue, with economic growth not picking up until after 2013 (CDP 2014, 2015b). Improved performance of the fishing industry and manufacturing sector as well as an influx of tourists from China in 2013 played parts in the recovery. The EU and Japan, two major donors to the Maldives, did not reduce ODA to the country after graduation, but plan to redirect more towards areas related to climate change. This decision would add budgetary pressures on the government to maintain the education and health sectors, which benefit most from ODA. The country was also immediately subject to preference erosion in Japan for its tuna exports after graduation in 2011. Imports by Japan declined in 2012 but significantly increased the following year, so the impact of higher tariffs was not significant. With preference erosion in Europe in 2014, the country did not see a major shift in tuna exports (CDP 2015b).

Cape Verde met the graduation criteria for the first time in 1994, though graduated from the LDC category 13 years later in 2007 due to structural vulnerabilities and dependence on ODA. Long-term national development strategies facilitated the country's progress by promoting economic transformation and poverty reduction. In the early 1990s, major structural reforms of the economy were targeted towards privatisation and trade liberalisation. Since 1996 private investment as a share of total investment has been exceeding 50 per cent (AfDB 2012). In 2003, the Economic Transformation Strategy that envisioned graduation from an LDC to an emerging economy was introduced (OECD and WTO 2010). National planning and revenue collection were improved with the introduction of an integrated system for budget and financial management in 2002 (UNCTAD 2016). A prosperous tourism industry boosted the competitiveness of the country's services sector and helped it integrate into the global economy. ODA and remittances also played a crucial role in the country's development. During the three years preceding graduation, on average 48.5 per cent of ODA was allocated towards social infrastructure development and 34.5 per cent was allocated towards economic infrastructure development (UNCTAD 2016). FDI also increased from 1.6 per cent of GDP in 2001 to 13.8 per cent in 2008 (OECD and WTO 2010). The Cape Verde government devoted substantial resources to education and health care during the period 1980–2010 amounting to, on average, around 16.7 per cent and 10.1 per cent of GDP respectively (AfDB 2012).

The Cape Verde government was aware of the consequences of losing LDC status in terms of forgoing support measures and phasing out development aid. In 2006, it established a Transition Support Group as a means to ensure smooth transition from the LDC category. It also negotiated a two-year extension on top of the standard practice of a three-year grace period under the EBA initiative. Cape Verde continued to perform well beyond graduation, though its pace slowed down owing to the global financial crisis and subsequent decline in tourism revenue. The government adopted counter-cyclical measures based on expansionary fiscal policies in response, but fiscal and current account deficits as well as the debt–GDP ratio increased as a result. As such, debt sustainability became a matter of concern. According to the IMF, the country's risk of debt distress changed from low to moderate. On the positive side, it qualified for the EU's enhanced Generalised System of Preferences plus (GSP plus) trade scheme in 2011 (CDP 2012b).

Botswana was the first country to graduate from the LDC category in 1994. While the country's success can, in part, be attributed to its luck of discovering substantial deposits of diamonds, a combination of prudent policies to capitalise on mineral resources, good governance, respect for the rule of law, effective macroeconomic policies to stimulate growth and adequate investment in human capital ensured a path towards graduation and sustainable development (Lewin 2011, Bose and Bose 2011, UNCTAD 2016). The country seems to have avoided the so-called 'resource curse'. Instead of conceding to the politics of rent seeking, corruption or efficiency losses, the government adopted effective industrial policies that resulted in private sector-oriented development of the mining sector. In 2000, over 70 per cent of the profits generated by the country's diamond industry were paid to the government, with this single industry contributing 60 per cent of total tax revenue (Hazleton 2002). Since the 1970s, the government revenue–GDP ratio averaged 50 per cent, resulting in budget surpluses. The government effectively channelled ODA into national development priorities through proactive engagement with development partners (UNCTAD 2016). It also devoted an increasing share of its budget to raising education standards, which increased school enrolment rates.

Following graduation, Botswana's economic growth slowed down from a five-year average of approximately 10.6 per cent to 5 per cent, but maintained large current account surpluses (UNCTAD n.d.). While FDI as a per cent of GDP increased, ODA as a per cent of GNI as well as remittances as a per cent of GDP decreased marginally. Tax revenue also decreased from an average of 26 per cent to 17 per cent (World Bank 2017b). Of the four former LDCs, Botswana managed its external debts after graduation most effectively. After years of stable debt levels, the government successfully brought down its external debt to an average of 15–17 per cent of GNI since 2008 through good planning and management.

Good practices and lessons

From former LDCs' experiences, good practices and lessons can be identified for the benefit of graduating countries. As far as pre-graduation experiences are concerned, the governments of former LDCs may not have explicitly targeted graduation as a goal, but rather began strategising when graduation was on the horizon. For most former LDCs, governance – prudent policies and improved management – was particularly strong in the run-up to transitions to non-LDC developing country status, which in turn translated into macroeconomic stability and prevailing environments that were conducive for private and foreign investment. Structural shifts towards productive and high value added industries were evident. Domestic resources were also duly mobilised. Governments were arguably successful in aligning LDC-specific benefits and ODA with national priorities. Infrastructure development and capital formation followed and sufficient efforts were made towards improving public education and health care. As a result, income increased and human assets improved significantly. Lastly, the governments were proactive in negotiating graduation-related terms and conditions before graduating.

Judging by former LDCs' post-graduation experiences, graduating does not guarantee a smooth transition. There are many formidable challenges that governments must manage to make transition as smooth as possible. Early negotiations with bilateral and multilateral trading partners on phasing out benefits following graduation are critical for facilitating transitions out of the LDC group. Experiences suggest that the identification of alternative financing is essential, especially alternative types of preferential access and concessional finance. Continued engagement with development partners can be useful in this regard. Further, former LDCs had difficulties in managing external debt – keeping both fiscal and current account deficits in check is important. Finally, strengthening regulatory frameworks is crucial for post-graduation stability and prosperity.

Concluding observations

Bangladesh, which is expected soon to graduate from the LDC category, has had an extraordinary developmental journey. Unlike countries that already graduated, it has a sizeable population and an expanding economy and does not have geographical constraints – it is neither a landlocked developing country nor SIDS. Bangladesh will likely be one of the first countries to graduate by meeting all three graduation criteria – the GNI per capita, the HAI and the EVI. As it approaches LDC graduation, the country should be acknowledged as already being an LMIC. The case of Bangladesh's journey towards becoming a non-LDC developing country can have significant appeal beyond domestic stakeholders. Concepts and comparative perspectives presented in this chapter can be used towards a universal approach to LDC graduation. As such, the concluding observations that follow are key takeaways arranged according to the research questions posed at the outset of the chapter.

A wide-ranging survey of relevant literature revealed that instead of an explicit theoretical framework underpinning the graduation paradigm, an eclectic mix of various schools of thought on growth and development informs the process. Indeed, the rationale for and determinants of LDC graduation are related to structuralist approaches, but go beyond neoliberal approaches to embrace heterodox thinking. Some of the common tenets of the approaches pertinent to LDCs are the need for positive structural change, productivity growth, capital investment and the enabling role of governments and institutions. Progress in terms of structural transformation, understood as the large-scale movement towards relatively more productive non-agricultural activities in the manufacturing and services sectors, is often used as a metric that can predict smooth transition from the LDC group.

Graduation from the LDC category is often confused with transition to MIC status, which can result in ineffective national planning and strategising. The two classifications differ in terms of parameters and motivations. Arguably, the UN's LDC classification is much more comprehensive than the World Bank's income-based classification in terms of scope and has the underlying objective of addressing countries' structural handicaps. The policy options for each country, especially one like Bangladesh that is transitioning through two development milestones, will vary. While there are a few LDCs in the high-income country group, most LDCs are part of the LIC group and must keep in focus the commonalities and differences in the policy challenges posed by separate transition processes.

Bangladesh's case also highlights the relevance of governance-related issues for structural transformation and LDC graduation, which does not involve any governance-related criteria. The country's apparently paradoxical development trajectory indicates that GNI per capita can be increased and structural indicators can be improved without discernible progress towards good governance. Acrimonious domestic politics aside, the national development agenda catalysed the emergence of RMG exports, growth in agricultural output fuelled by liberalisation, agri-input distribution, enhanced emphasis on education and expansion of the safety net for vulnerable segments of the population. Simultaneous efforts by the government, the private sector, national and international NGOs and development partners have been instrumental in achieving remarkable social development outcomes in the country. Still, economic growth has been largely non-inclusive and characterised by rising income and asset inequality. Bangladesh's experience demonstrates that economic growth is possible without governance-related reforms, but the quality of that growth may be inadequate. Governance is a missing key factor in LDC graduation parameters, one that is fundamental to a country's structural transformation and sustainable development.

A comparison with co-graduating countries provides insights regarding the areas where Bangladesh has done relatively well and where results have been inadequate. Bangladesh has outperformed co-graduating countries in various areas, but has lagged in others. While it is relatively less dependent on ODA, the country has not significantly improved domestic revenue mobilisation or attracted FDI. As far as structural change is concerned, the country has fared better in terms of increasing the share of value added manufacturing in GDP and the export basket. Nevertheless, labour productivity remains mediocre and exports remain highly concentrated in a few apparel products, which are negative indicators of structural transformation. An important takeaway for Bangladesh from the cross-country comparisons is the need to invest in enhancing productive capacities and promoting the skill set of the young labour force, which would not only facilitate the country's move up the global value chain, but also diversify the export basket for new markets.

Finally, Bangladesh can draw on the important lessons that emerged from the review of policy approaches towards graduation pursued by former LDCs, which also highlighted certain post-graduation challenges. Strong governance stands out as a key factor in graduation and smooth transition, with priorities being appropriate policies that promote prudent macroeconomic management, an enabling investment climate, investment in quality human assets, aptly aligned ODA disbursements and proactive management of trade relations affected by graduation. Post-graduation challenges include accessing alternative types of concessional finance, continuing engagement with development partners and cautiously managing external debt as well as fiscal and current account deficits.

Graduation from the LDC category is the beginning of another journey, the success of which is predicated on the quality of the transition process. A strategic outlook in this regard is essential when designing policy and institutional interventions. Such interventions should be adequately informed by trends at the global level and lead to positive structural change at the national level. While the promises of graduation can be uplifting for an LDC, the associated pitfalls remain quite real. Creative, coherent and contextualised national policymaking must address formidable global challenges, specifically those identified in the 2030 Agenda for Sustainable Development that promises to leave no one behind. Keeping the global level in view may open up new horizons for global partnership in favour of LDCs.

Annex

Table 2.a.1 Trends in gross fixed capital formation, gross domestic savings and external resource gaps as per cent of GDP in graduating LDCs

Graduating LDC	Gross fixed capital formation		Gross domestic savings		External resource gap	
	Average (2005–10)	Average (2011–16)	Average (2005–10)	Average (2011–16)	Average (2005–10)	Average (2011–16)
Bangladesh	25.92	28.53	20.42	22.18	–5.50	–6.35
Bhutan	46.64	57.55	38.61	32.94	–8.03	–24.61
Lao PDR	30.68	27.06	22.70	16.58	–7.98	–10.48
Myanmar	16.41	31.64	18.18	31.26	1.77	–0.37
Nepal	21.20	24.18	10.18	10.08	–11.02	–14.10
Graduating oil-exporting African LDCs	31.55	27.95	60.35	45.44	28.80	17.49
Graduating SIDS	29.38	25.73	5.33	6.78	–24.06	–18.96

Source: authors' calculations using data from UNCTAD (n.d.).

Table 2.a.2 Shares of total value added and employment by sector (%) in graduating LDCs

Graduating LDC	Reference Year	Agriculture		Industry		Manufacturing		Services	
		Share of total value added	Share of employment	Share of total value added	Share of employment	Share of total value added	Share of employment	Share of total value added	Share of employment
Bangladesh	Average (2005–10)	18.67	48.07	26.15	15.70	16.74	11.57	55.18	36.27
	Average (2011–16)	16.21	44.83	27.48	19.80	17.28	14.67	56.31	35.35
Bhutan	Average (2005–10)	19.96	65.53	42.31	6.27	8.30	3.52	37.72	28.22
	Average (2011–16)	17.26	58.37	43.58	9.83	8.61	6.03	39.16	31.85
Lao PDR	Average (2005–10)	26.55	75.62	28.59	6.63	10.84	4.17	44.86	17.75
	Average (2011–16)	20.17	65.42	32.95	9.30	9.62	5.47	46.89	25.32
Myanmar	Average (2005–10)	41.53	65.17	21.80	13.15	16.07	9.35	36.67	21.70
	Average (2011–16)	28.75	54.92	33.32	16.02	20.48	10.80	37.93	29.08
Nepal	Average (2005–10)	33.56	75.13	16.36	6.42	7.27	0.27	50.08	18.50
	Average (2011–16)	33.69	73.40	14.83	7.70	6.15	0.20	51.48	18.92
Graduating oil-exporting African LDCs	Average (2005–10)	3.32	47.51	67.20	8.48	9.25	2.73	29.48	44.03
	Average (2011–16)	4.41	52.48	57.97	8.52	12.04	2.68	37.62	39.06
Graduating SIDS	Average (2005–10)	20.18	53.93	22.91	9.80	3.98	4.67	56.91	36.30
	Average (2011–16)	19.98	47.90	22.83	10.71	4.29	4.87	57.19	41.42

Sources: authors' calculations using data from UNCTAD (n.d.) and ILO modelled estimates (ILO 2017).

Table 2.a.3 Changes in shares of total value added by sector (%) and shares of employment by economic activity (%) in former LDCs and comparison with Bangladesh

Country	Reference year	Agriculture		Industry		Manufacturing		Services	
		Share of total value added	Share of employment	Share of total value added	Share of employment	Share of total value added	Share of employment	Share of total value added	Share of employment
Botswana	Before graduation (5 years)	4.70	13.10	54.10	27.90	5.76	8.94	41.20	59.00
	After graduation (5 years)	4.03	17.70	47.66	23.90	5.95	9.16	48.31	58.40
Cape Verde	Before graduation (5 years)	12.39	36.30	22.53	15.30	6.30	4.55	65.08	48.30
	After graduation (5 years)	9.31	31.30	20.93	16.40	5.80	4.35	69.76	52.30
Maldives	Before graduation (5 years)	5.04	15.50	14.41	18.30	5.00	10.98	80.55	66.20
	After graduation (4/5 years)	3.73	13.80	17.82	14.80	5.26	11.11	78.45	71.40
Samoa	Before graduation (5 years)	9.77	37.10	25.56	12.80	11.10	5.78	64.68	50.10
	After graduation (1/2 years)	9.24	36.00	24.93	10.90	10.01	5.71	65.83	53.00
Bangladesh	Average (2005-10)	18.67	48.07	26.15	15.70	16.74	11.57	55.18	36.27
	Average (2011–16)	16.21	44.83	27.48	19.80	17.28	14.67	56.31	35.35

Sources: authors' calculations using data from UNCTAD (n.d.) and ILO modelled estimates (ILO 2017).

Notes

1 The conflation may not be unique to Bangladesh. Similar instances can be found in the media, if not in official statements, in other LDCs such as Bhutan and Laos.
2 The income-only criterion was introduced to address the situation where a country continues to fail in improving its structural indices, despite having sufficient income indicating governance concerns rather than structural ones.
3 In the cases of the Maldives and Samoa, graduation dates were deferred due to the unforeseen consequences of the 2004 and 2009 tsunamis, respectively.
4 The underlying assumption was that graduation thresholds would be fixed at the levels of the 2015 CDP review.
5 Averages were calculated for the five years preceding graduation and the five years, or as many years that have elapsed, after graduation. The reference periods were limited to five years in order to somewhat control for the effects of other variables and capture only the impact of graduation. The impact of graduation may not be fully realised until the end of the transition period.

References

Acemoglu, D., Johnson S. and Robinson, J. A., 2001. The colonial origins of comparative development: An empirical investigation. *American Economic Review*, 91 (5), 1369–1401.

AfDB, 2012. *Cape Verde: A success story* [online]. Abidjan: African Development Bank. Available from: www.afdb.org/fileadmin/uploads/afdb/Documents/Project-and-Operations/Cape%20Verde%20-%20A%20Success%20Story.pdf [Accessed 15 May 2017].

Ahmed, F. Z., Greenleaf, A. and Sacks, A., 2014. The paradox of export growth in areas of weak governance: The case of the ready made garment sector in Bangladesh. *World Development*, 56, 258–271.

Alonso, J. A., Cortez, A. L. and Klasen, S., 2014. *LDC and other country groupings: How useful are current approaches to classify countries in a more heterogeneous developing world?* CDP Background Paper 21. New York: United Nations Department of Economic and Social Affairs.

Anand, S. and Sen, A., 2000. Human development and economic sustainability. *World Development*, 28 (12), 2029–2049.

Asadullah, M. N., Savoia, A. and Mahmud, W., 2014. Paths to development: Is there a Bangladesh surprise? *World Development*, 62, 138–154.

Bangladesh Planning Commission, 2011. *Accelerating growth and reducing poverty*. Sixth Five Year Plan FY2011–FY2015. Dhaka: Ministry of Planning, Government of Bangladesh.

Bangladesh Planning Commission, 2015. *Millennium Development Goals: Bangladesh progress report 2015*. Dhaka: Ministry of Planning, Government of Bangladesh.

Barro, R. J., 1991. Economic growth in a cross section of countries. *Quarterly Journal of Economics*, 106 (2), 407–443.

Barro, R. J. and Lee, J-W., 1994. Sources of economic growth. *Carnegie-Rochester Conference Series on Public Policy*, 40, 1–46.

Basnett, Y., Keane, J. and te Velde, D. W., 2014. The Istanbul programme of action for LDCs: A monitoring and benchmarking exercise. *In: LDC IV Monitor, Istanbul programme of action for the LDCs (2011–2020): Monitoring deliverables, tracking progress – analytical perspectives*. London: Commonwealth Secretariat, 38–70.

Berthélemy, J-C., 2006. Convergence and development traps: How did emerging economies escape the underdevelopment trap? *In:* F. Bourguignon and B. Pleskovic, eds. *Growth and integration: Annual World Bank conference on development economics.* Washington, DC: World Bank, 127–156.

Bhattacharya, D. and Borgatti, L., 2012. An atypical approach to graduation from the LDC category: The case of Bangladesh. *South Asia Economic Journal,* 13 (1), 1–25.

Bertocchi, G. and Canova, F., 2002. Did colonization matter for growth? An empirical exploration into the historical causes of Africa's underdevelopment. *European Economic Review,* 46 (10), 1851–1871.

Bhattacharya, D. and Hossain, S. S., 2011. *Least developed countries in the next decade: What is there in the Istanbul programme of action?* International Policy Analysis. Geneva: Friedrich-Ebert-Stiftung, Geneva Office.

Bhattacharya, D. and Khan, T. I., 2014. The challenges of structural transformation and progress towards the MDGs in LDCs. *In:* LDC IV Monitor, *Istanbul programme of action for the LDCs (2011–2020): Monitoring deliverables, tracking progress – analytical perspectives.* London: Commonwealth Secretariat, 1–37.

Bhattacharya, D., Dasgupta, S. and Neethi, D. J., 2013. *Does democracy impact economic growth? Exploring the case of Bangladesh: a cointegrated VAR approach.* CPD-CMI Working Paper 5. Dhaka and Bergen: Centre for Policy Dialogue and Chr. Michelsen Institute.

Bhattacharya, D., et al., 2013. *Lagging behind: Lessons from the least developed countries for a development agenda post-2015* Perspective. Berlin: Friedrich-Ebert-Stiftung.

Blanton, R., Mason, T. D. and Athow, B., 2001. Colonial style and post-colonial ethnic conflict in Africa. *Journal of Peace Research,* 38 (4), 473–491.

Bose, A. and Bose, K., 2011. Botswana case study role of ICT in graduation from a least developed country to a developed country. *In:* P. Cunningham and M. Cunningham, eds. *IST-Africa 2011 conference proceedings,* 11–13 May 2011, Gaborone. Dublin: International Information Management Corporation, 1–10.

CDP, n.d. *LDC data* [online]. New York: Committee for Development Policy. Available from: www.un.org/development/desa/dpad/least-developed-country-category/ldc-data-retrieval.html [Accessed 12 December 2017].

CDP, 2012a. *Monitoring of graduated countries from the category of least developed countries: Maldives.* CDP2012/PLEN/12. New York: Committee for Development Policy.

CDP, 2012b. *Monitoring of progress of graduated countries: Cape Verde.* CDP2012/PLEN/11. New York: Committee for Development Policy.

CDP, 2014. *Note by the secretariat on monitoring of graduated countries from the category of least developed countries: Maldives.* CDP2014/PLEN/6. New York: Committee for Development Policy.

CDP, 2015a. *Report on the eighteenth session (14–18 March 2016).* E/2016/33. New York: Committee for Development Policy.

CDP, 2015b. *Monitoring of graduated countries from the category of least developed countries as a complement to the 2015 triennial review: Maldives and Samoa.* CDP2015/PLEN/8. New York: Committee for Development Policy.

CDP, 2016. *Monitoring of graduated countries from the category of least developed countries: Samoa, Equatorial Guinea, and Vanuatu.* CDP2016/PLEN5. New York: Committee for Development Policy.

CDP, 2018a. *Inclusion in the LDC category* [online]. New York: Committee for Development Policy. Available from: www.un.org/development/desa/dpad/least-developed-country-category/ldc-inclusion.html [Accessed 25 March 2018].

CDP, 2018b. *Graduation from the LDC category* [online]. New York: Committee for Development Policy. Available from: www.un.org/development/desa/dpad/least-developed-country-category/ldc-graduation.html [Accessed 25 March 2018].

CDP and UN DESA, 2015. *Handbook on the least developed country category: Inclusion, graduation, and special support measures*. 2nd edn. New York: Committee for Development Policy and United Nations Department of Economic and Social Affairs.

Chang, H.-J., 2003. Kicking away the ladder: Infant industry promotion in historical perspective. *Oxford Development Studies*, 31 (1), 21–32.

Chowdhury, A. M. R., et al., 2013. The Bangladesh paradox: Exceptional health achievement despite economic poverty. *Lancet*, 382 (9906), 1734–1745.

Collier, P., 2007. *The bottom billion: Why the poorest countries are failing and what can be done about it*. New York: Oxford University Press.

Cornia, G. A. and Scognamillo, A., 2016. *Clusters of least developed countries, their evolution between 1993 and 2013, and policies to expand their productive capacity*. CDP Background Paper 33. New York: United Nations Department of Economic and Social Affairs.

Cortez, A. L., 2011. *Beyond market access: Trade-related measures for the least developed countries. What strategy?* DESA Working Paper 109. New York: United Nations Department of Economic and Social Affairs.

Cortez, A. L., Kinniburgh, I. and Mollerus, R., 2014. *Accelerating development in the least developed countries through international support measures: Findings from country case studies*. CDP Background Paper 22. New York: United Nations Department of Economic and Social Affairs.

CPD, 2007. *Bangladesh Vision 2021: Prepared under the initiative of Nagorik Committee 2006*. Dhaka: Centre for Policy Dialogue.

CPD, 2018. *State of the Bangladesh economy in FY2016–17: First reading*. Dhaka: Centre for Policy Dialogue.

Dahlman, C. and Mealy, S., 2016. Obstacles to achieving the Sustainable Development Goals: Emerging global challenges and the performance of the least developed countries. *In*: LDC IV Monitor, *Tracking progress, accelerating transformations: Achieving the IPoA by 2020*. London: Commonwealth Secretariat, 49–61.

Drabo, A. and Guillaumont, P., 2016. Prospects of graduation for least developed countries: What structural change? *In*: LDC IV Monitor, *Tracking progress, accelerating transformations: Achieving the IPoA by 2020*. London: Commonwealth Secretariat, 30–38.

EPB, 2017. *Statistic data-2016–2017* [online]. Dhaka: Export Promotion Bureau, Ministry of Commerce, Government of Bangladesh. Available from: www.epb.gov.bd/site/files/51916ae6-a9a3-462e-a6bd-9ef074d835af/Statistic-Data-2016-2017 [Accessed 12 December 2017].

ESID, 2017. *The Bangladesh paradox: Why has politics performed so well for development in Bangladesh?* ESID Briefing 27. Manchester: Effective States and Inclusive Development Research Centre.

Faaland, J. and Parkinson, J. R., 1976. *Bangladesh: The test case for development*. London: C. Hurst & Co.

Frank, I., 1979. *The 'Graduation' issue in trade policy toward LDCs*. World Bank Staff Working Paper 334. Washington, DC: World Bank.

Guillaumont, P., 2009. *Caught in a trap: Identifying the least developed countries*. Paris: Economica.

Guillaumont, P., 2011. *The concept of structural economic vulnerability and its relevance for the identification of the least developed countries and other purposes (nature, measurement,* and evolution). CDP Background Paper 12. New York: United Nations Department of Economic and Social Affairs.

Guillaumont, P., Jeanneney, S. G. and Wagner, L., 2015. *How to take into account vulnerability in aid allocation criteria and lack of human capital as well: Improving the performance based allocation*. Working Paper 13. Clermont-Ferrand: Fondation pour les études et recherches sur le développement international.

Haq, K. and Kirdar, Ü., eds, 1987. *Human development, adjustment and growth*. New York: United Nations.

Haq, M. U., 1995. *Reflections on human development*. New York: Oxford University Press.

Hazleton, R., 2002. *Diamonds: Forever or for good? The economic impact of diamonds in Southern Africa*. Occasional Paper 3, the Diamonds and Human Security Project. Ottawa: Partnership Africa Canada.

Heath, R. and Mobarak, M., 2011. *Supply and demand constraints on educational investment: Evidence from garment sector jobs and the female stipend program in Bangladesh*. Working Paper 2(4). New Haven, CT: Yale School of Management.

ILO, 2017. *ILOSTAT* [online]. Geneva: International Labour Organization. Available from: www.ilo.org/ilostat [Accessed 20 November 2017].

Islam, N., 2003. *Making of a nation Bangladesh: An economist's tale*. Dhaka: University Press Limited.

Kabeer, N. and Mahmud, S., 2004. Globalization, gender and poverty: Bangladeshi women workers in export and local markets. *Journal of International Development*, 16 (1), 93–109.

Kang, D. C., 2002. *Crony capitalism: Corruption and development in South Korea and the Philippines*. Cambridge: Cambridge University Press.

Keane, J., Aldafai, G. and Arda, M., 2016. Structural economic transformation and export diversification in the least developed countries. *In*: LDC IV Monitor, *Tracking progress, accelerating transformations: Achieving the IPoA by 2020*. London: Commonwealth Secretariat, 17–29.

Khan, M., 2012. Beyond good governance: An agenda for developmental governance. *In*: J. K. Sundaram and A. Chowdhury, eds. *Is good governance good for development?* London: Bloomsbury Academic, 151–182.

Khatun, F., 2016. Development policies since independence. *In*: A. Riaz and M. S. Rahman, eds. *Routledge handbook of contemporary Bangladesh*. London and New York: Routledge, 131–143.

Klasen, S., *et al.*, 2016. *Trade preferences for LDCs. Are they effective? Preliminary econometric evidence*. CDP Policy Review 4. New York: Committee for Development Policy.

Kreft, S., *et al.*, 2015. *Global climate risk index 2016: Who suffers most from extreme weather events? Weather-related loss events in 2014 and 1995 to 2014*. Briefing Paper. Bonn and Berlin: Germanwatch.

Kundur, S. K., 2012. Development of tourism in Maldives. *International Journal of Scientific and Research Publications*, 2 (4), 1–5.

Kuznets, S., 1955. Economic growth and income inequality. *American Economic Review*, 45 (1), 1–28.

Kuznets, S., 1973. Modern economic growth: Findings and reflections. *American Economic Review*, 63 (3), 247–258.

Lewin, M., 2011. Botswana's success: Good governance, good policies, and good luck. *In*: P. Chuhan-Pole and M. Angwafo, eds. *Yes, Africa can: Success stories from a dynamic continent*. Washington, DC: World Bank, 80–90.

Lewis, W. A., 1954. Economic development with unlimited supplies of labour. *Manchester School*, 22 (2), 139–191.

Lin, J. Y., 2012. New structural economics: A framework for rethinking development. *In:* J. Y. Lin, ed., *New structural economics: A framework for rethinking development and policy.* Washington, DC: World Bank, 11–47.

Lin, J. Y. and Monga, C., 2012. The growth report and new structural economics. *In:* J. Y. Lin, ed., *New structural economics: A framework for rethinking development and policy.* Washington, DC: World Bank, 81–112.

Lin, J. Y. and Xu, J., 2016. *Applying the growth identification and facilitation framework to the least developed countries: The case of Uganda.* CDP Background Paper 32. New York: United Nations Department of Economic and Social Affairs.

McMillan, M., *et al.*, 2017. *Supporting economic transformation: An approach paper.* London: Overseas Development Institute.

McMillan, M. S. and Rodrik, D., 2011. *Globalization, structural change and productivity growth.* NBER Working Paper 17143. Cambridge: National Bureau of Economic Research.

Mahmud, W., Ahmed, S. and Mahajan, S., 2010. Economic reforms, growth, and governance: The political economy aspects of Bangladesh's development surprise. *In:* D. Brady and M. Spence, eds. *Leadership and growth.* Washington, DC: World Bank, 227–254.

Mahmud, W., Asadullah, M. N. and Savoia, A., 2013. *Bangladesh's achievements in social development indicators: Explaining the puzzle.* Research brief 13/0303. London: International Growth Centre.

Malesky, E. J. and Samphantharak, K., 2008. Predictable corruption and firm investment: Evidence from a natural experiment and survey of Cambodian entrepreneurs. *Quarterly Journal of Political Science,* 3 (3), 227–267.

Myrdal, G., 1957. *Economic theory and under-developed regions.* London: G. Duckworth.

Nunn, N., 2007. Historical legacies: A model linking Africa's past to its current underdevelopment. *Journal of Development Economics,* 83 (1), 157–175.

Nurkse, R., 1953. *Problems of capital formation in underdeveloped countries.* New York: Oxford University Press.

OECD and WTO, 2010. *Aid-for-trade case story: Cape Verde.* Paris and Geneva: Organisation for Economic Co-operation and Development and World Trade Organization.

Olson, M., Sarna, N. and Swamy, A. V., 2000. Governance and growth: A simple hypothesis explaining cross-country differences in productivity growth. *Public Choice,* 102 (3–4), 341–364.

Price, G. N., 2003. Economic growth in a cross-section of nonindustrial countries: Does colonial heritage matter for Africa? *Review of Development Economics,* 7 (3), 478–495.

Rahman, M. and Bari, E., 2016. *Escaping the middle-income trap: Perspectives from Bangladesh.* Dhaka: Friedrich-Ebert-Stiftung, Bangladesh Office.

Rahman, M., Khan, T. I. and Amin, M. A., 2014a. *The economy of tomorrow: How to produce socially just, sustainable and green dynamic growth for a good society case study of Bangladesh.* Berlin: Friedrich-Ebert-Stiftung.

Rahman, M., Khan, T. I. and Sadique, M. Z., 2014b. *Public expenditure trends in low-income countries in the post-MDG context* [online]. Background paper prepared for European Report on Development 2015. Available from: https://ec.europa.eu/europeaid/sites/devco/files/erd5-background-paper-public-expenditure-trends-2015_en.pdf [Accessed 2 April 2018].

Ranis, G., 2004. Arthur Lewis's contribution to development thinking and policy. *Manchester School,* 72 (6), 712–723.

Ranis, G., 2009. Reflections on Bangladesh in comparison to East Asia. *In*: Q. Shahabud-din and R. I. Rahman, eds. *Development experience and emerging challenges: Bangladesh.* Dhaka: University Press Limited, 27–31.

Ranis, G. and Fei, J. C., 1961. A theory of economic development. *American Economic Review*, 51 (4), 533–565.

Riaz, A. and Rahman, M. S., 2016. Introduction. *In*: A. Riaz and M. S. Rahman, eds. *Routledge handbook of contemporary Bangladesh.* London and New York: Routledge, 1–14.

Robinson, S., 1971. Sources of growth in less developed countries: A cross-section study. *Quarterly Journal of Economics*, 85 (3), 391–408.

Rodrik, D., 2007. *One economics, many recipes: Globalization, institutions, and economic growth.* Princeton, NJ: Princeton University Press.

Rodrik, D., Subramanian, A. and Trebbi, F., 2004. Institutions rule: The primacy of institutions over geography and integration in economic development. *Journal of Economic Growth*, 9 (2), 131–165.

Rosenstein-Rodan, P. N., 1943. Problems of industrialisation of eastern and south-eastern Europe. *Economic Journal*, 53 (210/211), 202–211.

Rostow, W. W., 1960. *The stages of economic growth: A non-communist manifesto.* Cambridge: Cambridge University Press.

Sen, K., 2013. The political dynamics of economic growth. *World Development*, 47, 71–86.

Shehabuddin, S. T., 2016. Bangladeshi politics since independence. *In*: A. Riaz and M. S. Rahman, eds. *Routledge handbook of contemporary Bangladesh.* London and New York: Routledge, 17–27.

Sobhan, R., 2010. *Challenging the injustice of poverty: Agendas for inclusive development in South Asia.* New Delhi: SAGE Publications India Pvt Ltd.

Stiglitz, J. E., 2016. *The state, the market, and development.* WIDER Working Paper 2016/1. Helsinki: United Nations University World Institute for Development Economics Research.

Stockemer, D., 2009. Does democracy lead to good governance? The question applied to Africa and Latin America. *Global Change, Peace and Security*, 21 (2), 241–255.

Sundaram, J. K., 2015. *Does good governance always boost development?* [online]. Available from: www.weforum.org/agenda/2015/06/does-good-governance-always-boost-development [Accessed 20 September 2017].

Thirlwall, A. P., 1979. The balance of payments constraint as an explanation of international growth rate differences. *Banca Nazionale del Lavoro Quarterly Review*, 32 (128), 45–53.

UNCTAD, n.d. *UNCTADstat* [online]. New York: United Nations Conference on Trade and Development. Available from: http://unctadstat.unctad.org [Accessed 25 March 2018].

UNCTAD, 2006. *Developing productive capacities.* The Least Developed Countries Report 2006. New York: United Nations Conference on Trade and Development.

UNCTAD, 2010. *Towards a new international development architecture for LDCs.* The Least Developed Countries Report 2010. New York: United Nations Conference on Trade and Development.

UNCTAD, 2014. *Growth with structural transformation: A post-2015 development agenda.* The Least Developed Countries Report 2014. New York: United Nations Conference on Trade and Development.

UNCTAD, 2016. *The path to graduation and beyond: Making the most of the process.* The Least Developed Countries Report 2016. New York: United Nations Conference on Trade and Development.

UNDP, n.d. *About human development* [online]. Available from: http://hdr.undp.org/en/humandev [Accessed 15 June 2017].

UNDP, 2011. *Supporting transformational change: Case studies of sustained and successful development cooperation*. New York: United Nations Development Programme.

UNDP, 2016. *Human development for everyone*. Human Development Report 2016. New York: United Nations Development Programme.

United Nations, 1971. *Identification of the least developed among the developing countries*. A/RES/2768(XXVI). New York: United Nations.

United Nations, 1991. *Report of the committee for development planning: Criteria for identifying the least developed countries*. A/RES/46/206. New York: United Nations.

United Nations, 2005. *Smooth transition strategy for countries graduating from the list of least developed countries*. A/RES/59/209. New York: United Nations.

United Nations, 2011. *Programme of action for the least developed countries for the decade 2011–2020*. A/CONF.219/3/Rev.1. New York: United Nations.

United Nations, 2013. *Smooth transition for countries graduating from the list of least developed countries*. A/RES/67/221. New York: United Nations.

United Nations, 2015. *Implementation, effectiveness and added value of smooth transition measures*. Report of the Secretary General. A/70/292. New York: United Nations.

UN-OHRLLS, 2016. *State of the least developed countries 2016: Follow up of the implementation of the Istanbul programme of action for the least developed countries*. New York: United Nations Office of the High Representative for the Least Developed Countries, Landlocked Developing Countries and Small Island Developing States.

World Bank, 2007. *Bangladesh: Strategy for sustained growth*. Bangladesh Development Series Paper 18. Dhaka: World Bank Office, Bangladesh.

World Bank, 2010. *Bangladesh country assistance strategy: 2011–2014*. Dhaka: World Bank Office, Bangladesh.

World Bank, 2017a. *World Bank country and lending groups* [online]. Available from: https://datahelpdesk.worldbank.org/knowledgebase/articles/906519-world-bank-country-and-lending-groups [Accessed 14 September 2017].

World Bank, 2017b. *World development indicators* [online]. Available from: http://data.worldbank.org/data-catalog/world-development-indicators [Accessed 12 December 2017].

Young, A. A., 1928. Increasing returns and economic progress. *Economic Journal*, 38 (152), 527–542.

Zafarullah, H., 2016. Public administration and bureaucracy. *In*: A. Riaz and M. S. Rahman, eds. *Routledge handbook of contemporary Bangladesh*. London and New York: Routledge, 94–108.

3 Structural transformation of Bangladesh economy

Role of smooth transition after graduation

Khondaker Golam Moazzem and Akashlina Arno

Introduction

Graduation from the least developed country (LDC) group would be an important 'milestone' in the process of development for Bangladesh. However, the economy would continue to face challenges of overcoming its development constraints. During the post-graduation period, the country would face challenges that could be aggravated by weakening capacities and a less favourable macroeconomic situation linked to reduced international support measures (ISMs). Such aggravation could have adverse consequences on its competitiveness in the global economy.

LDCs need to focus on structural transformation and economic diversification in order to enhance and maintain their global competitiveness and ensure sustainable economic growth and development. Given the problem of various structural handicaps confronted by LDCs (Drabo and Guillaumont 2016), irreversible progress needs to be made on at least two accounts – a positive structural change in favour of the sectors with relatively higher productivity and a strong improvement in human development indicators, particularly those related to health and education (Bhattacharya and Khan 2014). Structural transformation of LDCs could be both the means and outcome of the process of graduation from the LDC group.

The objective of this study is to examine the benchmark situation for Bangladesh's structural transformation and provide a better understanding of possible structural changes during the transition period towards graduation. It identifies the level of structural transformation required during the post-graduation period with a view to ensure smooth transition after graduation. Given the analysis of the benchmark situation and needed future levels of structural change in Bangladesh, the chapter outlines appropriate policies and measures to overcome expected challenges.

The contribution of the study to the existing literature on the development of LDC economies and their structural transformation is threefold. First, the chapter reviews relevant literature on the graduating LDC economies and other developing economies and their existing labour productivity. Considering the past literature, there is a lack of evidence that graduation from the LDC group, or excelling in any of the LDC graduation criteria, would lead to an efficient structural change in the economy, leading to sustained development in the long-run. Second, the lack of evidence between LDC graduation and structural transformation is strengthened through the panel regression analysis adapted from McMillan and Rodrik (2011). The chapter adapts the initial model to study the effect of the graduation criteria on productivity changes and finds that the relationship between them is insignificant. The final contribution of this chapter is the policy perspective in terms of Bangladesh's structural transformation.

The chapter comprises six sections. Following this introduction, the second section elaborates on conceptual issues related to graduation from the LDC category and structural transformation. The third section provides a benchmarking of Bangladesh's structural transformation with a view to determine its capacities and weaknesses that are relevant to a smooth transition after graduation. The chapter then explains the phase when Bangladesh would experience 'graduation-led structural transformation' to illustrate the required level of structural transformation at the time of expected graduation in 2024. Through quantitative analysis, the fifth section demonstrates which indicators, including the graduation criteria, would affect the process of structural transformation. It briefly projects the phase when Bangladesh may experience 'structural transformation-enabled graduation', in order to measure the economy's strength, to ensure a smooth transition. The final section addresses Bangladesh's existing policy framework and suggests policy changes to facilitate structural transformation of the economy.

Analytical framework and methodological approach

There are multiple connotations of the terms 'graduation' from the LDC category, and 'structural transformation'. Both issues are evolving and related measurable indicators are often debated. This section introduces an analytical framework to get a better understanding of the two issues, especially in the case of Bangladesh.

Concepts

Graduation and smooth transition after graduation

A related phrase is 'graduation with momentum' (UNCTAD 2016), which refers to a country's capacity for smooth transition following graduation from the LDC group. The post-graduation period is critical because the country confronts a number of challenges due to the expected heavy reduction of ISMs, including a reduction in external financing, loss of trade preferences and changes to other special and differential treatment (S&DT) provisions. According to the United Nations Conference on Trade and Development (UNCTAD), the loss of ISMs may reduce a country's competitiveness in the global economy and limit access to low-cost financial resources (UNCTAD 2016). In order to continue a country's progress towards economic growth and development following graduation, planning for a smooth transition is essential.

The smoothness of transition following graduation depends on the path the economy takes to graduate. Fulfilling the income-only criterion may indicate that a country has a relatively high gross national income (GNI) per capita; however, it does not ensure that the country has or will have made any progress in terms of the Human Assets Index (HAI) or Economic Vulnerability Index (EVI). Several LDCs in Sub-Saharan Africa and Asia that are heavily dependent on primary sectors are likely to struggle with the reduction in trade preferences after graduation (Swaray 2005). Similarly, meeting either or both the HAI and EVI criteria does not ensure sustainability in development after graduation. In order to measure whether a country can sustain growth and development following graduation, it is important to understand the structure of its economy (UNCTAD 2016). Among the EVI, while some of the indicators related to location and economic structure sub-indices capture some ideas about the structure of an economy, other indicators are needed to understand the structural adjustment that is required. Indicators such as the shares of workers employed in agriculture, manufacturing and services sectors as well as the urban and rural sectors help to understand a country's ability to experience a smooth transition.

Structural transformation

A common characteristic of a poor country is that a large share of its labour force works in the agriculture sector, which is an indicator of limited structural transformation (Caselli 2005). The term 'structural transformation' can be defined as the reallocation of economic resources to more productive economic activities (Kuznets 1966). Similar to the concept introduced by Lewis (1954), where the labour force shifts from the agriculture sector to the manufacturing sector due to increased productivity, the reallocation of the factors of production between the three sectors, agriculture, manufacturing and services, is expected to increase the productivity of a country and sustain higher growth. Kuznets (1971) identified structural transformation as one of the main features of modern economic growth. In the context of the LDCs, structural transformation ensures upgradation of a graduating country's economic activities, which enables its economy to become more resilient against exogenous shocks and thus continue progress towards sustainable economic growth and development (UNCTAD 2016).

Structural transformation of an economy is usually measured by the differences in productivity among different types of economic activity. Duarte and Restuccia (2010) studied the structural transformation experienced by the United States compared to developing countries and found that it is reflected in the productivity gap between developed and developing economies, particularly in the agriculture and services sectors. McMillan *et al.* (2014) identified structural transformation as one of the main factors that influenced Africa's labour productivity growth over the 2000–10 period.

McMillan and Rodrik (2011) divided a country's total labour productivity growth into two components, 'within sector' productivity growth and 'between sector' productivity growth. While the former measures the weighted sum of productivity growth within individual sectors, the latter measures the growth in productivity due to labour reallocation across sectors. Therefore, 'between sector' productivity growth, or the 'structural change', can be used to measure a country's structural transformation. Martins (2015) showed that developed countries which have already experienced significant structural transformation had structural change of around 0.2 per cent between 2002 and 2013, while African, Asian and Latin American countries had structural change of around 0.8 per cent, 1.6 per cent and 0.5 per cent, respectively. In most cases, developing countries suffer from lack of adequate capacity for structural transformation even though they may experience economic growth. Lack of capacity is due to a country's limited sources of growth, which might include a narrow product base, limited technological capabilities and human resources, limited investment and a less diversified export base.

A major challenge for most developing countries is to ensure better access to employment opportunities by maintaining high productivity both within and across sectors. The majority of LDCs suffer from severe transformation deficits. Often structural transformation and employment generation are considered when discussing the manufacturing sector. The services sector also needs to be considered for its potential for structural transformation, especially when considering its contribution to the global value chain. Economic diversification, both in the domestic market and export-oriented industries, is an important indicator when it comes to sustaining structural transformation. Diversification of a country's export base, along with upgrading the quality of different products, is expected to result in further reallocation of economic resources to more productive economic activities. According to the International Monetary Fund (IMF), product diversification in export-oriented industries depends on three interrelated aspects: frequency with which new products are introduced, the likelihood that they will survive and their growth prospects (IMF 2014).

Analytical framework

From conceptual and empirical aspects, graduation from the LDC group and structural transformation are expected to be linked. The aim of the chapter is to establish whether the graduation criteria positively influence structural adjustments. Keane *et al.* (2016) found that the majority of LDCs focusing on the graduation criteria struggle when it comes to improving structural transformation. While a few indicators under the graduation criteria could be linked to positive structural change, it is important to analyse whether these indicators have adequate influence or whether introducing structural transformation indicators, such as a certain level of structural change are necessary.

Graduation-led structural transformation

Graduation from the LDC group and strong structural transformation are both necessary for reducing structural handicaps to development (Drabo and Guillaumont 2016). According to Guillaumont (2014), however, the indicators under the current graduation criteria concentrate on reducing 'arbitrary' structural handicaps rather than 'relative' structural handicaps. Such emphasis means that the graduation criteria focus on improving very specific economic and societal issues, such as infant mortality rate and nutrition. While such issues are important for an economy, improving them does not necessarily affect the economy's output structure as a whole. Structural transformation implies improving labour productivity and increasing total output, which lead to upgradation of an entire economy. Changes in certain indicators under the graduation criteria, such as increasing the secondary school enrolment ratio in the HAI and reducing instability of agricultural production in the EVI, may contribute towards increasing labour productivity. However, whether these indicators affect 'between sector' productivity, thus facilitating structural transformation, is still in question. Even if an LDC scores relatively high on the graduation criteria, its economy may still suffer from weak structure.

Basnett *et al.* (2014), explores Nepal's structural transformation, which continues to be weak due to low and erratic productivity growth. Since 1995, the country's manufacturing sector has experienced average annual growth of only 2.5 per cent. In 2014, agriculture value addition accounted for 37 per cent of gross domestic product (GDP) – a decrease from 68 per cent estimated average in the 1960s, while manufacturing value addition was at 15 per cent of GDP – a fall from 20 per cent in the 1990s. The only sector that increased value addition is the services sector, which rose to 47 per cent of GDP in 2014 from an average of 16 per cent in the 1960s. While labour has moved from the agriculture sector, the move has been largely towards foreign labour markets rather than the more productive domestic manufacturing and services sectors.

Despite limited structural transformation, Nepal is expected to graduate from the LDC group in 2021 by meeting the HAI and EVI criteria (UNCTAD 2015). According to the 2009 data, Nepal had the fifth lowest EVI and twelfth highest HAI among the 48 LDCs. The country is expected to be the first to graduate without meeting the income criterion (Kawamura 2014). From this situational analysis of Nepal, it can be observed that meeting the graduation criteria is not sufficient to achieve structural transformation of an economy. In order to sustain growth and productivity, an LDC must focus on both indicators under the graduation criteria and structural transformation indicators.

Further, Sen (2016) studied the determinants of structural transformation in Asia by analysing the economic situations of China, India and Thailand. Not being LDCs, the aforesaid are developing countries experiencing high economic growth while attempting to overcome their structural handicaps to long-term development. In 2016, the shares of employment in the countries' agriculture sectors were 36.7 per cent, 51.1 per cent and 38.2 per cent for China, India and Thailand, respectively. Sen (2016) found that the three countries are lagging in productivity not only across sectors but also within sectors and identified government failures, specifically ineffective policies and labour market regulations, and market failures, such as coordination failures and the failure of credit markets, to be the main causes for the lack of structural change. In order to overcome barriers to structural transformation, concentrating on the graduation criteria is evidently not enough. An active development of effective labour, migration and land policies and better labour and product market regulations are necessary for sustainable development.

Structural transformation-enabled smooth transition after graduation

Achieving 'graduation with momentum' requires 'a shift of production towards more sophisticated goods and services through investment in technological upgrading of productive facilities and the establishment of new sectors and activities' (UNCTAD 2016). Momentum can be gained through producing better quality products that have higher value addition, as well as by improving forward and backward linkages. Domestic capacity is essential to cope with new and acute vulnerabilities to external risks and shocks, such as constraints to raising fiscal revenue and balance of payments problems due to reduced ISMs and other challenges, including environmental risks.

UNCTAD (2016) highlighted the importance of LDCs preparing for smooth transition following graduation. Graduation entails the loss of trade preferences, such as those of the European Union, and the loss of concessions, including those in the Global System of Trade Preferences among developing countries. Nicita and Seiermann (2016) estimated a loss of United States dollar (US$) 4.2 billion per year in exports if all the countries in the LDC group graduate. If each country is the only one to graduate from the LDC group, allowing all other remaining LDC members to retain and take advantage of their trade preferences, Ethiopia, Tanzania and Vanuatu would face large losses of nearly 8.7 per cent, 8.8 per cent and 17.4 per cent of their exports respectively. Countries that are dependent on primary sectors, such as exports of agricultural commodities, are expected to struggle more with the loss of trade preferences upon graduation (Swaray 2005).

To ensure sustainable growth and development, graduating countries need to analyse how they are achieving the graduation criteria and whether meeting them is sufficient to facilitate the structural transformation. McMillan *et al.* (2017) showed that structural transformation contributes to increasing the total productivity of an economy by increasing 'between sector' productivity. Hausmann and Klinger (2006) stated the importance of structural transformation for developing countries to move from simple goods towards production of complex products in order to compete with developed countries in the global economy. For a smooth transition, given the loss of trade preferences following graduation, a graduating country has to compete in global trade for which the capacity to produce more complex products and the allocation of labour towards more productive sectors are essential.

Following Sen (2016), policies that focus on managing government and market failures are necessary to promote structural change. For a government, labour policies such as protecting labour rights and implementing a minimum wage would have significant effects on labour productivity. Policies that encourage migration from rural to urban sectors also contribute to structural transformation. A government should adopt policies that encourage investment in the more productive sectors of an economy, such as better land policies and product market regulations. In order to eliminate market failures, better mechanisms for market coordination are needed and human capital formation should be increased by investing in skill-building initiatives.

McMillan *et al.* (2017) also outlined the policies required to promote structural change. This paper suggested several targeted interventions including the need for export-push policies (to encourage more international trade), exchange rate protection (to maintain an undervalued real exchange rate), selective industrial policies (to promote the most productive industries) and the formation of national development banks (to provide long-term credit for small and medium-sized enterprises). These policies all share a common goal to increase investment in the more productive sectors of an economy, such as the manufacturing sector, and restructure the labour force to increase the total labour productivity. Moreover, they noted that Bangladesh has gone through significant economic transformation, especially when the performance of the manufacturing sector is considered. However, issues such as political uncertainty, weak institutions, lack of skilled workers, unreliable energy supply and the unavailability of suitable land for industrialisation have discouraged investment. In order to develop targeted interventions that would encourage investment, particularly investment in export-oriented industries, these issues need to be addressed.

Methodology of the study

While a significant portion of the empirical analysis was based on Bangladesh's economic performance, the following sections attempt to provide empirical evidence on the general relationship between the graduation criteria and efficient structural transformation. The primary methodology is adapted from the paper by McMillan and Rodrik (2011).

The chapter measures Bangladesh's level of labour productivity by studying the 'within sector' and 'between sector' productivity growth of the country. The chapter also establishes the level of productivity of other emerging economies to allow benchmarking Bangladesh. Among the comparison of the emerging markets, Bangladesh is the only economy that is also an LDC, therefore allowing us to study whether the country is prepared to compete in the international market following graduation. The chapter conducts several projections of Bangladesh's prospects in labour productivity compared with the other economies.

The results show that the country is lagging behind in not only level of productivity but other significant factors in international trade such as export diversity measured by each country's value of the Herfindahl-Hirschman Index (HHI).

Following McMillan and Rodrik, the chapter performs random-effect regression analysis on the emerging markets to establish the relationship between graduation criteria and structural transformation. The independent variables chosen for the analysis are the three graduation criteria – GNI per capita and the EVI and HAI. Other relevant variables affecting international trade such as macroeconomic stability are also included as controls. The regression model uses data from 1992 to 2014.

Benchmarking structural transformation of Bangladesh's economy

This section provides an analysis of Bangladesh's present situation in terms of structural change and the preparedness of its economy to ensure smooth transition following graduation. First, Bangladesh's economic performance is reviewed, after which more perspective is provided on how that performance measures up with those of competing export-manufacturing countries.

Bangladesh's structural transformation

Contributions of various sectors to employment and GDP

Bangladesh has experienced slow progress in structural transformation. As shown in Figure 3.1, the share of labour force in agriculture decreased from 51.1 per cent in the fiscal year (FY)[1]1995–96 to 43.9 per cent in FY2014–15, with a change in the agriculture sector's contribution to GDP from 21.4 per cent to 15.5 per cent over the same period. The share of employment in industry increased from 12.7 per cent in FY1995–96 to 19.6 per cent in FY2014–15, while the share of employment in services only increased from 36.2 per cent to 36.5 per cent between those years (BBS 2015, 2017). Bangladesh's agriculture sector continues to have the largest share of the total labour force despite its low contribution to GDP, which indicates a low level of structural transformation over the years. Despite Bangladesh's exports being heavily reliant on industry, the average growth in the share of the labour force in that sector over the past two decades was particularly low at only 0.35 per cent per year (BBS 2015, 2017).

'Within sector' and 'between sector' productivity

In order to measure a country's level of structural transformation, this chapter adopts the methodology used by McMillan and Rodrik (2011), who analysed different economies' structural transformation by studying labour productivity changes in various sectors. The total labour productivity growth calculations are divided into two indicators, 'within sector' productivity growth and 'between

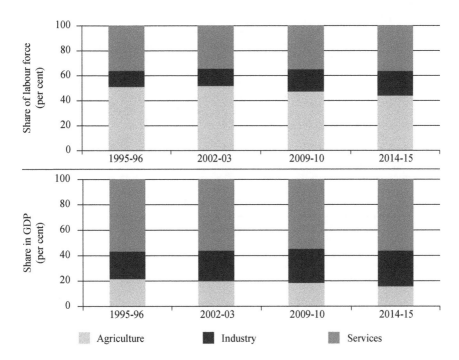

Figure 3.1 Share of labour force for each sector and contribution to GDP by each sector.
Sources: BBS (2015, 2017).

sector' productivity growth. The former measures the weighted sum of productivity growth within individual sectors, while the latter ('between sector' or
structural change) measures growth in productivity due to labour reallocation.

For Bangladesh, the total annualised growth in labour productivity was negative at –0.9 per cent in 1986 and significantly increased to 5.8 per cent in
2013–15 (Figure 3.2). Comparing the relative productivity of seven sectors in
Table 3.1 for the years 1985, 2000 and 2015, the agriculture sector dominated
in the share of employment, yet had the lowest level of productivity. The agriculture sector's relative productivity has been falling since 1985, yet the sector
continues to hold over 40 per cent of the total labour force. Sectors with higher
shares of relative productivity, such as manufacturing, hold relatively much
smaller shares of the total labour force. There have been limited changes in sectoral productivity and the movement of labour across sectors, which suggest that
structural transformation in Bangladesh is almost stagnant.

Figure 3.2 presents 'within sector' and 'between sector' productivity growth
during the 1985–2015 period using data from seven sectors: agriculture; mining
and utilities; manufacturing; construction; wholesale, retail and hotel; transport,
storage and communications; and others. Bangladesh experienced an average of
2.9 per cent of total labour productivity growth; however, the majority of

Table 3.1 Bangladesh's employment shares and relative productivity in different sectors, 1985–2015

Sector	Employment share (%)			Relative productivity (%)		
	1985	2000	2015	1985	2000	2015
Agriculture	57.67	62.15	43.88	52.15	40.00	37.92
Mining and utilities	0.32	10.62	13.18	81.85	115.42	115.97
Wholesale, retail and hotels	12.46	4.85	15.58	112.23	204.35	150.65
Manufacturing	9.28	12.12	14.02	143.20	210.59	152.65
Construction	1.90	7.31	0.48	264.02	333.47	593.60
Transport, storage and communication	4.04	0.83	5.07	236.54	268.77	179.24
Other	14.33	2.12	7.79	189.68	262.91	157.02
Total	100	100	100	–	–	–

Sources: BBS (2015, 2017) and Groningen Growth and Development Centre (2017).

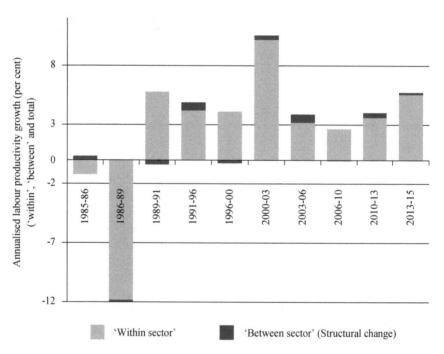

'Within sector'   'Between sector' (Structural change)

Figure 3.2 'Within' and 'between sector' productivity growth, 1985–2015.
Sources: United Nations (n.d.); BBS (2015, 2017).

growth was due to 'within sector' productivity growth rather than 'structural change'.

'Within sector' productivity growth increased from being negative at –1.2 per cent in 1985–86 to 5.6 per cent in 2013–15. The 'structural change', which represents the growth in productivity due to labour movement from one sector to another ('between sector' productivity growth, hereafter referred to as 'structural change') (McMillan and Rodrik 2011), actually decreased from 0.3 per cent in 1986 to 0.2 per cent in 2013–15, with the average structural change being 0.2 per cent for nearly three decades. Since 1989, Bangladesh has experienced positive labour productivity growth. However, the structural change has been volatile over the years. In 1989–91, 1996–2000 and 2006–10, the country experienced negative 'between sector' productivity growth despite having positive 'within sector' productivity growth. Bangladesh's structural transformation has evidently been slow, which raises the question whether the level of the structural change is adequate for smooth transition after graduation from the LDC group.

Export diversification

Despite Bangladesh's reliance on the export of products from its manufacturing sector, an indicator of weak structural transformation is a low level of export diversity. Diversification of a country's export base is considered critical for the manufacturing sector of an economy to expand and avoid exogenous shocks (IMF 2014). To calculate export diversity, this chapter uses the HHI, which measures a country's level of product concentration. With the HHI, a value closer to 1 indicates a high level of concentration on fewer products and thus a low level of export diversity in an economy. HHI values for selected countries are given in Table 3.2.

Considering the export diversity of developing countries excluding LDCs, all five selected countries were lagging behind. For each year, Bangladesh had the highest HHI score, which steadily rose from 0.33 in 1995 to 0.4 in 2015. There were significant differences between Bangladesh and the other selected countries, with the next highest HHI score in 2015 being only 0.2 for Pakistan and the lowest score being 0.12 for India. Table 3.3 compares Bangladesh's export diversity with that of other LDCs from Asia.

In 2015, Yemen and Myanmar had higher HHI scores than Bangladesh. Calculating averages for the past two decades, however, Bangladesh had an

Table 3.2 HHI values for selected developing countries

Year	Bangladesh	India	Indonesia	Pakistan	Vietnam	Average of developing countries
1995	0.33	0.14	0.14	0.23	0.20	0.09
2000	0.38	0.15	0.13	0.21	0.24	0.13
2005	0.38	0.13	0.13	0.23	0.23	0.13
2010	0.41	0.16	0.16	0.20	0.11	0.12
2015	0.40	0.12	0.14	0.20	0.16	0.09

Source: UNCTAD (n.d.).

Table 3.3 HHI values for selected Asian LDCs

Year	Afghanistan	Bangladesh	Bhutan	Cambodia	Laos	Myanmar	Nepal	Yemen
1995	0.34	0.33	0.29	0.4	0.31	0.3	0.39	0.81
2000	0.36	0.38	0.32	0.34	0.3	0.26	0.32	0.85
2005	0.27	0.38	0.3	0.36	0.27	0.34	0.14	0.82
2010	0.29	0.41	0.35	0.33	0.31	0.37	0.14	0.67
2015	0.27	0.40	0.39	0.31	0.27	0.41	0.14	0.53

Source: UNCTAD (n.d.).

average HHI score of 0.38, with only Yemen having a higher average score of 0.74. Regardless of the expectation that Bangladesh will graduate from the LDC group at the same time as most Asian LDCs, significant export diversification is necessary.

Macroeconomic stability

Macroeconomic stability and structural transformation are both considered essential factors for sustainable economic growth (Ocampo 2003; Balma and Ncube 2015). Asiedu (2006) identified that an unstable macroeconomic environment contributed significantly to the loss of foreign direct investment (FDI) in Sub-Saharan African countries. Reduced investment not only hampers economic growth but also total labour productivity, which limits opportunities for economies to experience structural change.

Table 3.4 shows that the majority of Bangladesh's macroeconomic indicators moved in favourable directions over the past two decades. Economic growth contributed to rises in GDP per capita – per capita income doubled in Bangladesh. Debt service (in terms of GNI) against long- and medium-term loans fell. The inflation rate was rather volatile, however. Notably, increasing trade openness significantly contributed to accelerating external trade and thereby facilitated participation in global value chains. Sen (2016) noted that a high unemployment rate points to a market failure in terms of labour allocation, which holds back the economy in terms of structural change. Despite the lack of skilled workers in the manufacturing and services sectors, Bangladesh failed to sufficiently increase human capital formation to provide either sector with the required labour. On the other hand, an increasing number of unskilled workers are either working in the less productive agriculture sector or unemployed.

Overall, Bangladesh has experienced slow progress in structural transformation over the last decades. The agriculture sector continues to have the largest share of the total labour force despite its low contribution to GDP, which indicates its lowest level of productivity. The manufacturing sector, upon which Bangladesh's exports are heavily reliant, has experienced low growth in the share of the labour force as well as low growth in productivity over the past two

Table 3.4 Bangladesh's major macroeconomic indicators, 1990–2015

Indicator	1990	1995	2000	2005	2010	2015
GDP growth	5.62	5.12	5.29	6.54	5.57	6.55
GDP per capita	400.26	446.97	510.46	600.72	760.33	972.88
Inflation	6.13	10.3	2.21	7.05	8.13	6.19
Total debt service (% of GNI)	2.3	1.9	1.4	1.1	0.9	0.7
Exports of goods and services (% of GDP)	5.91	10.86	12.34	14.39	16.02	17.34
Trade openness***	9.61	12.38	14.41	33.54	35.16	38.88
Total unemployment as % of total labour force	–	2.6*	3.4	4.3	4.5	4.5**

Sources: World Bank (2017a) and *World Development Indicators* (*WDI*). Data from: https://data.worldbank.org/country/bangladesh.

Notes
* Data from 1996;
** Data from 2013;
*** Trade openness calculated as total trade (imports + exports) as a percentage of GDP.

decades. Limited changes in sectoral productivity and movement of labour across sectors suggest that structural transformation in Bangladesh is almost stagnant. Bangladesh experienced an average of 2.9 per cent of total labour productivity growth. However, the majority of this productivity growth was due to 'within sector' productivity growth rather than 'between sector' productivity growth or 'structural change'. Low level of productivity has confined Bangladesh's export competitiveness to a limited number of products and the export basket has been overtly concentrated to fewer products. And fall of the export-diversity index behind those of other competing economies such as India, Indonesia and Vietnam and even those of most of the Asian LDCs (except Yemen) continued. The limited progress the economy has achieved so far is due to a favourable macroeconomic environment, which includes rise in per capita income, less volatile rate of inflation, gradual rise of trade openness and fall of debt services. Despite those positive macroeconomic changes, Bangladesh did not perform adequately in increasing human capital formation to provide manufacturing and services sectors with the required labour.

Prospects of structural change in Bangladesh's political climate

Since Independence, Bangladesh has shown significant progress in several development indicators despite suffering from 'bad' governance (Kabeer *et al.* 2012). The political environment of Bangladesh is plagued with uncertainty and corruption and suffers from bureaucrats that are rarely subject to scrutiny from the state or public elections. Despite the challenges, the manufacturing sector, especially the readymade garment (RMG) sector, has exhibited significant progress (Ahmed *et al.* 2014). Despite the political unsettlement, the

RMG sector has benefited from the government's commitment to expanding the sector and successive governments have maintained their commitment towards ensuring necessary policy supports for the industry. More importantly, the factories of the RMG industry as well as other export-oriented manufacturing industries did not face any unwanted pressure from the political parties during the time of political strikes, especially in the 1990s and 2000s. Such implicit understanding between businesses and political parties has positively contributed towards maintaining uninterrupted operation in the export-oriented industries even during the difficult political environment.

Entrepreneurs in the manufacturing industry had to work in an environment with significant 'governance deficit' while dealing with public offices. The extra costs related to corrupt practices not only increased the cost of doing business but also distorted the competitive environment. Moreover, such a weak governance environment has provided scope for entrepreneurs to by-pass compliance related rules and regulations and thereby created a less secure working environment in the manufacturing industry. In addition, it caused frequent accidents and worker casualties, even death, in the 1990s and 2000s. Since a large number of these enterprises operated under buyers' codes of conduct, third party monitoring and international compliance standards (ISO, SA), some of the components of compliance standards had been double-checked. Despite those activities, lack of physical and social compliance, unearthed during the time of monitoring fire, electrical and structural safety issues in RMG enterprises by the private sector led initiatives of 'Accord' and 'Alliance' as well as the public sector led 'National Initiative', is a major concern for manufacturing enterprises.

Over time, the level of competitiveness in major manufacturing industries has changed, which linked technological upgrading with social upgrading of the enterprises in the global value chains. In order to ensure an enabling environment for technological upgrading, businesses demand better in-land connectivity with major seaports, uninterrupted electricity and gas supply, easy availability of land with all kinds of facilities, availability of skilled professionals and workers, among others. On the other hand, social upgrading indicates decent jobs which include better employment facilities, decent wages, work place safety and security, and workers' rights. Both technological and social upgrading in the manufacturing value chains demand more in-depth involvement of the government and private sector including employers, workers, brands/buyers and international organisations towards ensuring better standards in order to maintain competitiveness.

Comparison of Bangladesh's structural transformation to that of emerging economies

A cross-country comparison with selected Asian emerging economies that have significant exporting manufacturing sectors illustrates Bangladesh's relative performance in terms of structural transformation. In 2015, apparel and clothing accessories consisted of 85 per cent of the total value exported by Bangladesh. On the other hand, Bangladesh along with four of its Asian competitors – India, Indonesia, Pakistan and Vietnam – were responsible for 18.2 per cent of the world's apparel exports that year (ITC 2017) and therefore can be considered direct competitors in the global economy. In order to remain competitive following graduation from the LDC group, Bangladesh has to have a similar or higher level of labour productivity, both in terms of 'within' and 'between sector' productivity.

According to International Labour Organization (ILO) data for the 1991–2015 period for the agriculture, manufacturing and services sectors of the five countries, Bangladesh stood at a similar level of structural transformation. Regarding the share of the labour force employed in the agriculture sector in 2015, Bangladesh had the highest share at 46 per cent with similar shares of 44 per cent, 43.5 per cent and 42.2 per cent in Vietnam, India and Pakistan respectively. Indonesia had the lowest share of the labour force employed in the agriculture sector at 33.5 per cent. Importantly, Figure 3.3 shows that Bangladesh had the lowest level of productivity among the five countries. More importantly, the gap in labour productivity between Bangladesh and those other countries, particularly India and Indonesia, widened.

Considering regional differences, Figure 3.4 compares Bangladesh's sectoral productivity with that of the two other South Asian countries, India and

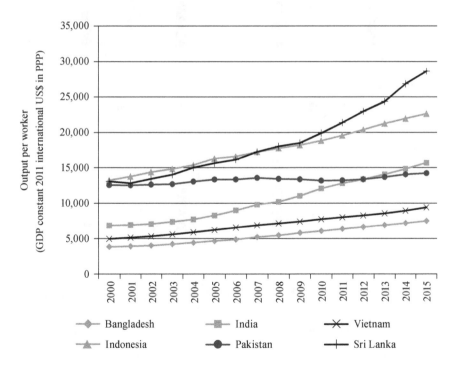

Figure 3.3 Labour productivity of Bangladesh and selected Asian emerging economies.
Source: ILO (2017).

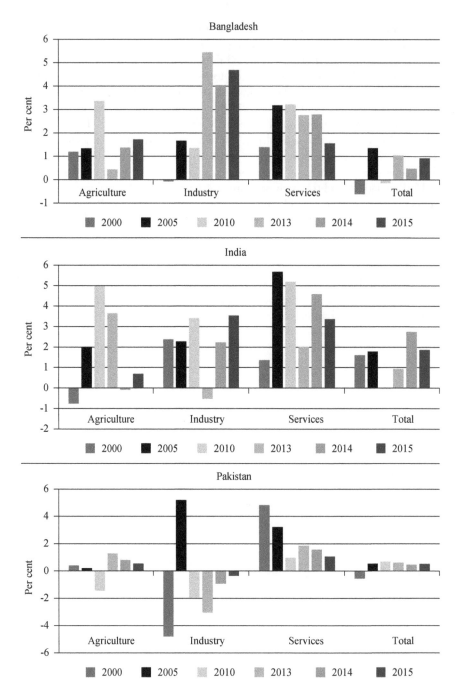

Figure 3.4 Relative growth of sectoral productivity of Bangladesh, India and Pakistan, 2000–13.

Sources: BBS (2015); Groningen Growth and Development Centre (2017).

Pakistan. While Bangladesh's economy is structurally similar to the two economies in terms of ranking of productivity of each sector, growth in relative productivity in the industry and services sectors was limited and volatile.

In order to measure the strength of structural transformation, Bangladesh's labour productivity growth (both 'within sector' productivity growth and the structural change) can be compared with that of the selected Asian emerging economies. Figure 3.5 shows average labour productivity growth for the five countries using data for the agriculture, industry and services sectors from 2011 to 2015. While Bangladesh experienced a high level of 'within sector' productivity growth, its structural change remained low, especially compared to India's and Vietnam's levels of structural changes. Bangladesh had relatively high labour productivity growth at an average of 4.39 per cent, which was higher than that of Pakistan and Indonesia, with its structural change at 0.83 per cent. While Pakistan suffered from a weak macroeconomic environment, Indonesia had already experienced significant structural change and therefore faced a slowdown. Given Bangladesh's macroeconomic environment, its economy is capable of a higher level of structural change and requires it to ensure smooth transition after graduation from the LDC group.

Better performances in terms of structural transformation by the other Asian emerging economies can be explained by better macroeconomic performances. Bangladesh is behind in the majority of macroeconomic indicators.

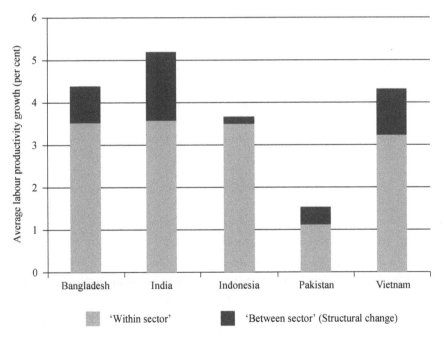

Figure 3.5 Average labour productivity growth of selected Asian emerging economies, 2011–15.

Source: World Bank (2017b).

Table 3.5 presents the macroeconomic situations of the five countries by providing the five-year average figures from 2001 to 2015. Compared to India, Indonesia and Vietnam – countries with significant exporting manufacturing sectors – Bangladesh has exhibited a lower export–GDP ratio in all three time periods. Till the period 2011–15, Bangladesh lagged behind all countries except Pakistan in terms of trade openness. While trade has a positive effect on economic growth, trade liberalisation does not necessarily induce growth (Rahman *et al.* 2010). It has been concluded that, in general, trade liberalisation has a negative effect on employment in the agriculture and manufacturing sectors, but a positive effect on employment in the services sector (Rahman *et al.* 2010). Bangladesh is the only country among the five to have a higher average unemployment rate in the period 2011–15 compared to the initial period of 2001–05.

There is evidence of structural transformation in Bangladesh through the decreasing trend of share of labour in the agriculture sector and an increasing share of labour in the manufacturing sector, although the progress is significantly slow. The majority of the increase in productivity has happened through an increase in 'within' productivity growth rather than through 'structural change'. Compared to other competing economies, Bangladesh has experienced limited growth in productivity. The country has also experienced less trade openness and export diversification, which highlights the importance of the economy to experience further structural change in order to remain competitive in the international export market.

Graduation-led structural transformation in Bangladesh

This section reflects on Bangladesh's pathway towards successful structural transformation, especially as the country nears graduation from the LDC group. The directions of several macroeconomic stability indicators are reviewed to analyse whether Bangladesh can sustain higher productivity in the future for structural change. The section lays out future trends of structural change, particularly in the context of expected graduation in 2024. These trends are compared to those of emerging economies to analyse how Bangladesh is expected to fare as graduation approaches.

Future trends of macroeconomic stability

Structural transformation has a broadly positive relationship with increases in productivity (IMF and IDA 2015). For a country to sustain productivity over the long-run, several macroeconomic factors need to be considered. In order to achieve macroeconomic stability, Bangladesh's Seventh Five Year Plan (7FYP) for FYs 2016–20 considered the future directions of several indicators including the inflation rate, debt level and GDP (Bangladesh Planning Commission 2015). Using the forecasts in 7FYP, this sub-section compares Bangladesh's macroeconomic progress between 2015 and 2021, when the country is expected

Table 3.5 Macroeconomic performances of Bangladesh and selected Asian emerging economies over time

Country	Year	GDP growth	GDP per capita (in US$)	Inflation	Total debt service (% of GNI)	Exports of goods and services (% of GDP)	Trade openness*	Unemployment rate**
Bangladesh	2001–05	5.09	556.03	5.13	1.11	12.55	0.24	3.94
	2006–10	6.07	695.69	7.66	0.98	16.79	0.35	4.2
	2011–15	6.32	882.06	7.53	1.07	19.19	0.51	4.34
India	2001–05	6.74	862.26	3.98	3.07	16.02	0.22	4.1
	2006–10	8.34	1,183.01	8.75	2.11	22.03	0.43	3.92
	2011–15	6.8	1,569.27	8.13	2.48	23.49	0.5	3.6
Indonesia	2001–05	4.73	2,343.59	9.33	8.61	31.65	0.26	9.56
	2006–10	5.74	2,866.6	7.85	5.48	26.36	0.39	8.56
	2011–15	5.53	3,551.74	5.76	5.25	23.93	0.48	6.34
Pakistan	2001–05	5.02	895.81	5.17	3.65	15.59	0.21	7.8
	2006–10	3.43	1,035.6	12.67	1.89	13.13	0.32	5.46
	2011–15	4.01	1,088.47	7.8	1.88	12.5	0.38	5.94
Vietnam	2001–05	6.9	924.3	4.53	2.41	57.98	0.69	2.32
	2006–10	6.32	1,214.32	10.94	1.55	68.64	1.31	2.46
	2011–15	5.91	1,533	7.87	3.28	83.85	2.03	1.96

Sources: World Bank (2017a) and ILO (2017).

Notes
* Trade openness calculated as total trade (imports + exports) as percentage of GDP;
** ILO estimated figures.

to be halfway to graduation. The trends of macroeconomic indicators are presented in Table 3.6.

As mentioned, Bangladesh's inflation rate has a volatile trend. In 2015, the country had an inflation rate of 6.5 per cent, which missed the target for inflation in the Sixth Five Year Plan for FY 2011 to FY 2015 by 0.5 per cent. However, 7FYP targets a downward trend in the inflation rate, which is expected to be at 5.5 per cent by 2020 and 5.2 per cent by 2021. The 7FYP expects not only a reduction of the inflation rate but also a continuous downward trend, which should support smooth transition after graduation.

Balma and Ncube (2015) empirically demonstrated a positive relationship between public investment and productivity as well as the importance of debt sustainability for long-term productivity growth. For Bangladesh, government spending was at 15.7 per cent of GDP in 2015 and is expected to increase to 25 per cent by 2021. The fiscal deficit was at 4.7 per cent of GDP in 2015 and it has been predicted to remain at 4.7 per cent till 2020. According to a debt sustainability analysis by the IMF and International Development Association (IDA), Bangladesh is on a sustainable path and at low risk of external public debt distress. Unsustainable public debt would be of concern because of short maturity periods, the tied nature of loans and currency mismatch risks. The debt sustainability analysis highlighted that in order to keep the debt level sustainable in the future, a permanent increase in government revenue, especially tax revenue, is needed (IMF and IDA 2016).

Further, Bangladesh's GDP growth was at 6.5 per cent in 2015 and is targeted to be at 10 per cent by 2021. However, given the targets set in both the Sixth Five Year Plan and 7FYP, the country has yet to meet any of the GDP targets for the past few years even though its GDP growth rate has been stable at over 6

Table 3.6 Macroeconomic indicators, 2015–21

Indicator	2015*	2021** (targets)
Real GDP growth (%)	6.5	10
Share of manufacturing in GDP (%)	17.8	27
Share of labour force in manufacturing sector (%)	15.4	20
GNI per capita (US$)	1,314	2,000
Exports (US$ billions)	31.7	82
Total government spending (% of GDP)	15.7	25
Consumer price index inflation (average)	6.5	5.2

Sources: World Bank (2017a), ILO (2017) and Bangladesh Planning Commission (2015).

Notes

* Some figures in 7FYP differ from available international statistics for 2015. From the World Bank's World Development Indicators database, the share of manufacturing in GDP was at 17.6 per cent, while GNI per capita and exports were at US$1,035.70 and US$27.6 billion, respectively. Other relevant statistics are: GDP growth (annual per cent) at 6.6 per cent and inflation (annual per cent) at 6.2 per cent (World Bank, 2017).

** The 2021 figures are targets set by the Government of Bangladesh rather than an economic forecasting based on existing data.

per cent since 2011. Since the 2021 figure is a target rather than a forecasted value, Bangladesh has to devise effective monetary and fiscal policies to ensure that the ambitious target is met. Figure 3.6 presents the directions of three national account indicators to illustrate the projected growth of productivity and infrastructure in Bangladesh.

Figure 3.6 shows that the national account indicators are moving in upward directions. The linear forecasting suggests that the indicators, especially gross capital formation and gross domestic savings, will continue the upward movement during the time period leading to Bangladesh's expected graduation from the LDC group in 2024. The projected trends are admittedly optimistic given the absence of exogenous shocks in the model. Notably, the upward trend of gross capital formation over the years could indicate a future increase in infrastructure, which would likely have a positive effect on productivity. The projected trend of the current account balance is positive and stable, which is encouraging for future investment.

At present, Bangladesh's macroeconomic and national account indicators reflect a stable position. According to the forecasts found in the two most recent five-year plans, Bangladesh is expected to make faster progress on structural transformation through increases in productivity and infrastructure. Since Bangladesh has so far struggled to achieve the targets for relevant macroeconomic stability indicators, it should prioritise efforts to improve on existing trends.

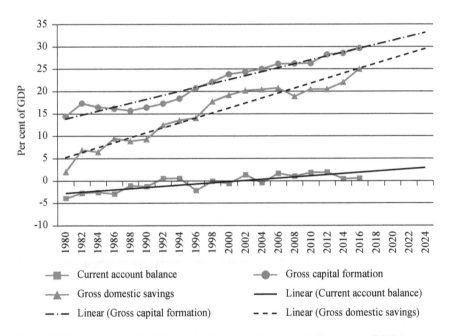

Figure 3.6 Projected trends of Bangladesh's national account indicators until 2024.
Source: World Bank (2017a).

Bangladesh's projected macroeconomic performance until 2024 will partly depend on global macroeconomic conditions in the coming years. Depressed global economic growth will likely continue because of the slow rises in economic growth in the major economies of Europe and North America. The rise of protectionist measures by a group of 20 countries may have a negative effect on Bangladesh's export trade environment (WTO 2016). Bangladesh's exports could suffer if the level of productivity continues to be stagnant, especially if the country graduates from the LDC group and loses access to trade preferences. Moreover, developing countries, which are both sources of raw materials for Bangladesh's industries and destinations for Bangladesh's products, are unlikely to confront sluggish economic growth, which would have consequences for Bangladesh's external trade and FDI inflow. Hence, the future trends of various indicators may be different from projected.

Projected trends of structural transformation: Bangladesh and selected emerging economies

This sub-section analyses whether the future trends of structural change place Bangladesh in a favourable position as the country nears expected graduation in 2024. In order to understand shifts in the country's labour market, ILO estimates of shares of the labour force employed in the agriculture, manufacturing and service sectors are analysed. The ILO data and estimates from 1991 to 2020 enable this sub-section to forecast trends in the labour market until 2024; Figure 3.7 illustrates labour movement across the three sectors.

As shown, the share of agriculture in total labour force is expected to gradually creep downward. An encouraging trend that emerges from the projection is the expected increase in the labour force in the manufacturing sector on which the economy's export industry heavily relies. Part of the manufacturing sector, the RMG industry accounts for approximately 80 per cent of Bangladesh's total exports and plays an important role in reducing rural and extreme poverty in the country (Bangladesh Planning Commission 2015). A shift of labour from the agriculture to the manufacturing sector could be a strong indicator of strong structural transformation. However, what is rather discouraging to note is that share of services sector in the labour force, a key indicator of structural transformation of the economy, does not show a significant rise. After the manufacturing sector's value addition at 17.6 per cent of GDP, the services sector provides Bangladesh with the highest value addition among the three sectors at 56.3 per cent of GDP (ILO 2017). Despite the productivity of the services sector, past progress and projected growth have been almost at a stagnant level. Given that it is expected to graduate in 2024, Bangladesh is expected to struggle with the present direction of structural change if the services sector experiences limited growth despite its high contribution to the economy's GDP.

While there is no set level of structural transformation required to achieve smooth transition after graduation, an analysis of Bangladesh's performance in terms of structural change can be carried out by comparing the country's position

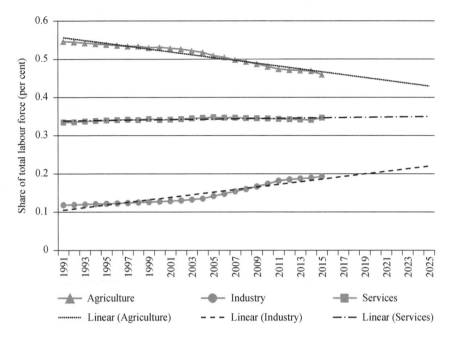

Figure 3.7 Projections for Bangladesh's labour force until 2024.
Source: ILO (2017).

and direction with those of emerging economies that are performing better. Forecasting of Bangladesh's structural change, which can be inferred from Figure 3.7 and illustrated in Figure 3.8, shows that while there has been no decrease in 'between sector' productivity growth, there has also been no significant increase. The set of graphs in Figure 3.8 enables the comparison of labour movement among the agriculture and manufacturing sectors to date and forecasts for emerging economies on average and shows more active structural change. Figure 3.8 also highlights structural change performances and forecasts for India and Pakistan, two emerging economies with an export-oriented manufacturing sector.

Emerging economies, as shown, are expected to experience significant structural change in the coming years. India and Pakistan, two of Bangladesh's regional competitors, are expected to experience even more rapid structural change compared to the emerging economies. While Bangladesh is not expected to exhibit a decline in the structural change, the pathway to structural transformation in 2024 is almost a flat line.

Indonesia and Vietnam exhibit a downward trend. However, given the two countries' superior performance in terms of productivity, it can be surmised that the economies have reached an already high level of structural change, leading to a slow-down of growth in further structural change. For Bangladesh, a low level of structural change is expected to occur until and after graduation from

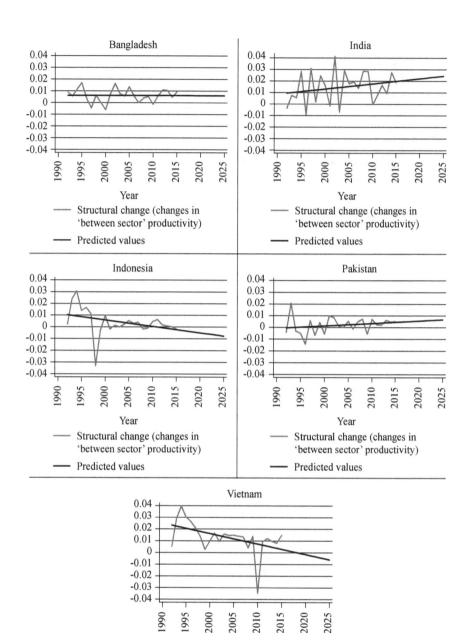

Figure 3.8 Linear forecasting of structural change (Bangladesh, India, Indonesia, Pakistan and Vietnam).

Source: authors' own estimation.

the LDC group. Even with macroeconomic indicators moving in favourable directions and a relatively high level of labour productivity, the potential for higher structural change seems to be limited.

Overall, Bangladesh experiences weaker structural change compared to the competing emerging economies. More importantly, the gap in labour productivity between Bangladesh and those other countries has widened. In case of graduation-led structural transformation till 2024, the majority of national account indicators are moving in upward directions and linear forecasting suggests that they will remain this way for gross capital formation and gross domestic savings. For Bangladesh, a low level of structural change is expected to occur until and after graduation from the LDC group. Even with macroeconomic indicators moving in favourable directions and a relatively high level of labour productivity, the potential for higher structural change appears limited. Compared to Bangladesh, emerging economies are advanced in terms of structural change and are expected to experience a significant rise in the coming years. The level of structural change is quite high in Bangladesh's major competing countries, especially India and Vietnam, which can be explained by their better macroeconomic performances such as high trade openness, better export diversification, less unemployment and efficient allocation of labour. Emerging economies are expected to continue their better performance in structural change in the coming years.

Structural transformation-enabled smooth transition after graduation

This section analyses how structural transformation and graduation from the LDC group are connected. A quantitative analysis to understand the impact of the graduation criteria indicates that the indicators under the three criteria are not sufficient to facilitate successful structural change in an economy. The section then goes on to study countries that have achieved graduation without experiencing adequate structural change. It is observed that the transition to graduation is difficult in the absence of structural transformation, especially when countries lose trade preferences and other S&DT provisions.

Post-graduation experiences of selected countries

In the experiences of the recently graduated countries from the LDC group, Cape Verde, the Maldives and Samoa, structural transformation was crucial for a smooth transition (UNCTAD 2016). Before graduation, Cape Verde was characterised by its dependence on external financing, especially official development assistance (ODA) and remittances. After graduation, it had to develop economically and allocate more labour towards its more productive service sector, notably the tourism industry, in order to sustain itself after the loss of preferences. The Maldives' tuna industry was significantly impacted after the loss of trade preferences through the Generalised System of Preferences (GSP) following graduation. The country now has a robust tourism industry but is vulnerable to exogenous shocks. Given its transition to graduation, a better allocation of labour would have benefited the economy. Samoa struggled with the transition period to graduation due to its heavy dependence on the export of primary products such as fish, honey, vanilla and cocoa. The country could have benefited from more developed manufacturing and services sectors after graduation.

Hartmann *et al.* (2016) compared the structural transformation of Latin American and the Caribbean countries and high-performing Asian economies and used product space to measure structural change, and revealed the gap in productive capacity between the two country groups. Asian economies with more diverse products and more productive manufacturing sectors did significantly better in terms of economic growth and reducing income inequality than the less diversified Latin American and the Caribbean countries.

Analysis of the relationship between structural transformation and graduation

In order to establish the relationship between structural transformation and graduation from the LDC group, a panel data analysis was carried out to study the effects of selected indicators under the graduation criteria on the structural change term. Adopting the methodology used by McMillan and Rodrik (2011), random-effect regression analyses allow the study of the determinants of structural change.

McMillan and Rodrik (2011) selected indicators that affect an economy's productivity to be independent variables. The significant variables were agricultural share in employment, raw materials' share in exports, the undervaluation index and the employment rigidity index. The regression results for these variables showed that structural transformation is dependent not only on a country's trade performance but also on labour productivity. Raw materials' share in exports, which had a negative coefficient, indicates a country's level of comparative advantage and trade diversity, while the undervaluation index indicates the country's trade practices, which affect its economy's level of efficiency in trade. Undervaluation of currency is expected to promote growth in exports. The employment rigidity index is expected to have a negative effect on labour productivity. Therefore, a decrease in rigidity is expected to contribute positively towards structural change.

This sub-section analyses how the graduation criteria affect the level of labour productivity caused by labour movement between sectors. The independent variables chosen are the three graduation criteria – GNI per capita, the EVI and HAI. For control variables, share of the agriculture in employment and two macroeconomic indicators, inflation and private investment, were chosen. The dependent variable is the same as that selected by McMillan and Rodrik (2011) – the structural change using data for the agriculture, manufacturing and services sectors in an economy. Random-effect regression analyses were performed on the data collected for five Asian countries: Bangladesh, India, Indonesia, Pakistan and Vietnam. The regression model uses data from 1992 to 2014. The regression results are presented in Table 3.7.

Table 3.7 Determinants of structural change in selected Asian countries including Bangladesh

Dependent variable: structural change	(1)	(2)	(3)	(4)	(5)	(6)	(7)	(8)
Share of agriculture in employment	0.05 (0.000)***	—	—	—	—	—	0.06 (0.016)**	0.036 (0.005)***
Private investment	—	0.041 (0.027)**	—	—	—	—	0.063 (0.019)**	0.046 (0.001)***
Inflation	—	—	-0.061 (0.000)***	—	—	—	-0.007 (0.809)	-0.051 (0.001)***
GNI per capita	—	—	—	-0.0002 (0.244)	—	—	0 (0.391)	—
EVI	—	—	—	—	-0.007 (0.488)	—	0.007 (0.449)	—
HAI	—	—	—	—	—	-0.008 (0.348)	-0.013 (0.21)	—
Constant	-1.731 (0.011)	-0.267 (0.601)	1.232 0.000	1.123 (0.004)	1.147 (0.01)	1.331 (0.034)	-3.594 (0.038)	-1.836 (0.019)
R^2	0.151	0.098	0.131	0.026	0.04	0.005	0.19	0.273
N	230	230	230	230	206	230	206	230

Source: authors' estimation.

Note
The p-values in parentheses.
, * represent significance at 5% and 1% levels, respectively.

From the analysis of the results given above, three conclusions can be drawn. First, starting at a high level of labour employed in the agriculture sector can mean more opportunity for structural change. The share of agriculture in employment is constantly significant with a positive coefficient. Similar to the findings by McMillan et al. (2014), if a country has stable macroeconomic indicators, a large share of labour employed in the agriculture sector would mean that the country's economy should experience higher structural change in the future. However, McMillan et al. (2014) marked that the variable agricultural share in employment remained significant only when paired up with other variables influencing labour productivity. This finding emphasises that while a country starting with a large share of agriculture in employment may see convergence in the labour market that leads to a more productive labour force, the process is not automatic and is supported by other factors affecting an economy's level of labour productivity.

Second, macroeconomic stability is crucial for structural transformation. The two macroeconomic stability indicators, inflation and private investment, are both significant. Inflation has an expected negative coefficient, while private investment has a positive coefficient. Aspe (1992) emphasised the importance of controlling inflation and stabilising other macroeconomic variables in Mexico to achieve structural change of its economy. Investment, especially FDI, is heavily related to increasing a country's productivity. For a country to experience structural change and subsequently sustainable economic growth, it is crucial to stabilise macroeconomic indicators.

Third, the graduation criteria – GNI per capita, HAI and EVI – have little effect on structural transformation. Perhaps the most surprising result in the analyses is that no graduation criteria have a direct impact on the structural change term. The result does not necessarily mean that the indicators under the graduation criteria have no impact on structural transformation. Rather, meeting the graduation criteria is not adequate for successful structural transformation in the future. As mentioned, Guillaumont (2014) described the indicators under the graduation criteria as concentrating on targeting 'arbitrary' structural handicaps. Therefore, in order to systematically achieve structural change, the route to graduation needs to consider other criteria that directly affect the structural transformation of an economy.

Overall, structural transformation-enabled smooth transition after graduation has been analysed by examining the relationship between structural transformation and graduation from the LDC group by adopting random-effect regression analysis based on McMillan and Rodrik (2011). Three conclusions can be drawn based on the analysis (i) starting at a high level of labour employed in the agriculture sector can mean more opportunity for structural change, (ii) macroeconomic stability related indicators, particularly inflation and private investment, are crucial for structural transformation, and (iii) the graduation criteria – GNI per capita, HAI and EVI – have little effect on structural transformation. In other words, meeting the graduation criteria is not adequate for successful structural transformation in the future.

Policy perspectives on graduation and the post-graduation period

This section reviews the national and sectoral economic policies that are currently being implemented with a view to assess their relevance and effectiveness for accelerating graduation-led structural transformation and structural transformation-led graduation during the post-graduation period. It considers the policy analysis presented in Bangladesh's 7FYP for the FYs 2016–20. Existing national policy documents do not provide policy perspectives beyond 2021. This section fills the gap by outlining policies towards expected graduation from the LDC group in 2024 and afterwards.

Policies for graduation-led structural transformation

Although the majority of its macroeconomic indicators are moving in favourable directions, Bangladesh currently has an almost stagnant level of 'between sector' productivity growth. Timmer and Akkus (2008) considered structural transformation to be a powerful tool for the alleviation of poverty in developing countries. However, structural change policies must target a country's poor and concentrate on developing their skills.

While the RMG industry makes up an important part of the country's manufacturing sector, Bangladesh's government encourages little labour movement from the agriculture sector to the manufacturing sector. Fernandes (2008) studied the total factor productivity of Bangladesh's firms from 1999 to 2003 and found that it suffered due to the lack of adequate infrastructure, heavy bureaucracy, high crime rates and limited global integration. Ahmed (2009) demonstrated how Bangladesh's RMG industry struggled due to the loss of guaranteed markets when the Multi-Fibre Arrangement was abolished and emphasised the need for upgradation in terms of technology and labour to sustain the manufacturing sector, following the loss of preferential market access due to graduation from the LDC group.

Bangladesh's labour market continues to be characterised by low-skilled labour, which hinders the progress that can be made by the manufacturing sector. Bangladesh's manufacturing sector, including the RMG sector, continues to be reliant on the low-technology sectors, sectors which produce traditional and conventional goods that are expected to require no or an extremely limited level of technological innovation. In 2015, the country's low-technology manufacturing sector exports in the global value added decomposition of exports were at approximately United States dollar (US$) 30.5 billion, while medium- and high-technology manufacturing sector's value added decomposition of exports were at only US$609 million. Comparatively, export-oriented Vietnam had figures of about US$46.3 billion for low-technology manufacturing sector value added decomposition of exports and around US$15.9 billion for medium- and high-technology manufacturing sector (ADB 2016). The lack of skilled labour and medium and high technology in the manufacturing sector could restrict productivity increases and thus make sustaining the sector difficult over the long-run.

The 7FYP delineated a number of policies that target different levels of upgradation and structural transformation of Bangladesh's economy. These policies focus on three key areas: industry-related policy and strategy, infrastructure-related policy and strategy, and development of the information and communication technology (ICT) industry. If implemented, these policies and strategies could significantly boost the economy in the run-up to graduation and beyond. According to 7FYP, Bangladesh's government plans to promote structural transformation by developing the manufacturing and services sectors. With such concentration on these sectors, the economy can increase total productivity and experience strong structural change. Continued development of the country's infrastructure is important for the export-oriented industries.

Annex Table 3.a.1 outlines existing labour, land, product market and infrastructure policies and strategies implemented to address specific market and government failures and bring about structural change. Policies have the objective of increasing investment that targets productivity increases in all factors of production, including skilled labour and better infrastructure for key sectors and industries. Encouraging investment is necessary to increase and direct FDI towards the manufacturing sector, particularly its export-oriented industries. FDI not only increases in the private investment required to increase productivity but also enables the 'spillover effect'. This effect happens through transfer of better technology and better managerial skills from the countries that provide investment. Improvements in technology and skills are expected to increase total productivity as well as sectoral productivity to encourage structural change.

To sustain long-term structural change in the services sector in particular, it has to be modernised in terms of both technology and skills. Bangladesh struggles to export services due to productivity challenges, especially in the cases of professional and skill-intensive industries such as banking, finance, ICT, and aviation. The country's services sector is dominated by relatively low-skilled sectors such as trade, transport and personal services.

The 7FYP focuses on the development of three industries within the service sector – international transport, tourism and international ICT services. Regulatory and incentive policies need to be implemented to boost growth of these industries. According to 7FYP, Bangladesh's government intends to implement a deregulation plan to encourage private investment in traditionally public industries such as education, ICT services, aviation and electricity. The plan encourages investment to upgrade education and training quality and emphasises expanding tertiary education.

The overall goals are to significantly raise the three industries' shares of employment and GDP, improve small-scale enterprises' access to financial services and increase integration with global value chains. A major focus of the policies is to support domestic technology development, research and innovation by ensuring a conducive policy environment via industrial diversification and value addition to commodities. Accelerating the use of ICT and providing universal and affordable access to the internet are other major goals.

Policies for structural transformation-enabled smooth transition after graduation

Graduation from the LDC group would cause Bangladesh to lose a significant proportion of the ISMs it currently enjoys as an LDC. At present, Bangladesh is eligible to receive dedicated funds through ODA. LDCs are eligible to receive 0.15 per cent to 0.20 per cent and above of a donor's GNI in assistance and Bangladesh, which receives 4.9 per cent of its economy's gross capital formation in ODA, is one of the largest recipients of funds (World Bank 2017a). After graduation, Bangladesh would lose GSP facilities, which would impact trade relationships with major countries. Unless Bangladesh becomes more competitive in terms of exports, it is expected to lose 5.5 per cent to 7.5 per cent of its exports (UNCTAD 2016).

It is important to rethink whether meeting the graduation criteria or other development criteria would be sufficient to provide a level of structural transformation that would ensure smooth graduation during the post-graduation period. Despite Bangladesh's success on several development indicators, its economy has experienced a low level of structural change. In order to overcome the challenges following graduation, the countries have to articulate policies to significantly increase labour productivity and sectoral productivity to be prepared to compete in the global economy.

Cross-country perspectives

Major developing countries which experienced significant economic progress over the last decades have put emphasis on structural transformation of their economies. Although the areas of emphasis are the same for most of the countries, such as agriculture, industry and services, the specific focus under these areas and instruments used for intervention are rather different. A cross-country examination of structural transformation of China, India, Korea and Vietnam found in Annex Table 3.a.2 reveals that all three sectors have got emphasis in core policies related to structural transformation in these economies. In the case of transformation of the agriculture sector, there is a major focus on enhancing productivity in crops, breeds of livestock, better extension services, better credit support, participation of women in farming, different types of subsidies, market-based trading of agricultural products, farmland protection, upgraded agricultural technologies and agricultural insurance. On the other hand, transformation in the industry sector is highlighted through: promoting domestic industries' supportive tariff policies; enhancing capabilities in export-oriented industrialisation; creating global brands; strengthening linkages between small and medium enterprises (SMEs) and FDIs; putting emphasis on establishing the complete value chain; ensuring technology transfer from foreign sources; and diversifying the industrial base by developing traditional industries such as shipbuilding, automobiles, iron and steel, petrochemicals, light industry and textiles. Besides, future pillars of industry focus on energy conservation, IT, high-end manufacturing equipment; developing new clusters for industries, and acquisition of modern management practices; setting up high-tech industries in special economic zones (SEZs); and shifting the focus from pro-business to pro-market policies. On the other hand, transformation of the services industry has been promoted through expansion of the insurance sector in new areas, further enhancement of rural banking and introducing competition policy for the services sectors, etc.

Action points

Bangladesh needs to undertake time-bound measures which will help to develop a strong foundation of structural transformation based on which it would be able to ensure smooth transition after graduation. Bangladesh's core focus of building a strong foundation on structural transformation should be on raising productivity – both 'within' and 'between sector' productivity – thereby being able to reduce the productivity gap with its peers and competing countries. Given the time-bound process of graduation, future initiatives should be taken in a time-specific manner. These proposed initiatives should focus on government policies and measures as well as private sector initiatives. A part of these initiatives has been reflected in the strategy document of the 7FYP; however, given its reference period till 2021, future courses of action should be more forward-looking. More importantly, the strategies are by default prepared without taking into cognisance the challenges for Bangladesh under a regime of no/limited preferential status. Taking all these issues into account, following are the areas where Bangladesh should put emphasis with regard to structural transformation over the next decade. Major actions are required in three areas such as macroeconomic management, setting sectorial priorities and strengthening institutional governance. Annex Table 3.a.3 provides the list of activities and required policy instruments to attain the target.

Note

1 The fiscal year in Bangladesh runs from 1 July to the next 30 June.

Annex

Table 3.a.1 Policies and strategies for structural change

Policy and strategy		Objective	Result and implementation
Labour policies and strategies			
Labour market regulation	National Social Security Strategy safety net programmes	• The National Social Security Strategy intends to improve Bangladesh's safety net programmes. • Contributory social insurance and employment regulations are expected to improve workers' rights.	• The safety net programmes are expected to allow workers to develop skills and move to more productive sectors, facilitating structural change. • Increase in productivity at the national level is difficult without a national policy on protecting workers' rights.
	Chittagong Development Authority strategies	• Improve Chattogram infrastructure. • Improve the living conditions of RMG industry workers and promote the development of Chattogram's RMG sector.	• The Chittagong Development Authority's strategy promotes structural change only in the city.
Labour migration policies	Technical and Vocational Education and Training programmes	• Technical and Vocational Education and Training programmes intend to increase technology available in rural areas and improve rural workers' skills. • With increased opportunities in rural areas, urban–rural migration is expected to fall.	• Technical and Vocational Education and Training programmes are not designed with the various requirements of the manufacturing and services sectors in mind. • Curricula need to concentrate on the sectors employing labour. • No adequate plans to encourage the manufacturing and services sectors to expand into rural areas, thus limiting opportunities for structural change.

continued

Table 3.a.1 Continued

Policy and strategy	Objective	Result and implementation
Land policies and strategies		
Land regulation Establishment of digital land management system	• Use of land information system to facilitate quick capturing, retrieval and querying of different cartographic information. • Use of land information system for recording and maintaining records is expected to minimise tampering of records.	• Better land policies are expected to make the agricultural, manufacturing and service sectors more attractive to external investors, which is especially important after graduation due to the positive impact on the level of external financing. • For land policies to be effective, adequate infrastructure has to be developed.
Land reform Economic Zone Act (2010)	• The Economic Zone Act is expected to ease land-related problems faced by potential investors. • The Act provides a legal basis for the establishment of economic zones in all potential areas including rural and underdeveloped regions.	
Product market policies and strategies		
Export diversification Protection policy	• The anti-trade and anti-export regime has been slowly dismantled since 1990. • Substantial anti-export bias remains in trade policy for protection of domestic markets.	• Given the loss of trade preferences following graduation, measurements for export diversification are necessary to remain competitive. • While market diversification is important, policies that facilitate product diversification are equally important.

Industrial policies	Moving into non-traditional markets for exports	• Explore economies with sizeable GDP for potential demand.*
	Exchange rate management	• For export diversification, the target is to avoid rigidity or appreciation of the real effective exchange rate. • A moderate depreciation of the real effective exchange rate is encouraged to sustain competitiveness of exports, particularly non-RMG exports.
	Fiscal policy	• All exporters benefit from a duty drawback scheme. • RMG exporters pay only a nominal income tax on their earnings that is fixed at 0.6% of total export earnings.
	FDI to stimulate exports	• FDI, associated with better technological and managerial skills and knowledge about international marketing conditions, is expected to improve the productivity and export performance of Bangladesh's firms. • Spillovers, especially technological spillovers, due to FDI improve the productivity of domestic firms.

• Existing industrial policies depend on attracting new foreign investors who would be crucial after the loss of trade preferences following graduation.

• Infrastructure needs to be simultaneously developed to support increases in firms' capacities and total labour productivity.

continued

Table 3.a.1 Continued

Policy and strategy		Objective	Result and implementation
Infrastructure policies and strategies			
Energy and electricity	Power System Master Plan (2010)	• Capacity targets are set for 23,000 megawatts of electricity by FY2020 (the end of 7FYP), 24,000 megawatts by 2021 and 37,000 megawatts by 2030.	• Development of infrastructure is a fundamental part of structural change and smooth transition following graduation.
	Renewable Energy Policy (2008)	• The Renewable Energy Policy expected 5% of total energy generation from renewable sources by 2015 and 10% by 2020.	• Infrastructure not only determines existing productivity of various sectors but also future investment opportunities.
	Power trade	• Increase power trade between Bangladesh and its northeastern neighbours. • Power trade allows access to electricity at a relatively low average cost, especially in the face of primary energy constraints.	• While several infrastructure plans were developed to improve the overall investment climate, development plans based on the most productive sectors could also lead to increased structural change.
	Efficient operation and maintenance	• The loss rate after adopting efficient operation and maintenance could be lowered to 5% or 500 megawatts of electricity from the previously expected 22%.	
	Domestic coal use	• High-quality domestic coal produced by the Barapukuria Coal Mine could be used for higher value-added processes.	

| Transport | Investment priorities | • The Sixth Five Year Plan included a long list of uncompleted transport projects.
• The Roads and Highways Department's Annual Development Plan has tended to spread the budget over an impractically large number of projects, without proper prioritisation.
• Prioritisation of projects is important for effective completion of key transport projects. |

Source: Bangladesh Planning Commission (2015).

Note

* The BRICS (Brazil, Russia, India, China and South Africa), Japan, Australia and South Korea are Bangladesh's fastest growing RMG export markets.

Table 3.a.2 Policies for enhancing structural transformation in selected economies of Asia

Country	Main policy	Policy component
South Korea	Agricultural policy	• Developing IT convergence business models including those for remote greenhouse control, quality management and traceability, and interactive R&D (research and development) road maps for farmers and the public.
		• Inducing Korea's sixth industrialisation by integrating agriculture with processing and tourism industry and advancing the livestock industry into a sustainable, eco-friendly industry by promoting use of animal waste as resources.
		• Alleviating management instability by expanding agriculture disaster insurance and introducing revitalisation programmes, while innovating agricultural management to induce cost reduction.
		• Fostering joint management bodies with village farming cooperatives, and development of professional management organisations by creating a range of non-agricultural income sources, such as processing and tourism.
		• Providing social welfare supports such as pension, health insurance and basic livelihood security system, and enabling farmers to better prepare for retirement with direct payment for farming transfer and farmland pensions.
		• Expanding town and township based public services (rural child care facilities) and village living infrastructure (communal homes, joint meal service facilities and establish rural traffic systems to connect such facilities).
		• Ensuring customised welfare for rural villages by establishing the 'Safety Management and Disaster Prevention Guarantee for Farmers Act', expanding farmland pensions for the aged, and strengthening support for the settlement of multi-cultural families in rural areas.
		• Invigorating local communities under local initiatives of local residents and support of urban residents through nationwide expansion of the 'Rural Village Campaign for All'.
		• Making a distribution environment where farmers receive more and consumers pay less, by reducing distribution stages through expanding consumer-participatory direct dealings and systemisation of distribution systems to a more producers' centred one.
		• Setting price stabilisation bands for key items, while refraining from direct market intervention, at time of excess in price on the basis of the price band.
		• Maintaining a close cooperation structure between the Prime Minister's office and relevant ministries, such as a standing committee, to prepare a joint response manual for food safety accidents.
		• Implementing a general food information network through cooperation with related government agencies, such as the Korea Food and Drug Administration, and establishing a network for real-time information on food traceability.

Industrial policy		• Protecting domestic industry by direct import controls.
		• Permitting imports on the basis of the 'positive list' system.
		• Instituting incentive structures that favoured use of imported capital and intermediate goods to develop efficient export industries at home.
		• Abolishing tariff exemptions on some types of capital goods imported, creating at the same time capital funds to support domestic producers.
		• Discovering latent and potential comparative advantages through experimentation and international benchmarking.
		• Positive reinforcement of successful experiments and phasing out unsuccessful experiments by providing performance-based rewards.
		• Conducting systematic study to understand what has to be done to fill the missing links in the domestic value chain and moving up the quality ladder, and making concerted efforts to aim for international competitiveness from the outset.
		• Taking strategic risks, weighing the challenges of skill accumulation, scale economies and complementary investments against the possibility of capacity underutilisation and financial distress.
		• Promoting upstream industries with large spillovers ('Big Push' through coordinated domestic industrialisation).
		• Retaining the ownership of export-oriented industrialisation and progressively developing capabilities to add value and manage risks by active learning from, and engaged with, the outside world.
Public service		• Consolidating overlapping functions; entrusting certain functions to the private sector; expanding out-sourcing.
		• Transferring central government function to local government.
		• Organising a result-oriented administration system.
		• Creating an open personal management system.
India	Agricultural policy	• Introduction of productivity increasing varieties of crops, breeds of livestock, strains of microbes and efficient packages of technologies, particularly those for land and water management, for obviating biotic, socio-economic and environmental constraints.
		• Introduction of yield increasing and environment-friendly production and post-harvest and value addition technologies.
		• Reliable and timely availability of quality inputs at reasonable prices, institutional and credit supports, especially for small and resource-poor farmers, and provide support to land and water resources development.
		• Ensuring supply of effective technology, and availability of extension system involving appropriate linkages and partnerships with an emphasis on reaching the small farmers.
		• Improved institutional and credit support and increased rural employment opportunities, including those through creating agriculture-based rural agro-processing and agro-industries, improved rural infrastructures, including access to information, and effective markets, farm to market roads and related infrastructure.
		• Special attention to be provided to the needs and participation of women farmers.

continued

Table 3.a.2 Continued

Country	Main policy	Policy component
	Industrial policy	• Strengthen global strategic linkages by creating global brands out of India, strengthening linkages between Indian and global SMEs and intensifying FDI. • Increasing the number of global-Indian firms to those in the Fortune-500 category. • Establishment of complete value chains, within India or across countries, in selected sunrise sectors like renewable energy, food processing, electronics etc. • Increasing the share of India in sourcing of top brands in sectors where India enjoys a distinct comparative advantage such as apparel and footwear. • Improving competitiveness by reducing the cost of infrastructure such as power, logistics, easing the regulatory/compliance burden, reducing the cost of capital and improving labour productivity. • Enabling an ecosystem for technology adoption and innovation. • Adoption of the right models of technology transfer to ensure that the transferred technology is enhanced and customised for Indian conditions. • Addressing the issue of academia – research institutions – industry linkages. • Promoting innovation by Indian firms by increasing their R&D spending and filing high-quality patents that can be commercialised. • Encouraging a start-up ecosystem plays a key role in Indian industry.
	Services policy	• Opening some segments of insurance sector like health insurance and removing the 10 year disinvestment clause. • Liberalising foreign investment in rural banking with the help of mobile technology. • Relaxing the minimum area norm in the construction sector. • Raising the foreign investment cap for uplinking news and current affairs TV channels from 26 % to 49%. • Addressing the issue of multiple levies and duties in telecom. • Rationalising taxes in the shipping sector. • Introducing an electronic system of tax payment for tourist vehicles. • Encouraging venture capital in services. • Operationalising offshore financial centres. • Removing the unnecessary regulations under the Banking Regulation Act. • Effective implementation of competition policy for services and regulatory body for services other than banking, insurance, telecom and ports.

China	Agricultural policy	• Introduction of three types of subsidies – direct cash payment, providing improved seed varieties and agricultural machinery.
		• Abolishing agricultural taxes.
		• Introduction of market-based trading of agricultural products – e.g. fully lifted control over purchase and sale of grain.
		• Reformed tenure in collective forests to encourage rural people to plant trees and protect forests.
		• Reformed mechanisms to ensure funding for compulsory education in rural areas.
		• Strengthening the social safety net in rural areas to ensure basic livelihood for the rural population.
		• Abolishing unfair policies and restrictions so that rural migrant workers may receive fair treatment.
		• Implementation of the strictest possible farmland protection and water resource management systems.
	Industrial policy	• Promoting the traditional industries such as – equipment manufacturing, shipbuilding, automobiles, iron and steel, nonferrous metals, building materials, petrochemicals, light industry and textiles.
		• Promoting industries which have hi-tech or environmental focus. These include energy conservation and environmental protection, new-generation IT, bio-tech, high-end manufacturing equipment, new energy (including nuclear and renewable energy), new materials and new-energy automobiles.
		• Experiment and acquisition of modern technology and management expertise.
		• Creation of economic links to the domestic economy with Hong Kong (close to Shenzhen), Macao (close to Zhuhai), Taiwan (close to Xiamen) and overseas Chinese communities (Shantou).
		• Setting up a link between the economic hinterland and overseas.
		• Transferring high-tech industries into the SEZs.
	Services policy	• Improvement of pricing of energy, water and other natural resources so as to gain resource efficiency and reduction of pollution.
		• Ensuring strong environmental standards and sound urban planning.
		• Improvement of water management through effective water allocation regimes and management arrangements and increasing water-use efficiency.
		• Raising the proportion of people connected to water supply and sanitation.
		• Implementation of higher resource taxes and introduction or pollution tax.
		• Replacement of business tax with value added tax on services.

continued

Table 3.a.2 Continued

Country	Main policy	Policy component
Vietnam	Agricultural policy	• Promotion of investment in the agriculture sector particularly for machinery and equipment. • Facilitating the access to commodity markets. • Supporting farmers to access agricultural input. • Limiting land use for agriculture (one household can use more than 3 ha land for agriculture and forestry). • Supporting 70% of the research funding for development of new technology. • Exemption and reduction of tax on agriculture land use. • Exemption of irrigation fee. • Reduction of corporate income tax for companies producing machinery and equipment for agriculture and irrigation.
	Industrial policy	• Shifting the focus from 'pro-business' to 'pro-market' industrial activities. • Providing support for development of the agro-processing, apparel, leather and footwear, electronics and ICT, some specific mechanical engineering industries. • Selectively develop some projects in petroleum, metallurgic, machinery, basic chemistry, construction material industries. • Strongly develop the high-tech industry particularly heavy and machinery industries. • Development of large industrial clusters and establishment of open economic zones particularly heavy and machinery industries. • Putting priorities for development of following industries: high-tech, textile and apparel, motorcycle, chemical, mechanical engineering, agro-processing: tobacco, rice, maize, soybean, peanut, automotive, ICT, pharmaceutical, energy. • Proper Master Plans for development of the following industries: electronics, steel, supporting industries, leather and footwear, beverages, dairy, pulp and paper, construction materials, mineral processing and synchronous equipment production.

Source: prepared by authors.

Table 3.a.3 List of required level of activities and policy instruments

Sector	Area	Activity	Measure to be taken
Macroeconomic management	GDP growth, public and private investment	• Maintain a sustained rate of GDP growth (preferably over 7%) beyond 2024 when the country is likely to graduate from the LDC category. • Promoting public investment in infrastructure building, for building necessary logistics and other facilities for domestic and international trade. • More investment in social sectors particularly education and health sectors in order to develop skilled and healthy workforce and professionals.	
	Inflation, interest rate and exchange rate	• Try to maintain sustained level of inflation which would be favourable both for producers and consumers. • Commercial borrowing from banks should not be too high and costly for doing business in the country. • Exchange rate should not discourage investment and export.	
	Debt burden	• Neither overall nor external debt burden should be high.	
Sectoral priorities	Agriculture	• Rise in productivity, cost efficiency in rice production. • Further mechanisation of rice cultivation. • Enhance capacity to export rice. • Prioritising high value non-crop cultivation. • Addressing the climatic changes in case of crop production. • Shifting priorities to livestock and fish production and attaining the capacity to export meat and fish following international standards. • Ensure maximum return per unit of land used for agricultural activities. • Promote contractual farming. • Further strengthen the agriculture supply chain between urban sales centres and rural markets. • Put emphasis on quality of seeds, products, post-harvest storage facilities.	• Provide necessary budgetary support to promote non-traditional non-crop agricultural activities. • Budgetary support for further mechanisation of agricultural activities. • Provide necessary training for developing entrepreneurs in poultry, livestock and fisheries sub-sectors. • Introduce special crop insurance schemes through private sector.

continued

Table 3.a.3 Continued

Sector	Area	Activity	Measure to be taken
	Off-farm activity	• Enhance productivity and cost efficiency and ability to produce quality products and services. • Promote activities in such a way that they could develop as supplementary/part of the broader value chain in formal industrial and service sectors.	• Provide necessary credit at a low interest rate to support their vertical expansion. • Formal private sector should develop networking with informal off-farm enterprises.
	Manufacturing	• Promote diversification of export-products both in RMG and non-RMG products putting more emphasis on increasing the export share of high value products. • Increased firm level productivity by applying more advanced technologies as well as increasing workers' skills. • Putting focus on more export of non-RMG products in non-traditional markets. • Gradually restructuring the manufacturing sector from low-tech to medium- and high-tech industries including production of raw materials, intermediate products and machinery. • Promoting use of ICT in improving efficiency in production. • Promoting backward and forward linkage industrial activities. • Promoting domestic labour-intensive manufacturing activities. • Encouraging entrepreneurship development in the country. • Promoting industries to produce quality products following international standards. • Complete formalisation of small and medium enterprises. • Creating a domestic base for skilled industrial workers and management, engineers and other professionals for catering to the needs of medium- to high-tech industries. • Promote FDI in medium- to high-tech manufacturing industries.	• Use target specific fiscal, monetary and budgetary tools to promote different types of activities. • Large group of companies should develop supply chain by integrating SMEs with similar activities. • Provide special incentives to the private sector which promote inclusive business. • Government should discourage non-complaint industrial activities in terms of worker-related and environment-related issues. • Putting priorities to basic primary, secondary and tertiary level of education keeping in view the skills requirement of the industry. • Further strengthening vocational education.

	Services	• Formalisation of informal service-related activities. • Promoting value added services particularly high value commercial services. • Develop skilled professionals who could cater to the needs of the domestic services sector. • Gradually strengthen domestic service industries to cater to the needs of the international market. • Further integration between manufacturing and services sector activities.	• Take necessary regulatory measures to formalise informal manufacturing enterprises. • Take necessary regulatory measures to formalise informal service sector related activities.
Governance	Institutions	• Strengthening the public sector with the ability to provide necessary services for ensuring a better business environment in the country. • Public sector should be able to play a supportive role for developing the private sector in the country. • Make supportive laws and rules with a view to meeting the needs of the private sector. • Ensure transparency and accountability in dealing with the private sector. • Ensure time-bound operation for the private sector. • Decentralisation of administrative responsibilities to ensure better service for the business.	• Necessary reform in public administration. • Enhance regulatory reform. • Strengthening the activities of the anti-corruption commission. • Make public all business-related dealings. • Increase use of ICT in public sector-related services. • Maintain standard operating procedures to provide transparency in public sector-related activities.

Source: prepared by authors.

References

ADB, 2016. *Key indicators for Asia and the Pacific 2016.* 47th edn. Manila: Asian Development Bank.

Ahmed, F. Z., Greenleaf, A. and Sacks, A., 2014. The paradox of export growth in areas of weak governance: The case of the ready made garment sector in Bangladesh. *World Development*, 56, 258–271.

Ahmed, N., 2009. Sustaining ready made garment exports from Bangladesh. *Journal of Contemporary Asia*, 39 (4), 597–618.

Asiedu, E., 2006. Foreign direct investment in Africa: The role of natural resources, market size, government policy, institutions and political instability. *World Economy*, 29 (1), 63–77.

Aspe, P., 1992. Macroeconomic stabilization and structural change in Mexico. *European Economic Review*, 36 (2–3), 320–328.

Balma, L. and Ncube, M., 2015. *Macroeconomic challenges of structural transformation: Public investment, growth and debt sustainability in Sierra Leone.* IMF Working Paper 15/164. Washington, DC: International Monetary Fund.

Bangladesh Planning Commission, 2015. *Seventh Five Year Plan FY2016 – FY2020.* Five Year Plan. Dhaka: General Economics Division, Planning Commission, Government of Bangladesh.

Basnett, Y., *et al.*, 2014. *Structural economic transformation in Nepal: A diagnostic study submitted to DFID Nepal.* London: Overseas Development Institute.

BBS, 2015. *Report on labour force survey Bangladesh 2013–2014.* Dhaka: Bangladesh Bureau of Statistics.

BBS, 2017. *Quarterly labour force survey Bangladesh 2015–2016.* Dhaka: Bangladesh Bureau of Statistics.

Bhattacharya, D. and Khan, T. I., 2014. The challenges of structural transformation and progress towards the MDGs in LDCs. *In:* LDC IV Monitor, *Istanbul programme of action for the LDCs (2011–2020): Monitoring deliverables, tracking progress – analytical perspectives.* London: Commonwealth Secretariat, 1–37.

Caselli, F., 2005. Accounting for cross-country income differences. *In:* P. Aghion and S. Durlauf, eds. *Handbook of economic growth.* Amsterdam: North-Holland, 679–741.

Drabo, A. and Guillaumont, P., 2016. Prospects of graduation for least developed countries: What structural change? *In:* LDC IV Monitor, *Tracking progress, accelerating transformations: Achieving the IPoA by 2020.* London: Commonwealth Secretariat, 71–103.

Duarte, M. and Restuccia, D., 2010. The role of the structural transformation in aggregate productivity. *Quarterly Journal of Economics*, 125 (1), 129–173.

Fernandes, A. M., 2008. Firm productivity in Bangladesh manufacturing industries. *World Development*, 36 (10), 1725–1744.

Groningen Growth and Development Centre, 2017. *The database.* Available from: www.rug.nl/ggdc/productivity/10-sector/ [Accessed 15 March 2017].

Guillaumont, P., 2014. *A necessary small revision to the EVI to make it more balanced and equitable.* Policy Brief B98. Clermont-Ferrand: Fondation pour les études et recherches sur le développement international.

Hartmann, D., *et al.*, 2016. The structural constraints of income inequality in Latin America. *Integration and Trade*, 20 (40), 70–85.

Hausmann, R. and Klinger, B., 2006. *Structural transformation and patterns of comparative advantage in the product space.* CID Working Paper 128. Cambridge, MA: Center for International Development, Harvard University.

ILO, 2017. *ILOSTAT* [online]. Geneva: International Labour Organization. Available from: www.ilo.org/ilostat/faces/wcnav_defaultSelection;ILOSTATCOOKIE=Afw38wfm47yYkx tljOOi2MITtPbBFAwxWfVR06nXLW-VOETUk51w!-453176760?_afrLoop=172845895 114396&_afrWindowMode=0&_afrWindowId=null#!%40%40%3F_afrWindowId%3 Dnull%26_afrLoop%3D172845895114396%26_afrWindowMode%3D0%26_adf.ctrl-state%3D4mcq8xoj2_4 [Accessed 15 March 2017].

IMF, 2014. *Sustaining long-run growth and macroeconomic stability in low-income countries: The role of structural transformation and diversification.* IMF Policy Paper. Washington, DC: International Monetary Fund.

IMF and IDA, 2015. *Bangladesh: fifth and sixth reviews under the extended credit facility arrangement – debt sustainability analysis.* IMF Country Report 15/304. Washington, DC: International Monetary Fund, International Development Association.

IMF and IDA, 2016. *Bangladesh: Staff report for the 2015 article IV consultation.* IMF Country Report 16/27. Washington, DC: International Monetary Fund, International Development Association.

ITC, 2017. *Trade map* [online]. Geneva: International Trade Centre. Available from: www.trademap.org [Accessed 29 April 2017].

Kabeer, N., Mahmud, S. and Castro, J. G. I., 2012. NGOs and the political empowerment of poor people in rural Bangladesh: Cultivating the habits of democracy? *World Development*, 40 (10), 2044–2062.

Kawamura, H., 2014. *The likelihood of 24 least developed countries graduating from the LDC category by 2020: An achievable goal?* CDP Background Paper 20. New York: United Nations Department of Economic and Social Affairs.

Keane, J., Aldafai, G. and Arda, M., 2016. Structural economic transformation and export diversification in the least developed countries. *In:* LDC IV Monitor, *Tracking progress, accelerating transformations: Achieving the IPoA by 2020.* London: Commonwealth Secretariat, 17–29.

Kuznets, S., 1966. *Modern economic growth: Rate, structure and spread.* New Haven, CT: Yale University Press.

Kuznets, S., 1971. *Economic growth of nations: Total output and production structure.* Cambridge, MA: Harvard University Press.

Lewis, W. A., 1954. Economic development with unlimited supplies of labour. *Manchester School*, 22 (2), 139–191.

McMillan, M. S. and Rodrik, D., 2011. *Globalization, structural change and productivity growth.* NBER Working Paper 17143. Cambridge: National Bureau of Economic Research.

McMillan, M., Rodrik, D. and Verduzco-Gallo, Í., 2014. Globalization, structural change, and productivity growth, with an update on Africa. *World Development*, 63, 11–32.

McMillan, M., *et al.*, 2017. *Supporting economic transformation: An approach paper.* London: Overseas Development Institute.

Martins, P. M. G., 2015. *Sub-regional perspectives on structural change.* CREDIT Research Paper 15/3. Nottingham: Centre for Research in Economic Development and International Trade, University of Nottingham.

Nicita, A. and Seiermann, J., 2016. *G20 policies and export performance of least developed countries: Policy issues in international trade and commodities.* Research Study Series 75. New York: United Nations.

Ocampo, J. A., 2003. *Structural dynamics and economic growth in developing countries.* Santiago: United Nations Economic Commission for Latin America and the Caribbean.

Rahman, M., Shadat, W. and Raihan, S., 2010. *Trade liberalisation, manufacturing growth and employment in Bangladesh.* Geneva: International Labour Organization.

Sen, K., 2016. *The determinants of structural transformation in Asia: A review of the literature*. ADB Economics Working Paper Series 478. Manila: Asian Development Bank.

Swaray, R. B., 2005. Primary commodity dependence and debt problems in less developed countries. *Applied Econometrics and International Development*, 5 (4), 131–142.

Timmer, C. P. and Akkus, S., 2008. *The structural transformation as a pathway out of poverty: Analytics, empirics and politics*. CGD Working Paper 150. Washington, DC: Centre for Global Development.

United Nations, n.d. *UNdata* [online]. New York: United Nations. Available from: http://data.un.org [Accessed 29 April 2017].

UNCTAD, n.d. *UNCTADstat* [online]. New York: United Nations Conference on Trade and Development. Available from: http://unctadstat.unctad.org [Accessed 29 April 2017].

UNCTAD, 2015. *Transforming rural economies*. The Least Developed Countries Report 2015. New York: United Nations Conference on Trade and Development.

UNCTAD, 2016. *The path to graduation and beyond: Making the most of the process*. The Least Developed Countries Report 2016. New York: United Nations Conference on Trade and Development.

World Bank, 2017a. *World development indicators* [online]. Washington, DC: World Bank. Available from: http://data.worldbank.org/data-catalog/world-development-indicators [Accessed 29 April 2017].

World Bank, 2017b. *Data blog* [online]. Washington, DC: World Bank. Available from: https://data.worldbank.org/indicator/SL.GDP.PCAP.EM.KD?view=chart [Accessed 15 March 2017].

WTO, 2016. *Report on G20 trade measures (mid-October 2015 to mid-May 2016)*. Geneva: World Trade Organization.

4   Pathways to Bangladesh's sustainable LDC graduation

Prospects, challenges and strategies

Mustafizur Rahman and Estiaque Bari

Introduction

Building on its impressive success of the past years, Bangladesh has now arrived at a point where it has met eligibility criteria for least developed country (LDC) graduation for the first time in March 2018 at the triennial review by the Committee for Development Policy (CDP), a subsidiary advisory body of the United Nations Economic and Social Council (UN ECOSOC). Since the 1980s, Bangladesh has been able to accelerate its gross domestic product (GDP) growth by about 1 per cent every decade. Indeed, Bangladesh was able to post an annual GDP growth of over 6 per cent over the past decade (BBS 1990, 1996, 2005, 2017). Introduction of high yielding crop varieties and the resultant productivity and production gains have enabled Bangladesh to ensure food security for its citizens (Rahman 2010). Growth of the domestic market allowed many small and medium enterprises to cater to the rising demand of the population, creating job opportunities in the manufacturing and services sector (Bakht and Basher 2015). Thanks to supportive trade policies pursued by Bangladesh, and by taking advantage of the global special and differential support measures enjoyed as an LDC in the areas of market access and other areas, the country was able to significantly enhance its global exports (Love and Chandra 2005, Dawson 2006). This success is particularly visible in the case of apparels where Bangladesh is currently the second largest exporter after China (ITC 2017). The sector employs about four million people, about 65 per cent of whom are women (Haque and Bari 2015). A significant rise in remittance inflows, averaging about United States dollar (US$) 10.9 billion over the past decade, contributed to a rising per capita gross national income (GNI), which allowed recipient households, mostly low income and rural, to raise living standards and invest more in health and education (De Bruyn and Kuddus 2005, Hatemi-J and Uddin 2014, BMET 2017). Successful low cost interventions and solutions in the health sector and programmes geared to expand primary school enrolment, particularly of girl children, have given excellent returns to Bangladesh in terms of social indicators (Ahmed and Del Ninno 2002, Chowdhury et al. 2002, 2013, Ahmed and Arends-Kuenning 2006). Microcredit programmes and non-state actors have played a critically important role in this regard (Zohir 2004). Wide ranging social safety net programmes have contributed to reducing vulnerabilities of the marginalised sections of the population (World Bank 2005). Bangladesh's growing strength in terms of key socio-economic indicators has enabled the country to achieve an increasingly high score in view of almost all of the sub-indicators under the three pillars associated with LDC graduation. While Bangladesh has a long way to go, and the country faces manifold challenges in going forward, its achievements have given the economy a good foundation to move towards smooth LDC graduation.

Bangladesh's graduation from the LDC category would justifiably be perceived as an important achievement attributable to Bangladesh's sustained national efforts and international support measures (ISMs) that favour LDCs. Indeed, Bangladesh's graduation would claim some distinction – it will be remarkable in the sense that it would take one of the largest LDCs, and some would say the 'outlier', out of the category. As authors' calculations suggest (after smoothing for 2011–15 averages, by using data from the *World Development Indicators* (WDI) database (World Bank 2017a)), considering the combined population, GDP and exports of all 47 LDCs, Bangladesh alone accounts for 17.3 per cent, 18.3 per cent and 13.6 per cent shares, respectively. The issues of Bangladesh's graduation and its sustainability are thus of interest both from the national vantage point and in terms of its global significance.

Bangladesh's graduation would create formidable challenges that must be addressed and opportunities that should be harnessed. Any graduation strategy will have to be informed on both counts. The identification of an appropriate strategy for Bangladesh's sustainable graduation, which motivates this study, is evidently a crucial exercise. For Bangladesh, an added challenge is that there is no going back once it graduates. In 1991, the CDP determined that countries with a population exceeding 75 million shall not be considered for inclusion on the LDC list (CDP and UN DESA 2015). With a population of approximately 160 million, Bangladesh's transition will entail a permanent graduation.

Objectives and structure

The overarching objective of the study is to articulate key elements of a graduation strategy for Bangladesh. Following this introduction, this chapter reviews Bangladesh's track record in terms of various indicators and sub-indicators as the country moved towards graduation eligibility. It then examines the prospects for its sustainable graduation on the basis of projections of the graduation criteria and thresholds. The next section analyses the costs and benefits that would result from graduation. The chapter then presents elements of a strategy for sustainable graduation that should inform Bangladesh's efforts going forward. The final section provides some concluding remarks.

Newness of the study

A number of studies have tried to anticipate the implications of graduation of the LDCs and come up with recommendations to enable the LDCs to cope with the attendant challenges, and move towards sustainable graduation (Audiguier 2012, Kawamura 2014, Cariolle *et al.* 2016). However, these studies have looked at the relevant issues and concerns from broader, LDC-wide perspectives while specific country-centric concerns were not addressed in detail. There is no denying the fact that each country has its distinct ramifications originating from LDC graduation. The advantages, vulnerabilities, concerns and challenges, as also the solutions, had to be different (UNCTAD 2013, 2014, 2015, 2016). For example, whilst preferential treatment accorded to LDCs is applicable to all LDCs as a group, different countries have actually been able to take advantage of those at different degrees. This depended on the extent to which particular LDCs were able to build up the required supply-side capacities and were able to translate preferential market access into competitive advantage by addressing other relevant factors. If the LDC had been able to take greater advantage of the ISMs, the likelihood of the disadvantages originating from LDC graduation may be to that extent higher. Thus, it is important to examine the relevance of particular ISMs in a country-specific setting to estimate the impact of preference erosion. This evidence is also important to identify concrete steps which the particular LDC would need to take during the transition phase of six years, and also to negotiate with the preference-offering countries for any possible extension of the support measures.

The newness of the present study is that for the first time an in-depth examination of the distinctive nature, specificities, implications and coping strategies have been carried out in the particular context of Bangladesh. The study has made projections to arrive at forecasted values as regards expected progression in terms of the various involved graduation indicators, attempted to measure sector-specific implications of phasing out ISMs, identified concrete strengths and vulnerabilities and, based on the analysis, has proposed a set of specific recommendations. The objective was to recommend pathways for Bangladesh's LDC graduation that would be with momentum and be sustainable. It is hoped that the study will contribute to the design of a sustainable graduation study for Bangladesh, a task that the country's policymakers will need to carry out in view of the graduation. Concerned stakeholders in Bangladesh, both state and non-state, will be able to draw on the findings and recommendations of the study to better understand what graduation will entail for the country, in specific areas, and where policies, incentives, institutions and initiatives will need to be geared to ensure that Bangladesh's graduation process is smooth and it is sustained over time.

Methodology of the study

The study draws on review of secondary literature and experiences of graduated countries, descriptive analysis of global datasets and quantitative analysis based on country-specific and globally available secondary data sources. The study has also benefited from inputs received at a national dialogue where an earlier draft was presented for comments and discussion.

For projections concerning Bangladesh's likelihood of LDC graduation, authors have estimated values for the GNI per capita, the Human Assets Index (HAI) and the Economic Vulnerability Index (EVI). For calculating GNI per capita for Bangladesh, authors have followed the World Bank's step-by-step method. Detailed methodology of projecting GNI per capita for Bangladesh is explained in Annex 4.1 using assumptions mentioned in Annex 4.2, and trend analysis presented in Annex Figure 4.a.1. Forecasted values for sub-indicators of HAI and EVI were estimated using trend analysis. Details of estimating the HAI have been presented in Annex 4.3. It is to be noted that, as the thresholds of HAI and EVI criteria are fixed at the level of 2012 by CDP (CDP and UN DESA 2015), authors have estimated the sub-indicators following past trends without modelling for external shocks. Based on the estimates of trend analysis, the final index values for HAI and EVI were calculated by using the max–min procedure developed by the CDP.

To capture the likely implications of the loss of ISMs consequent to LDC graduation, loss in terms of export revenue was estimated by using a gravity model. Detailed methodology and results of the gravity type regression model are presented in Annex 4.4 and Annex Table 4.a.1. A distinctive feature of this analysis is that it has gone beyond the common practice (Aiello and Cardamone 2007, Vanhnalat *et al.* 2015) and has considered disaggregated level tariff data for purposes of regression analysis. Results of the estimates for all explanatory variables were presented as appropriate in different sections of the chapter.

Bangladesh's journey towards graduation

As it stands, 16 countries are on track for graduation from LDC status by 2024 (UNCTAD 2016). Among these countries, Equatorial Guinea already graduated in June 2017 (UN DESA 2017a).[1] Another nine LDCs are predicted to graduate by 2021, followed by six, including Bangladesh, in 2024 (UNCTAD 2016). Among these LDCs, Angola is predicted to graduate on the basis of the income-only criterion of GNI per capita and 11 countries are predicted to graduate according to different combinations of two out of the three graduation criteria. Only Bangladesh, Djibouti and Yemen[2] are expected to graduate according to all of the three criteria (UNCTAD 2016). At the 2015 CDP review, for the second consecutive time Kiribati met both the income and HAI criteria, but the CDP deferred its decision on graduation until the 2018 triennial review due to the country's extreme vulnerability. Similarly, Tuvalu's graduation was deferred by the UN ECOSOC because of its high EVI (UNCTAD 2016). What emerges is that, while meeting the graduation criteria is necessary, for an LDC to actually graduate it needs to demonstrate that it is on track in terms of all three criteria in order to ensure that graduation would be sustainable.

From the perspective of sustainable graduation, it is important to demonstrate constant progress towards achieving threshold(s) when two criteria or only the income criterion have already been met. An examination of graduation history indicates that the majority of LDCs have fallen short of sustainable graduation despite crossing the graduation requirements. In other words, even when graduation criteria have been met, vulnerabilities may continue to afflict graduated countries. This insight is corroborated by the track records of the five graduated countries – Botswana, Cape Verde, the Maldives, Samoa and Equatorial Guinea – whose performance was mainly underpinned by earnings from natural resources, remittances, tourism and higher official development assistance (ODA) (UNCTAD 2016). Graduation was not accompanied by structural transformation and broad-based economic development founded on economic diversification, manufacturing growth, broad-basing of exports and higher levels of employment generation (Bhattacharya and Khan 2014).

At the 2015 CDP review, five countries met the graduation criteria for the first time – Bhutan, Nepal, São Tomé and Príncipe, the Solomon Islands and Timor-Leste (UNCTAD 2016). Of which, CDP had recommended Bhutan, São Tomé and Príncipe, and the Solomon Islands for graduation in its 2018 review (UN DESA 2017a). Although Nepal and Timor-Leste have met the criteria for graduation for the second time, CDP did not recommend these two countries on the ground of economic and political challenges (UN DESA 2017a). At the 2018 CDP review, Bangladesh alongside the Lao PDR and Myanmar were considered to have met the LDC graduation criteria, for the first time. As was anticipated, global economic slowdown resulted in a lower graduation threshold in terms of GNI per capita, from US\$1,242 in 2015 to US\$1,230 in 2018 (UN DESA 2017b). At the time of the 2018 CDP review, Bangladesh's GNI per capita was calculated to be US\$1,274 – higher than the threshold (Table 4.1). Bangladesh's score for HAI was calculated to be 73.2, well above the graduation threshold of 66 or above (Table 4.2). The EVI score remained more or less at the same level (indeed, dropping to an insignificant margin, from 25.1 in 2015 to 25.2 in 2018). Actual EVI, thus, was at a significant distance from the thresholds of 32 or below (Table 4.3). Crossing the thresholds for all three graduation criteria, with significant comfort margins in HAI and EVI, makes Bangladesh's eligibility for LDC graduation a more balanced one among all candidate LDCs.

The above observation is corroborated by the exercise carried out by the authors based on a comparison of the relative performance of the candidate

Table 4.1 Actual and projected GNI per capita of Bangladesh in US\$

Year of CDP review	Graduation threshold	Scenario A	Scenario B	Scenario C	Scenario D
2018 (actual)	1,230	1,274			
2021	1,245–1,270	1,735	1,660	1,730	1,730–1,780
2024	1,345–1,375	2,340	2,280	2,340	2,260–2,500

Sources: authors' projection for 2021 and 2024 based on World Bank and UN DESA methodology (see details in Annexes 4.1 and 4.2).

Table 4.2 Actual and projected values of HAI by indicator in years of CDP review

Indicator	Actual value		Projected value	
	2015	2018	2021	2024
Population undernourished (%)	16.7	15.1	18.1	20.4
Under-five mortality rate (per 1,000)	41.0	34.2	29.3	26.6
Gross secondary school enrolment ratio (%)	53.6	63.5	73.6	87.2
Adult literacy rate (%)	58.8	72.8	79.2	86.0
Maternal mortality ratio (per 100,000)	–	176.0	119.5	72.3
HAI (by using max-min procedure)	63.8	73.2	79.2	86.3

Sources: authors' projections for 2021 and 2024 based on UN DESA methodology (see details in Annex 4.3).

Table 4.3 Actual and projected values of EVI by indicator, sub-index in years of CDP review

Indicator/sub-index	Actual value		Projected value	
	2015	2018	2021	2024
Population (in million)	156.5	162.9	166.2	172.3
Remoteness (0 to 100 scale)	38.9	38.5	38.5	38.5
Merchandise export concentration (0 to 1 scale)	0.37	0.41	0.41	0.42
Share of agriculture, forestry and fishing (%)	17.0	15.4	13.0	11.5
Share of population in low elevated coastal zones (%)	8.9	8.9	8.9	8.9
Exposure index (by using max-min procedure)	22.7	22.8	22.4	22.2
Instability of exports of goods and services (standard error value of regression)	6.7	7.1	7.3	7.3
Victims of natural disasters (%)	4.7	4.0	3.5	3.7
Instability of agricultural production (%)	3.3	3.1	2.8	2.7
Shock index (by using max-min procedure)	27.5	27.6	27.1	27.1
EVI (by using max-min procedure)	25.1	25.2	24.8	24.7

Sources: authors' projections for 2021 and 2024 based on UN DESA methodology (see details in Annex 4.3).

LDCs in terms of the three graduation criteria. Bangladesh is by far the most populous LDC with sizeable shares of GDP and exports when compared to the other 15 prospective LDC graduates. As Figure 4.1 shows, Bangladesh's population, GDP and exports (averages for 2011–15) are respectively 47.8 per cent, 38.4 per cent and 25.3 per cent of the combined values for these three indicators for the 15 candidate LDCs that are predicted to be graduated by 2024.

The performance of earlier graduates and current candidate LDCs reveals that previous and prospective LDC graduates that have sizeable populations were far off the GNI per capita graduation threshold with the exception of Angola.

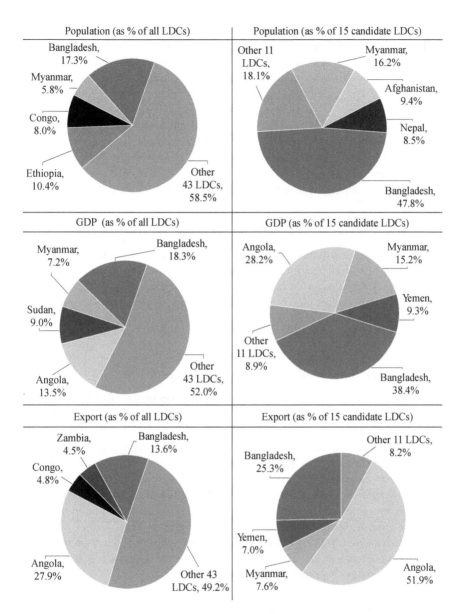

Figure 4.1 Bangladesh's population, GDP and exports as shares of all LDCs and 15 candidate LDCs.

Source: authors' calculations based on WDI data, World Bank (2017a).

However, Angola performed poorly with regard to the other two criteria and it is predicted to graduate only in terms of the income criterion in 2021. Bangladesh's dispersion in terms of GNI per capita was similar to that of Nepal and Myanmar, countries with far smaller population sizes. This exercise demonstrates that in spite of the additional challenges that a densely populated country faces, Bangladesh is progressing towards graduation with commendable strength.

Similarly, many candidate LDCs, which had relatively high GNI per capita, did not meet the HAI criterion. Moreover, the majority of the earlier five graduated countries and current candidate LDCs did not meet the EVI criterion in 2018. Dispersion (deficit) between the threshold and actual score on EVI for most countries, especially small island countries, was high. It is to be conceded that a high GNI per capita with relatively low HAI and EVI or a relatively low GNI per capita with high HAI and EVI might put under question the long-run sustainability of LDC graduation of a country. Therefore, for an LDC, the relative advantage of a more balanced pathway to graduation, with a good track record in terms of all the three criteria, cannot be overemphasised. From this perspective, Bangladesh, that has met all three graduation thresholds, maintaining a significant comfort margin, is on a firm footing. This scenario demonstrates the strength of Bangladesh's economy as the country prepares to graduate in 2024 following two successive triennial reviews.

Prospects for Bangladesh's sustainable graduation

As Bangladesh has been found eligible for graduation in the 2018 CDP review, the issue of sustainable graduation from the LDC category will likely – and justifiably – gain increasing attention. There are several reasons for this. First, Bangladesh needs to keep up its momentum so that it distances (improves) itself further from thresholds, which would create a buffer zone that protects the country from external shocks. Second, the experiences of some graduated countries show that, in spite of having crossed the thresholds once, vulnerabilities can continue and lead to deferred graduation. Third, the interregnum years between graduation consideration and final graduation – the 2018–24 period in Bangladesh's case – provide a breathing space for taking necessary preparations for sustainable graduation. Thus, the identification of weak points that require corrective measures becomes critical.

This section presents a sensitivity analysis that was undertaken by the authors to forecast the likelihood of Bangladesh's sustainable graduation by projecting the values of the three graduation criteria at two points in its pathway to graduation – 2021 and 2024. These values were projected under various assumptions and likely scenarios.

Projections of GNI per capita were undertaken in four scenarios, assuming no external shocks, using the World Bank's Atlas method: (i) scenario A: Bangladesh achieves the relevant GDP growth targets in accordance with the Seventh Five Year Plan (7FYP) (Bangladesh Planning Commission, 2015);

(ii) scenario B: the International Monetary Fund's (IMF) growth projections for Bangladesh are used; (iii) scenario C: the projected remittance inflow and foreign direct investment (FDI) inflow on the basis of past trends are used; (iv) scenario D: Bangladeshi taka (BDT)/US$ exchange rate depreciation/ appreciation by ±1 taka (e.g. ±7.7 per cent) of the annual average exchange rate for Fiscal Year (FY) 2016 over the period of 2017–22. The projections are presented in Table 4.1.[3]

According to the projections, over the next two consecutive CDP reviews, Bangladesh is projected to meet the GNI per capita graduation threshold (a moving target) with a significant margin assuming that Bangladesh is able to attain the targets set by 7FYP, and is also able to sustain this beyond the 7FYP period without any major external shock.

However, Bangladesh's journey towards graduation is taking place at a time of considerable global uncertainty arising from slow recovery of global trade after the prolonged financial crisis,[4] protectionist threats, stagnation in World Trade Organization (WTO) negotiations and shifts in global financing modalities. The global trading scenario is likely to be affected by restrictive trade practices by developed countries, the United Kingdom's (UK's) prospective exit from the European Union (EU) and its impacts on the UK's trade with Europe, the increasing presence of mega-regional trading blocs and the weakening of the WTO as the global multilateral institution governing trade rules. While the adverse effects of the global financial crisis on Bangladesh were rather limited, such developments are likely to have greater impacts in the future as Bangladesh's economy becomes increasingly integrated with the global economy (Rahman and Bari 2016). In view of this situation, exchange rate management to support trade policy will play a significant role during the graduation process. This insight is corroborated by the estimates of the analytical (regression) model[5] used in this study. The results of the regression estimates suggest that a 1 per cent depreciation in the exchange rate in BDT raises the export value of the 40 selected partner countries by 0.09 per cent; the relationship is statistically significant at the 1 per cent level (column 6 of Annex Table 4.a.1).

In addition, the slowdown in remittance growth and the global migration crisis may have adverse impacts on Bangladesh's growth performance. Economic slowdown in major remittance-sending countries, low oil prices and depreciated currencies of many receiving countries contributed to this decrease. Remittances to developing countries are expected to increase annually by approximately 4 per cent in 2016–17, but decreases in remittances from Gulf Cooperation Council countries linked to low oil prices, increasing black market premia and capital controls could limit remittance inflows through formal channels in some countries (Ratha *et al.* 2016). The global migration crisis could also limit access to concessional ODA. A number of projections indicate that protectionist policies being threatened by the new United States administration and the fallout of the UK's prospective exit from the EU could slow down the global economy.

These developments are likely to adversely impact Bangladesh's economy, particularly exports. Estimates carried out by the authors suggest that a 1 per cent increase in GDP per capita of countries where Bangladesh has preferential market access would increase Bangladesh's export revenue by 0.25 per cent (column 6 of Annex Table 4.a.1). Slowdown of the global economy could have a detrimental impact on Bangladesh's exports – export growth of FY2017 was only 1.2 per cent, well below the annual target of 8.0 per cent (EPB 2017).

Projections made by the authors as regards the HAI sub-indices indicate that Bangladesh will continue to progress with regard to indicators of social development including those relating to reducing the under-five mortality rate and improving the gross secondary school enrolment ratio and the adult literacy rate. In 2015, the CDP decided that, in future reviews, it will include maternal mortality ratio (MMR) as a fifth indicator for the HAI (CDP and UN DESA 2015). The projection carried out for this study (linear and non-linear) suggests that inclusion of this indicator will further improve Bangladesh's score in HAI (Table 4.2).[6] In contrast, trend analysis indicates that Bangladesh's performance with regard to undernourishment could remain a concern if appropriate measures are not taken. Even if this indicator is factored into the equation, the overall HAI scores are projected to be 79.2 and 86.3, respectively, at the time of the 2021 and 2024 CDP reviews (Table 4.2). These values are well above the graduation threshold of 66 or above.

There is a caveat, however. While Bangladesh has made commendable progress on many of the related HAI and EVI indicators (see Tables 4.2 and 4.3), trend analysis may not necessarily generate accurate projections. Projections in this study were based on past values when Bangladesh made good progress compared to the correspondingly low reference points of the past. Going forward, building on past performance could become more difficult as hard-to-reach areas and communities would be targeted. To achieve further progress in terms of social development indicators, the solutions are likely to be more capital intensive than the many low-cost solutions of the past and present (Rahman and Bari 2016).

In view of ongoing volatility in the global economy, with slowdowns in both goods and services markets, Bangladesh needs to pay closer attention and make the best use of windows of opportunity in two key areas: taking advantage of preferential market access currently available to it as an LDC and undertaking structural changes to make its economy more competitive. As the regression analysis shows, the advantage in terms of additional export earnings from preferential market access is quite evident for Bangladesh when export earnings in markets with high preferential access are juxtaposed with the markets where Bangladeshi goods enter on the basis of paying most favoured nation (MFN) tariffs and when goods receiving duty-free access are juxtaposed with goods that do not receive such access.

While Bangladesh has demonstrated significant success in disaster management (Karim and Mimura 2008), natural disasters are an uncertain variable in any development equation. In addition, Bangladesh continues to be a considerably challenged country in terms of climate vulnerabilities (Brouwer *et al.* 2007). Mitigating and adapting to climate change should remain high on

Table 4.4 LDC graduation procedure to be followed

Timeline	LDC graduation procedure
The 2018 CDP review in March	• CDP found Bangladesh eligible for graduation from the LDC category for the first time. Following that, United Nations Department of Economic and Social Affairs (UN DESA) to notify its initial findings to Bangladesh.
Between next two CDP reviews (2018–21)	• United Nations Conference on Trade and Development (UNCTAD) to prepare a vulnerability profile and hand over the report to Bangladesh. • UN DESA to prepare an *ex-ante* impact assessment and hand over the findings to Bangladesh. • Bangladesh expected to provide comments on the UNCTAD report and findings of UN DESA assessment (optional).
The 2021 CDP review	• UN DESA to confirm Bangladesh's eligibility for graduation from the LDC category for the second time and submit the CDP recommendations to UN ECOSOC, taking into account fulfilment of graduation criteria and other information (country statements, UN DESA's assessment, UNCTAD report on vulnerability profile). • UN ECOSOC likely to endorse the CDP recommendations. • United Nations General Assembly (UNGA) to take note of the CDP recommendations.
Between subsequent two CDP reviews (2021–24)	• Bangladesh to set up a consultative mechanism and prepare a transition strategy. Bangladesh to report to CDP on the preparation of the strategy (optional). • United Nations Development Programme (UNDP) expected to facilitate the consultative group and provide support upon request. UN system expected to provide targeted assistance and capacity building support upon Bangladesh's request. • Development and trading partners expected to participate in the consultative mechanism with Bangladesh's policymakers. • CDP to continue monitoring Bangladesh's development progress during the interim period and report annually to UN ECOSOC.
The 2024 CDP review	• Graduation becomes effective and Bangladesh graduates permanently out of the LDC category.
Following Graduation (2024–27)*	• Bangladesh expected to implement and monitor the transition strategy. Bangladesh to volunteer to submit to CDP progress reports on the implementation of the strategy on an annual basis for the first three years after graduation and at the two subsequent triennial reviews. • Bangladesh to receive support from development and trading partners in implementing the transition strategy. However, the onus will mainly be on Bangladesh to mobilise resources towards smooth transition. • CDP to monitor Bangladesh's socio-economic progress. Bangladesh to report to UN ECOSOC annually for the first three years after graduation and at the two subsequent triennial reviews.

Source: authors' compilation following the CDP's graduation framework, UN DESA (2017b).

Note

* There is no fixed period for a smooth transition given the phasing out of ISMs. A smooth transition will depend on negotiation by the concerned LDC with providers of LDC-specific support.

Bangladesh's policy agenda because graduation from the LDC category is likely to adversely affect Bangladesh's possibility of receiving climate finance on preferential terms from global sources such as infrastructure development funds, climate change adaptation funds and the technology-related Green Climate Fund (Rai *et al.* 2014). Improvement in standards of living through higher GNI per capita would better equip people to address natural disasters. The parameters of GNI per capita, HAI and EVI are correlated with strengthening Bangladesh's capacities in various areas. The resulting resilience would enable the country to prepare for graduation from a position of strength.

In the interim period, between 2018 and 2024, several developments will require the close attention of policymakers. Reactive initiatives and proactive measures are necessary in going forward. Table 4.4 outlines the journey ahead and the graduation eligibility procedure. To prepare for this journey, Bangladesh needs to be cognisant of both challenges and opportunities.

Costs and benefits of Bangladesh's LDC graduation

It is important to understand the costs and benefits associated with LDC status in order to design an appropriate graduation strategy for Bangladesh. The Support Measures Portal for LDCs, established and maintained by the Secretariat of the CDP, lists 136 LDC-specific ISMs across the fields of development finance, trade, technology and technical assistance (UNCTAD 2016). However, utilisation of these ISMs varies significantly depending on specific needs of a particular LDC, capacity to export, capacity to use and manage available resources and the actual extent of support promised by development partners. As mentioned, Bangladesh is expected to graduate from the LDC category in 2024 and will no longer be able to enjoy LDC-specific ISMs following the three-year period of smooth transition that ends in 2027.

Bangladesh has been eligible for LDC-specific ISMs for more than four decades. Although it has not been able to take advantage of all the ISMs, it is one of only a few LDCs that has reaped benefits from many of them (Cortez *et al.* 2014). Bangladesh's successful utilisation of preferential market access for LDCs is a case in point. The country has also been able to make good use of concessional finance and the WTO's Aid for Trade and technical assistance. However, Bangladesh has not been able to take full advantage of the Doha Declaration on the Agreement on Trade-Related Aspects of Intellectual Property Rights (TRIPS) and Public Health that offered preferential treatment for production and export of pharmaceuticals by LDCs (Cortez *et al.* 2014). The loss of eligibility for ISMs would have a number of consequences for Bangladesh's economy as a whole and many specific sectors. At the same time, graduation from the LDC category would have positive ramifications in terms of branding Bangladesh as a success story and increasing FDI inflow, which are likely to be reflected in credit ratings and subsequent access to commercial loans at preferential interest rates. It is crucial to identify implications in this context in order to be able to adequately prepare a graduation strategy.

Concessional financing

In the cases of all five graduated countries (Botswana, Cape Verde, the Maldives, Samoa and Equatorial Guinea), ODA had played an important role in their economies. Given these countries' small populations, per capita ODA was relatively high[7] and a large share of concessional finance was in the form of grants. In contrast, Bangladesh's dependence on ODA has gradually declined over time – compared to the early 1990s when the ratio of ODA to exports of goods and services was 1:1, the ratio became 1:16 in 2015 (World Bank 2017a). ODA as a percentage of GDP has decreased from 8 per cent to less than 2 per cent over the same period. Per capita ODA in Bangladesh currently stands at less than US$20 (average ODA received in the period of FY2011–FY2015). A large part of the ODA received is in the form of loans. Over the 2012–15 period, Bangladesh's share of the ODA received by the LDCs as a group was 7 per cent, which was higher than the previous two successive five-year averages (OECD.Stat 2016).

The Istanbul Programme of Action (IPoA) for LDCs had set a target of 0.15–0.20 per cent of donor GNI to be provided as aid to LDCs (United Nations 2011). This percentage range would be equivalent to US$67 to 89 billion (in 2014 value) (United Nations 2017). Though many donor countries are yet to meet this target, some have – the share of aid to LDCs reached 0.10 per cent of GNI in 2013, but fell back to 0.09 per cent in 2014 and 2015 (OECD.Stat 2016). For Bangladesh, ODA constitutes about one-third of Annual Development Programme financing and remains important for social sectors and infrastructure. In recent years, compared to the other LDCs, the share of grants declined for Bangladesh. An increasingly larger share of ODA came in the form of loans.

Bangladesh received the equivalent of approximately US$3.3 billion in ODA in 2016, of which 34.7 per cent was in the form of grants and the rest came in the form of loans (Table 4.5). This scenario was almost the opposite in 2011. Concessional loans are expected to decline further as Bangladesh transitions from International Development Association (IDA) – only to blended and,

Table 4.5 Flow of ODA to Bangladesh, 2011–16

ODA indicator	2011	2012	2013	2014	2015	2016
Gross disbursement of ODA (in US$ million, constant 2016 value)	1,953.4	2,621.3	3,075.6	2,872.1	3,210.2	3,266.0
Commitments (% of ODA)	40.0	105.1	62.6	56.9	63.9	80.0
Grants (% of ODA)	59.8	44.7	44.9	41.3	35.5	34.7
Loans (% of ODA)	40.2	55.3	55.1	58.7	64.5	65.3
IDA (% of loans)	40.1	44.1	35.9	43.2	42.8	47.9

Sources: authors' calculations using the database of Creditor Reporting System (CRS) and OECD. Stat (2018).

then blended to International Bank for Reconstruction and Development (IBRD) assistance only. At present, Bangladesh receives 40 per cent of its concessional loans in the form of IDA loans, the 'soft window' of the World Bank that has a very low interest rate of 0.75 per cent, long repayment period of 20–30 years and grace period of five to ten years. According to the World Bank Atlas method, Bangladesh's GNI per capita of US$1,330 (in 2016) means that the country surpassed the IDA-only operational threshold of US$1,165 (in FY2018). Bangladesh is now eligible for blended financing. In FY2018, the blend operation threshold was US$1,905. If current GNI per capita growth rates are sustained, Bangladesh may cross that threshold by the time it, most likely, graduates in 2024.[8]

As was noted earlier, Bangladesh's LDC graduation prospects coincide with its middle-income journey. This would mean that, at a time when Bangladesh will be undertaking its post-LDC development pathway, it will be required to borrow on non-concessional terms as a lower middle-income country (LMIC). As a graduated LDC, Bangladesh would need to adjust to new realities where it is eligible for blended and IBRD financial assistance only. In the process, borrowing costs may rise significantly as Bangladesh gets used to receiving ODA with shorter repayment periods and at higher interest rates. In addition, Bangladesh would incur higher debt service payments. While its debt service record is one of the best and debt service payments as a percentage of foreign exchange earnings remain very low, costs would be on the rise.

However, following the transition from IDA – only to blended and afterwards to IBRD assistance, Bangladesh's economic strength as a non-LDC would have to be seen from the perspective of the country's improved creditworthiness. Graduation could unlock a broad range of development financing options, albeit at a price. The Chinese proposal of US$25 billion with an interest rate of 2 per cent,[9] the Russian loan of US$11.4 billion with an interest rate of 4 per cent for the Rooppur Nuclear Power Plant and Indian lines of credit[10] at concessional interest rates are early signs of such options (CPD 2017). On the other hand, securing loans, either by the public sector (issuing sovereign bonds) or private sector (raising commercial loans), would be possible at relatively lower interest rates given better credit ratings. To the extent that LDC graduation reflects strength of an economy and its embedded capacities, it is also expected that investors' interest in a country would rise.[11] In 2015, Bangladesh received FDI of US$2.2 billion, which was its highest annual figure to date – 44.1 per cent higher compared to 2014 and almost double compared to the US$1.1 billion received in 2011 (UNCTAD 2017).

According to scores pertaining to IDA credit ratings, Bangladesh has performed relatively better in terms of indicators of economic management and policies for social inclusion when compared to the 15 candidate LDCs for graduation by 2024.[12] However, with respect to indicators such as implementing structural policies and public sector management and institutions, Bangladesh's performance was relatively weak.[13] Overall, Bangladesh's credit rating in terms of managing IDA loans was similar to those of the 15 prospective LDC graduates, though lower than those of the five graduated countries. A graduation strategy would need to be cognisant of these assessments.

Preference erosion and loss of preferential treatment

Once graduated from the LDC category, Bangladesh would lose LDC-specific tariff preferences enjoyed by its exports. The country currently has preferential market access – of varying degrees and extent – to more than 40 countries. Unless it manages to renegotiate access through bilateral free trade agreements (FTAs) or as part of regional trade agreements (RTAs), Bangladesh would face MFN rates for exports beyond 2027. Estimates carried out for this study suggest that at prevailing MFN rates, taking into account markets and products, Bangladesh's exports would face an additional 6.7 per cent tariff on average once it graduates. The regression results indicate that a 1 per cent increase in the LDC-specific tariff rate would lead to a decrease in Bangladesh's exports of 1.9 per cent in the selected 40 countries[14] (column 6 of Annex Table 4.a.1).[15] For FY2015, Bangladesh's export value for selected 40 countries was US$21.3 billion. Thus, this decrease could result in an estimated loss of around US$2.7 billion for Bangladesh in view of potential export earnings, or nearly 8.7 per cent of Bangladesh's global export value of US$31.2 billion in FY2015. This result is fairly consistent with United Nations Conference on Trade and Development (UNCTAD) estimates that indicate Bangladesh's exports may fall by 5.5–7.5 per cent due to loss of preferential access (UNCTAD 2016). Estimates of UNCTAD also indicate that the potential effects on the LDCs from losing LDC-specific preferential access to Group of Twenty countries were equivalent to a reduction of 3 to 4 per cent of their earnings from merchandise exports. If extrapolated for all 48 LDCs (including Equatorial Guinea), this reduction would amount to a loss of more than US$4.2 billion per year (UNCTAD 2016). However, these effects may decrease over time given the extent that MFN tariffs are brought down and also when LDCs become part of various RTAs, which would reduce LDCs' preference margins in the markets concerned and thus lead to a reduction in the costs of losing preferential market access upon graduation (UNCTAD 2016). On the other hand, other competing LDCs of Bangladesh such as Cambodia are also expected to graduate, which would somewhat reduce the extent of potential losses for Bangladesh.

For Bangladesh, since the Generalised System of Preferences (GSP) scheme of the US[16] does not cover apparels, mainly other markets are of concern from the vantage point of preference erosion (Ahmed 2009). At present, according to the authors' estimates, the share of goods that receive preferential treatment in the EU is 97.8 per cent. The share of goods receiving such treatment in selected non-EU countries in which Bangladesh gets partial or full tariff preference is 80.6 per cent (Annex 4.4 and Annex Table 4.a.2). The authors' analysis of tariff rates, market share and preferences shows that at current MFN rates, Bangladesh's exports would face an 8.7 per cent tariff increase on average in the EU three years after graduation from the LDC category. Similarly for selected non-EU countries, the tariff increase would be 3.9 per cent (Annex 4.4 and Annex Table

4.a.2).[17] It is clear that in both the EU and selected non-EU countries, Bangladesh's export basket contains high shares of products that receive LDC-specific preferential treatment and, thus, export preference erosion is anticipated to be significant, particularly in the EU. Estimates also suggest that for some non-EU countries such as Canada, where the average preference margin is 7.3 per cent, tariff preference erosion would likely also be high. Preference erosion would likely negatively affect Bangladesh's exports and, consequently, GDP growth and other socio-economic indicators such as poverty alleviation, industrialisation and employment generation. A recent study estimated that the withdrawal of GSP plus concession by the EU led to a fall in both Sri Lanka's GDP by 0.58 per cent and employment by 1.09 per cent (Bandara and Naranpanawa 2015).[18]

As per the 2005 Hong Kong Ministerial Decision of the WTO, LDCs have been promised duty-free quota-free treatment for all exports originating from all LDCs by all developed countries and developing countries in a position to do so (if unable, then for at least 97 per cent of tariff lines). The WTO's dedicated window, the Enhanced Integrated Framework, also provides trade-related financial and technical support to LDCs. Also, they have been promised support for implementing commitments under the WTO's Trade Facilitation Agreement. The special and differential treatment (S&DT) provisions in the WTO provide various types of support to LDC members of the WTO. While many of the initiatives are shrouded under the grab of 'best endeavour' clauses[19] and financial support has not been forthcoming as promised, these could be important supportive measures if they were realised.

As is known, intellectual property rights regulations are not strictly enforced in the case of the LDCs. For example, the WTO's Doha Declaration on the Agreement on TRIPS and Public Health allows LDCs waivers in terms of patenting and licensing requirements. Bangladesh has been enjoying this waiver since 2001, the year the declaration was adopted. Bangladesh will not be able to enjoy this benefit once it becomes ineligible for the ISMs, although the eligibility period has recently been extended for the LDCs until December 2032.[20]

Once graduated from the preferential market access regime, Bangladesh would no longer be able to benefit from any progress made in the context of the WTO decision on Services Waiver for the LDCs that is geared to provide preferential access to service exports from the LDCs.[21] The scope for climate-related technology transfer would also be narrowed down.

Other support measures for LDCs

Through Aid for Trade and in many other ways, LDCs receive preferential treatment to enhance their supply-side capacities in trade-related areas (Melo and Wagner 2016). Once graduated, Bangladesh will no more be eligible to seek assistance from the Enhanced Integrated Framework Trust Fund that helps LDCs incorporate trade into national development plans and translate trade priorities into bankable projects for broader Aid for Trade funding. It would lose support for project preparation, feasibility studies and funding of smaller projects (including seed projects). It would be ineligible for concessional finance related to science, technology and innovation provided to LDCs (UNCTAD 2016).

As may be recalled, the IPoA had promised to set up a Technology Bank to facilitate technology transfer to LDCs. Some progress has been made in this connection – a Governing Council of the Technological Bank was constituted and held its first meeting in July 2016. And in December 2016 the United Nations General Assembly (UNGA) officially endorsed the establishment of the Technological Bank (UN-OHRLLS 2017).

Being an LDC, Bangladesh is entitled to send nominations, on gratis basis, to three national training and technical assistance activities per year, in addition to regional courses (compared to two for developing countries). In addition, budget caps for LDCs' contributions to regular budgets of the UN, International Labour Organization (ILO), UN Industrial Development Organization etc., as well as access to special travel funds and free tickets to UN and WTO meetings, will also not be applicable for Bangladesh (UNCTAD 2016). Appropriate budgetary allocations would need to be made towards these foregone benefits.

Thus, being one of the few LDCs which has been able to take significant advantage of the various support measures in favour of the LDCs, it is extremely important that Bangladesh takes the necessary preparations when preferential and S&DT will no longer be available to the country in order to ensure that its graduation is sustainable.

Elements of a sustainable graduation strategy

As UNCTAD (2016) rightly observed, graduation is the first milestone in the marathon of development, not the winning post of a race to leave the LDC category. That Bangladesh is on track for eligibility for graduation is indicative of its robust performance on some key macroeconomic and sectoral indicators (Economic Relations Division 2016a). Meeting the three graduation criteria and maintaining stamina and momentum would demonstrate the underlying strengths of the country's economy and a certain degree of resilience. Yet, it can be argued that the graduation criteria limit countries to focusing on only some selected indicators, albeit important ones. Graduation with stamina, momentum and resilience requires looking beyond an 'instrumentalist' approach to graduation to adopt a broader approach to structural economic transformation in line with the Sustainable Development Goals (SDGs).

It is clear from the analyses above that even if the remit of analysis is limited to threshold scores, LDC graduation would likely have serious implications for Bangladesh from a number of vantage points – market access, trade-related support, access to concessional finance, technology transfer, access to climate finance and more stringent compliance with standards, certification, intellectual property rights regimes and labour standards. Bangladesh needs to design a well-thought-out graduation strategy to be pursued during the interim period between graduation eligibility in 2018 and permanent graduation likely in 2024. Bangladesh also needs to learn from the experiences of countries that have already graduated. In view of the above, what follows are elements of a strategy for Bangladesh's sustainable graduation from the LDC category.

Reporting requirements as a motivation for designing a transition strategy

As Bangladesh has become eligible for graduation, UNCTAD will prepare a vulnerability profile for the country that identifies areas which require particular attention to enable smooth transition. The United Nations Department of Economic and Social Affairs (UN DESA) will prepare an *ex-ante* impact assessment before the 2021 CDP review. Bangladesh should take the optional opportunity to prepare comments on these documents, which can get the ball rolling on preparing a transition strategy. The consultative mechanism that would follow LDC graduation should be a good opportunity to seek global support for helping Bangladesh implement various components of the strategy. Reporting to the CDP and UN ECOSOC should also be seen from the perspective of mobilising global support. If Bangladesh prepares a graduation strategy based on addressing challenges and accessing opportunities, it will be in an advantageous position both in terms of preparing domestically and mobilising globally.

Structural transformation of the economy

Despite Bangladesh becoming eligible for LDC graduation in 2018, roughly 40 million people will still be living below the national poverty line (half of whom will be living below the extreme poverty line). The Lewisian 'turning point' of the economy (with a significantly more prominent role for the manufacturing sector) will continue to be in the making, and supply-side diversification and shifting from factor-driven to productivity-driven production practices will remain formidable challenges. In policymaking and policy implementation, Bangladesh needs to prioritise technology upgradation, skills endowment, productivity enhancement and higher competitiveness. Institutions, incentives, fiscal and monetary policies need to be geared towards this. The country will need to take advantage of the benefits of digital transformation of the economy by taking appropriate actions. Adequate resources should be mobilised and high-quality implementation should be ensured. In the era of the SDGs, which involve triangulating economic development, social inclusiveness and environmental sustainability, Bangladesh's transition needs to be tuned to their concerns. If the country graduates under a business-as-usual scenario, it will be susceptible to vulnerabilities. Thus, more emphasis needs to be put on drivers of structural transformation of the economy and sustainable development.

Strengthening market access

As mentioned, one of the major implications of Bangladesh's graduation would be the loss of LDC-specific tariff preferences. MFN rates for a country's key exports are high, so preference erosion and the resulting loss of competitiveness could be significant if corresponding measures towards enhancing competitiveness are not undertaken. In view of this, Bangladesh needs to deploy renewed efforts on raising export competitiveness as well as product and market diversification. In the readymade garment (RMG) sector where Bangladesh has a proven global foothold, intra-RMG diversification by putting emphasis on quality, fashion and design will need to be prioritised. Bangladesh must take advantage of the increasing South–South trade opportunities, particularly in the regional markets of India and China, through targeted product diversification and by attracting FDI.

It may be recalled that the 2005 resolution adopted by UNGA came up with a number of propositions to help LDCs ensure smooth transition towards graduation. The UN resolution urged all development partners to support the graduating LDCs in implementing their respective transition strategies by avoiding sudden reduction of ODA or technical assistance. The resolution invited all members of WTO to consider extending the existing S&DT and exemptions for LDCs beyond graduation (United Nations 2005). It also invited development and trading partners of graduating LDCs to reduce country trade preferences 'in a phased manner in order to avoid their abrupt reduction' (United Nations 2005). Aligning its policies to this call in support of smooth transition, the EU has already extended its preferences for LDCs under the Everything But Arms (EBA), by an additional three years following graduation. A number of Organisation for Economic Co-operation and Development (OECD) countries has also provided support to LDC graduates, to varying degrees. Regrettably, WTO rules have not been revised in a way that could have enabled graduated LDCs to continue to receive support under the S&DT provisions, at least for some time after graduation. Bangladesh should also explore how best it can take advantage of preference schemes available for the developing countries.

Bangladesh needs to be ready to take innovative approaches to strengthen market access as a non-LDC. It remains one of the few countries in the region that is yet to sign a bilateral FTA. The time has come to selectively sign bilateral FTAs and comprehensive economic partnership agreements which have the potential to benefit Bangladesh. Negotiating such arrangements in a smart way, taking into consideration the rules of origin, sensitiveness of particular items for the economy, various standards to be maintained and non-tariff measures to be put in place, is important.

With regard to export destinations, Bangladesh needs to explore how it can take advantage of non-LDC-specific preferential arrangements such as various GSP schemes for developing countries. In the context of the EU, which is Bangladesh's major export destination, Bangladesh should explore opportunities to have preferential access under either the 'GSP plus' or 'Standard GSP' scheme. A country, to apply to the EU to enjoy preferential treatment under 'GSP plus', must first fulfil the precondition of being beneficiaries of the Standard GSP. The precondition is the following: according to World Bank classification a country must not have been classified as an upper-middle or high-income country for three consecutive years. Since Bangladesh is unlikely to cross the lower threshold of an upper middle-income country (GNI per capita of US$3,956 in 2018 value) by the time of graduation in 2024, it should be eligible to apply for GSP standard.

To become eligible for the EU's GSP plus scheme a country also must be determined economically vulnerable in terms of a low level of economic diversification and integration with the global economy. Currently, there are two vulnerability indicators. First, a country's seven largest sectors (GSP-covered product sections) must account for at least 75 per cent of the value of their total GSP-covered exports to the EU. Bangladesh's exports to the EU are highly concentrated in apparels, whose share was 91.8 per cent of its total export to the EU (EPB 2016).[22] Second, a country's GSP-eligible exports to the EU must represent less than 6.5 per cent of the value (three years' average) of the EU's total GSP imports under the GSP coverage from all GSP beneficiary countries (European Commission 2015). According to authors' calculations, Bangladesh's three years' average (2014, 2015 and 2016) export to the EU under GSP coverage was about 24.2 per cent of the EU's total GSP covered import from all GSP beneficiary countries; respective average values were euro (EUR) 14 billion and EUR 57.9 billion (European Commission 2018). Thus, Bangladesh may not be eligible for GSP plus under this condition. The current GSP rules are stated to expire in 2023. Bangladesh will need to carefully monitor any possible changes to the GSP rules following this timeline. Also, Bangladesh should follow the developments in EU rules and regulations following Brexit (in March 2019). Thus, Bangladesh should be ready to apply for 'GSP Plus' conditionalities if it becomes eligible. In this regard, being ready by meeting the non-economic condition to be eligible for GSP plus is also important.

To apply for GSP plus preferential benefits, a country must ratify and implement 27 specified international conventions in the fields of human rights (seven UN conventions on human rights), labour standards (eight fundamental ILO conventions on labour rights), sustainable development (eight international conventions on environmental protection and climate change) and good governance (four UN conventions). Bangladesh has already ratified or acceded to all but the ILO convention concerning Minimum Age for Admission to Employment (No. 138, 1973). Simple ratification is not enough – what matters is the enforcement of all conventions. In respect to the EBA arrangement, it is encouraged but not a binding requirement for GSP plus.

One recalls that Bangladesh was mentioned under a special paragraph in the June 2016 ILO review because of labour rights concerns; indeed, the observations were repeated in the subsequent review held in July 2017. The EU has raised serious concerns about trade union rights and the enforcement of ILO conventions in Bangladesh's apparels industry. With a forward-looking perspective, Bangladesh should pay more attention to enforcing ILO conventions at both the industry and enterprise levels. Such efforts will be well-rewarded when Bangladesh graduates from the LDC category and decides to apply for GSP plus. Since GSP plus could provide duty-free access for a large number of items including apparels, ensuring eligibility ought to receive high priority in the graduation strategy.

Getting ready for the emerging global trading scenario

The global trading scenario is expected to become even more challenging when Bangladesh will most likely graduate. Moving away from a multilateral trading discipline under the WTO towards a system anchored by mega-regional arrangements like the Comprehensive and Progressive Agreement for Trans-Pacific Partnership, Regional Comprehensive Economic Partnership and Transatlantic Trade and Investment Partnership is already an emerging trend (Rollo *et al.* 2013, Rahman and Ara 2015, Elliott 2016, Jungbluth *et al.* 2016, Lakatos *et al.* 2016). The number of cross-regional FTAs, like that between India and the ten members of the Association of Southeast Asian Nations, the India–EU FTA and the Canada–EU FTA, will likely grow and increasingly dominate global trade. A potential US–Vietnam FTA has come under discussion following the decision of the US not to be part of the Comprehensive and Progressive Agreement for Trans-Pacific Partnership. The US may enter into bilateral FTAs with Bangladesh's competitors. This emerging scenario has implications for Bangladesh's trade and economic interests. While Bangladesh's products will have to enter the markets of many RTA member countries by paying MFN tariffs, these countries will enjoy duty-free market access to their respective partners' markets, which will have adverse impacts on Bangladesh's competitiveness in those markets. In view of this scenario, Bangladesh should pursue highly proactive trade promotion efforts including negotiating membership in RTAs, which will require adequate preparations.

Bangladesh should not lose hope in multilateralism and the WTO. There are 145 S&DT provisions in the WTO for developing countries and LDCs, of which 16 are specific to LDCs (UNCTAD 2016). Many of the 125 provisions for which Bangladesh will be eligible following graduation are 'best endeavour' provisions. Bangladesh should continue playing a proactive role within the WTO to advance the interests of LMICs. Bangladesh should also negotiate as a group with other LDCs (at least with prospective LDC graduates) to maintain the existing preferential treatments received as an LDC (such as TRIPS) which extends beyond the timeline of LDC graduation. However, given the stalemate in WTO negotiations and the move towards plurilateralism within the ambit of the WTO, Bangladesh must pursue its demands through all possible channels.

At the same time, Bangladesh must deepen trade and economic relations with countries in its region. Strengthening cooperation through promoting multi-modal, seamless connectivity between the Southeast Asian, South Asian and sub-regional levels is critical. Investments in trade facilitation, the establishment of a single window for handling export and import procedures, electronic data interface facilities for export–import related information sharing at custom points, harmonisation of standards and certification, and the design of standard operating protocols are required if initiatives such as the Bangladesh–China–India–Myanmar Economic Corridor and Bangladesh–India–Nepal

Motor Vehicles Agreement are to be realised (Bhutan is expected to join in the near future). Along with strengthening its participation in existing RTAs such as the South Asian Free Trade Area and Bay of Bengal Initiative for Multi-Sectoral Technical and Economic Cooperation Free Trade Area, Bangladesh needs to broaden the horizon of partnership. Cooperation with countries of the Bay of Bengal region demands particular attention in view of exploring potential opportunities of the 'Blue Economy' – an emerging global initiative on ocean sustainability. Here, the opportunities emanating from Japan's Bay of Bengal Industrial Growth Belt initiative ought to be prioritised. All efforts will require a renewed emphasis on attracting FDI by harnessing opportunities presented by public–private partnerships in addition to country partnerships and collaborations.

Getting ready for the new aid landscape

Graduation from the LDC category will lead to significant changes in the terms and conditions of aid received by Bangladesh from international organisations and multilateral institutions. Bangladesh's LDC graduation will be accompanied by graduation from the IDA and Asian Development Fund (Davies 2016). Also mentioned, Bangladesh will likely transition from IDA to blended and then to IBRD assistance. Three types of Asian Development ment Funds are now available – Group A (concessional assistance only), Group B (ordinary capital resources blend) and Group C (ordinary capital resources only). Bangladesh is currently classified in Group B as a 'blend country' based on GNI per capita and creditworthiness and thus receives a blend of Asian Development Fund resources and ordinary capital resources (Davies 2016).

Bangladesh needs to address a number of issues, specifically the rising cost of assistance, its increasing external debt burden, how to access new financing opportunities including at the Asian Infrastructure Investment Bank and New Development Bank, and raising capital through issuing sovereign bonds on the international market. Meanwhile, appropriate utilisation of approximately US$21.8 billion aid in the pipeline should be prioritised, since terms will likely become stringent with graduation (Economic Relations Division 2016b). Negotiating bilaterally with development partners for assistance on favourable terms even after graduation will remain a possibility that ought to be explored. Maintaining and deepening bilateral relations with key development partners is paramount. While fully avoiding suppliers' credit types of financial flows may not be possible, negotiating softer terms (interest rates, repayment and grace periods, procurement conditionalities) and untying of assistance should remain high on the policy agenda. Bangladesh needs to get ready to gradually shift to capital-account convertibility by giving due importance to exchange rate management and good governance.

Learning from graduated countries

Finally, Bangladesh must learn from the experiences of graduated countries. Three key observations can be made. First, all five graduated countries have small, vulnerable economies that remain susceptible to vulnerabilities despite meeting the graduation criteria. Being conscious of this susceptibility, these countries pursued policies to reduce specific vulnerabilities. Certain countries adopted initiatives to strategically reposition their economies as part of post-LDC development trajectories. Botswana pursued policies to diversify its economy from overdependence on diamond mining and, at the same time, deployed earnings from mining to invest in education, infrastructure, economic corridors (the country is landlocked) and industrialisation. Cape Verde, which does not have mineral resources, pursued prudent macroeconomic management and harnessed the power of the private sector by developing the tourism sector, encouraging remittance flows and attracting FDI. Second, some countries, like the Maldives, tried to cope with graduation prospects and emergent challenges by requesting deferment of graduation (UNCTAD 2016).

Third, and importantly, some countries tried to ensure a soft landing by renegotiating access to 'soft loans' and preferential market access. Cape Verde, which has remained significantly dependent on aid,[23] negotiated status as a 'blend country' and access to concessional finance from multilateral institutions such as the World Bank and African Development Bank (UNCTAD 2016). It also negotiated, as did Samoa, an additional three-year transitional period for accessing support from the Enhanced Integrated Framework of the WTO, with a provision of an additional two years (subject to approval by the Enhanced Integrated Framework Board). In 2011, the Maldives negotiated an extension of the EBA arrangement by another three years. Similarly, Cape Verde negotiated GSP plus market access in the EU once it was no longer eligible for market access on EBA terms. However, it had to take active measures to implement and enforce 27 core international conventions to meet the eligibility criteria. Countries, such as Samoa, also negotiated special treatment with China, Japan and other countries as part of which they receive preferential, non-reciprocal market access (UNCTAD 2016).

The lessons from these experiences for Bangladesh are twofold. First, adequately prepare to reduce vulnerabilities and facilitate the necessary structural transformation of the economy. Second, explore windows of opportunity for preferential treatment through smart negotiations and proactive engagement with international organisations including the WTO and multilateral institutions such as the World Bank, the ADB and regional financial entities.

A supportive political environment

The return to democracy in the 1990s was crucial to Bangladesh's considerable development success in the backdrop of which it has been considered for LDC graduation in 2018. It is important to remember that Bangladesh's progress in the context of LDC graduation owes much to the relative political stability the country has enjoyed since the early 1990s, allowing the country to undertake and implement programmes towards its socio-economic development (Mahmud *et al.* 2008).

As far as sustainable graduation is concerned, the next decade will be critically important for Bangladesh as the country first crosses the transition period, and then gets on with the initial period of life after LDC graduation. During this period Bangladesh will need to maintain political stability and have a supportive political environment to be able to pursue the graduation strategy (Rahman and Bari 2016). Experience shows that several LICs, following initial success in terms of socio-economic parameters, had fallen backward because of political instability and involvement in regional conflicts (Alesina *et al.* 1996, Sab 2014). This then not only led to the destruction and damage of what was achieved in the past but also led to diversion of valuable limited resources to non-development activities and undermined development efforts. Bangladesh's key stakeholders will, thus, need to be aware of such possibilities and demonstrate due vigilance to maintain political stability to ensure that there is good governance and a supportive political environment to implement its sustainable graduation strategy.

Concluding remarks

This chapter highlights a number of distinctive features that define the pathway to Bangladesh's sustainable LDC graduation and comes up with elements of a smartly crafted graduation strategy to ensure that Bangladesh graduates with stamina, momentum and resilience. It outlines a number of important transitions that inform Bangladesh's graduation process. Graduation from the LDC category will commence following the recent graduation of Bangladesh from low-income to LMIC. In terms of market access, the country will transition from LDC-specific preferential treatment to MFN-based market participation. In the context of aid, it will transition from concessional to blended finance. Additionally, Bangladesh's graduation journey will be taking place at a time when the global trading scenario is changing fast and during the era of the SDGs. This pathway entails addressing formidable challenges and realising opportunities linked to graduation. The authors argue in favour of designing an appropriate, multi-faceted graduation strategy going forward.

The authors observe that meeting the graduation criteria in 2018 speaks of Bangladesh's success and strong performance on some key macroeconomic and sectoral indicators. It is also anticipated that Bangladesh will be able to finally graduate in 2024 by maintaining its record of meeting all the three graduation criteria. However, this evidence does not in any way indicate that all vulnerabilities have been dealt with, that there is no sliding back or that the country is adequately equipped to undertake the post-LDC journey. Still to be addressed are the issues of poverty, inequality, structural economic transformation, creation of decent jobs, supply-side diversification, export product and market diversification, shifting from factor-driven to productivity-driven production practices, accessing opportunities presented by the digital economy, the information technology-enabled service economy and new knowledge eco-systems, and integration into regional markets and the global economy. These issues call for Bangladesh to make conscious policy choices and boost its implementation capacities.

The authors argue that Bangladesh's graduation strategy should involve appropriate policies, institutions, development practices and incentives to address the challenges. Since there is a six-year period between graduation eligibility and graduation from the LDC category, such a strategy would enable Bangladesh to be well-prepared in view of the anticipated post-LDC journey. Experiences of other graduating and graduated countries indicate that some LDCs have been successful by taking appropriate measures while others have deferred graduation given susceptibility to vulnerabilities. By designing and implementing a comprehensive graduation strategy, Bangladesh should be able to smoothly transition through LDC graduation. Graduation for Bangladesh will be permanent on account of the population threshold. It is therefore particularly important that the country adequately prepares a well-thought-out graduation strategy.

The study has put forward a number of recommendations in view of the proposed LDC graduation strategy. First, Bangladesh should take the reporting requirement seriously. It will necessitate Bangladesh's policymakers to articulate the anticipated challenges and inform UN DESA about the initiatives it is contemplating to take in this regard. This homework will help Bangladesh to get ready for its post-LDC journey. Second, as part of this exercise, the experiences of graduated countries should be thoroughly examined to draw appropriate lessons for Bangladesh's graduation strategy. This exercise will also give insights as regards negotiating with development partners for continuation of some of the preferential and S&DT provisions for Bangladesh. Third, the graduation strategy will need to identify drivers of structural transformation of the economy and suggest how these drivers are to be deployed to bring about the needed changes. Fourth, in view of the serious implications for market access emanating from Bangladesh's graduation, the graduation strategy will need to come up with concrete measures to ensure its competitive strength in the global market. Fifth, in view of the dynamics of change in the evolving global trading scenario, anticipated in the study, the strategy will have to come up with adequate response measures to address these challenges. Sixth, in the context of Bangladesh's double graduation – LDC graduation and (lower) middle-income graduation – the strategy ought to include measures to prepare for the emerging aid scenario confronting Bangladesh with the attendant high cost non-concessional loans. The authors have also put emphasis on the overriding importance of a conducive political environment to pursue the proposed graduation strategy. Such a strategy will also help Bangladesh to mobilise global support towards its sustainable LDC graduation.

Annexes

Annex 4.1 Methodology for GNI per capita projections

To carry out projections to determine Bangladesh's likelihood of meeting the LDC graduation criteria, the authors estimated certain values. Relevant data were taken from various sources including the IMF database, the WDI database (World Bank 2017a) and Bangladesh's 7FYP (Bangladesh Planning Commission 2015) (historical exchange rate data from Excel Clout (n.d.) were used). To make projections on GNI per capita, the authors followed the World Bank's Atlas method (World Bank n.d.a). In order to reduce the impact of short-term exchange rate fluctuations, GNI is calculated from national accounts data converted into US$. Later, GNI per capita is calculated by dividing GNI in US$ by the annual population of a country. To calculate GNI in US$, the World Bank uses the Atlas conversion factor instead of exchange rates to reduce the impact of exchange rate fluctuations in cross-country comparisons of national incomes. In order to calculate GNI per capita following the World Bank's step-by-step method, Special Drawing Rights (SDR) values must first be calculated (World Bank n.d.b). Effective from 1 October 2016, the SDR basket consists of the US$, EUR, Japanese yen (hereafter referred to as Yen), British pound (GBP) and newly added Chinese renminbi (hereafter referred to as Renminbi) (IMF 2015, 2016). The respective weights of the US$, EUR, Renminbi, Yen and GBP are fixed at 41.73 per cent, 30.93 per cent, 10.92 per cent, 8.33 per cent and 8.09 per cent until the next review scheduled for 2021. The value of the SDR is the arithmetic sum of these currency weights: US$ (0.58252), EUR (0.38671), Renminbi (1.0174), Yen (11.9) and GBP (0.085946) (IMF 2016). To carry out the calculations (forecasting) of the SDR deflator using World Bank methodology, exchange rates were assumed to be fixed until 2022. In addition, the IMF-estimated GDP deflator and inflation data were used to forecast the rates of the SDR deflator. Quarterly exchange rate data from Excel Clout (n.d.) were used for projections. Both linear and non-linear trend analyses were carried out to forecast the future trends of exchange rates up to 2022. Model specifications in cases of trend analyses were considered based on the highest value of goodness of fit (R^2). As this study used the World Bank's Atlas method to calculate GNI per capita (three-year average), the value and weight of the newly introduced Renminbi for the 2013–15 period were assumed to be equivalent to those of the 2016–20 period. To adjust for statistical discrepancies due to differences between IMF and World Bank methodologies, the projected SDR deflator values were multiplied by a margin of statistical error of 16 per cent. After calculating SDR values, the authors built four scenarios under different assumptions to forecast GNI per capita up to FY2024 using equations (i) and (ii) below:

$$e_t^* = \frac{1}{3}\left[e_{t-2}\left(\frac{P_t}{P_{t-2}} \middle/ \frac{P_t^{SDR\,\$}}{P_{t-2}^{SDR\,\$}}\right) + e_{t-1}\left(\frac{P_t}{P_{t-1}} \middle/ \frac{P_t^{SDR\,\$}}{P_{t-1}^{SDR\,\$}}\right) + e_t\right] \tag{i}$$

e_t^* – Atlas conversion factor for year t using direct quote $\left(\dfrac{national\ currency}{US\$}\right)$

$\dfrac{P_t}{P_{t-2}}, \dfrac{P_t}{P_{t-1}}$ – proxy for domestic inflation;

$\dfrac{P_t^{SDR\,\$}}{P_{t-2}^{SDR\,\$}}, \dfrac{P_t^{SDR\,\$}}{P_{t-1}^{SDR\,\$}}$ – proxy for international inflation

$$y_t^\$ = \frac{Y_t}{N_t} \Big/ e_t^*$$

(ii)

$y_t^\$$ – Atlas GNI per capita in US\$ in year t

Y_t – Atlas GNI per capita in US\$ in year t

N_t – midyear $(1\ \text{July})$ population for year t

Annex 4.2 Assumptions used to project GNI per capita values by following the World Bank's Atlas method

Scenario A: using macroeconomic targets in 7FYP

In scenario A, the value of GDP at current prices in BDT was forecasted for the next six years (2017–22) on the basis of the actual value for FY2016 using the targets for macroeconomic indicators, specifically GDP growth and inflation, set by the Government of Bangladesh (GoB) in its 7FYP. The targets for 2021 and 2022 were assumed to be the same as those for 2020, since FY2020 is the final year of the 7FYP period. The exchange rate was assumed to be fixed at BDT 80 per US\$. Annual population growth was assumed to be 1.2 per cent. After forecasting GDP values at current prices using these assumptions, in accordance with the targets of the 7FYP the value of remittances was added and the value of FDI was subtracted. Other secondary payments and incomes were adjusted to calculate the value of GNI at current prices in BDT. Finally, Atlas GNI per capita in US\$ in year t was calculated using equation (ii) (Annex 4.1).

Scenario B: using the IMF's growth projections for Bangladesh

In scenario B, the IMF's growth projections for Bangladesh were used, specifically projections of GDP growth, GDP deflator, inflation and population growth. The growth rates for these indicators in 2022 were assumed to be the same as those for 2021. The exchange rate was assumed to be fixed at BDT 80 per US\$. After forecasting the GDP values at current prices using these assumptions, the values of factor income inflow and outflow were adjusted to calculate GNI at current prices in BDT. Later, Atlas GNI per capita in US\$ in year t was calculated using equation (ii) (Annex 4.1). The linear trend analysis was calculated over 20 years to find the gap between GDP per capita and GNI per capita for Bangladesh after adjusting the values for remittance inflow and FDI inflow. It is assumed that the discrepancy will follow a linear trend over the 2017–22 period.

Scenario C: using projected remittance and FDI values

In scenario C, the value of GDP at current prices in BDT was forecasted for the next six years (2017–22) on the basis of the actual value for FY2016 using the targets for macroeconomic indicators, specifically GDP growth and inflation, set by the GoB in its 7FYP. The targets for 2021 and 2022 were assumed to be the same as those for 2020, since FY2020 is the final year of the 7FYP period. The exchange rate was assumed to be fixed at BDT 80 per US\$. Annual population growth was assumed to be 1.2 per cent. The value of remittance inflows in BDT thousand billions was projected using the third order polynomial trend analysis (Annex Figure 4.a.1). Later, these values were adjusted by the fixed exchange rate. Similarly, the value of FDI inflows in US\$ billions was projected by using second order polynomial trend analysis (Annex Figure 4.a.1). In both cases, the best model for trend analysis was determined on the basis of the highest value of R^2. Once forecasted, GDP values at current prices were adjusted by the values of factor income inflow and outflow to calculate GNI at current prices in BDT by using equation (ii) (Annex 4.1).

Scenario D: annual exchange rate depreciation/appreciation by ±1 taka

In scenario D, all assumptions from scenario C were kept the same except the assumption about the exchange rate. In this scenario, the BDT/US\$ exchange rate depreciates/appreciates by ±1 taka (e.g. ±7.7 per cent) of the annual average exchange rate for FY2016 over the period of 2017–22.

Annex 4.3 Methodology for HAI and EVI projections

The forecasted values for HAI and EVI were calculated by using the max–min procedure developed by the CDP (CDP and UN DESA 2015). Max–min values are subject to change according to changes in global dynamics. However, for simplicity of calculation, max–min values used in this study were assumed to be constant at 2015 reference level. HAI and EVI were then calculated for Bangladesh by following the methodology developed by the CDP (CDP and UN DESA 2015). The results are presented in Annex Figure 4.a.2.

To make projections for HAI indicators, the WDI dataset was used for percentage of population undernourished, under-five mortality rate and adult literacy rate (World Bank 2017a). In addition, UNESCO (2017) and WHO (2015) databases were used for gross secondary enrolment ratio and MMR, respectively. Linear and non-linear trend analyses were undertaken to project values up to FY2024. The best model for projection was selected by considering the highest value of R^2 (see Annex Figure 4.a.2).

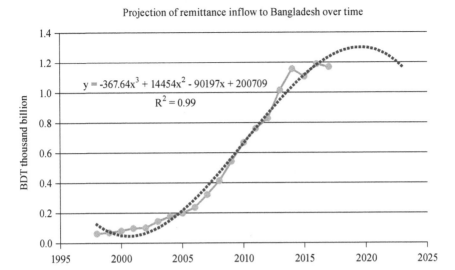

Projection of remittance inflow to Bangladesh over time

$$y = -367.64x^3 + 14454x^2 - 90197x + 200709$$
$$R^2 = 0.99$$

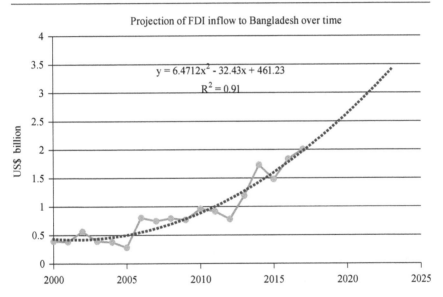

Projection of FDI inflow to Bangladesh over time

$$y = 6.4712x^2 - 32.43x + 461.23$$
$$R^2 = 0.91$$

Figure 4.a.1 Trend analyses of remittance inflow and FDI inflow for Bangladesh.

Source: authors' projections using the data from Bangladesh Bank (2017).

In order to project the values of EVI indicators and sub-indices, the following data sources were used: UN System of National Accounts Main Aggregates database for data on population; share of agriculture, forestry and fisheries; instability of exports of goods and services; and trade remoteness (UNSC 2017). Others sources include the UNCTAD database for data on merchandise export

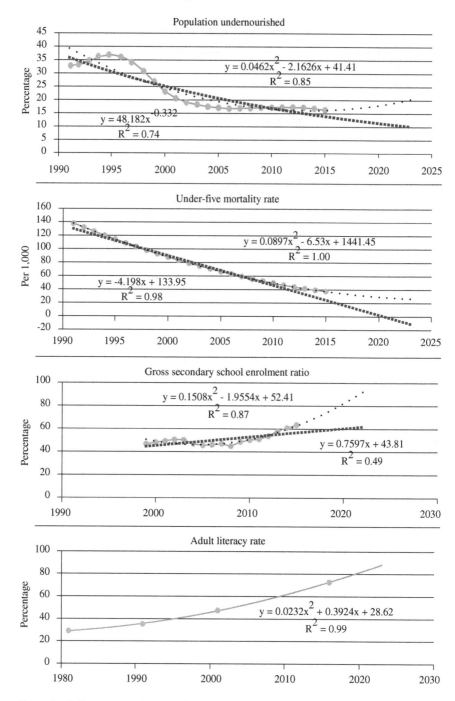

Figure 4.a.2 Projections of HAI indicators.

Source: authors' projections.

concentration (UNCTADstat 2017); Center for International Earth Science Information Network dataset for data on share of population in low elevated coastal zones (CIESIN 2017); Emergency Events Database for data on victims of natural disasters (CRED 2017), and Food and Agricultural Organization Statistics for data on instability of agricultural production (FAOSTAT 2017).

Multiple assumptions were made to project EVI indicators and sub-indices. The score calculated by max–min procedure for population is expected to remain zero for Bangladesh during next three CDP triennial reviews as the size of its population (160 million and more) is significantly higher than the CDP's upper bound of 100 million (i.e. it is improbable to fall below the upper threshold by the next decade). Regarding the share of population in low elevated coastal zones (defined as below five metres), the average value of previous data points was estimated to be 8.93 with a variance of 0.003. Consequently, the value for share of population in low elevated coastal zones in Bangladesh is assumed to be constant at 8.93 for the next three CDP reviews. In addition, to avoid complexities arising from making projections of remoteness due to data inconsistencies, remoteness for Bangladesh is assumed to be constant at the 2018 level for the next three CDP reviews. Apart from these three indicators under EVI, indicators and sub-indices were projected following the detailed methodology developed by the CDP (CDP and UN DESA 2015). Again, linear and non-linear trend analyses were used to project values up to FY2024. The best model for projection was chosen by considering the highest value of R^2.

Annex 4.4 Methodology, equation and results of the regression models

At present, being an LDC, Bangladesh enjoys LDC-specific preferential market access to more than 40 countries. It will lose tariff preferences enjoyed by its exports when it graduates from the LDC category. To estimate the change in export revenue once Bangladesh graduates, the authors adopted widely used gravity regression models (Filippini and Molini 2003, Baldwin and Taglioni 2006, Hatab *et al.* 2010, Davies and Nilsson 2013, Nguyen 2013, Bianco *et al.* 2016, Nicita and Seiermann 2016). To conduct analysis at a disaggregated product level (HS-6 level: total of 7,427 products), the authors analysed data for 40 countries – Australia, Canada, Chile, China, India, Japan, Norway, New Zealand, Russia, South Korea, Switzerland, Turkey and 28 EU members – that provide Bangladesh with full or partial preferential tariff rates for being an LDC (specific duties imposed on products were not considered; the rules of origin criteria at product level were also not considered in these regressions). Six regression models were used in the estimation process to avoid model misspecification error. Among these models, on the basis of post-estimation results (after controlling for model specification test, heteroscedasticity tests and multicollinearity tests) the model in equation (iii) was found to be best fit.

Disaggregated export data by country and product level (six-digit Harmonised System code) were collected from Bangladesh's Export Promotion Bureau

(EPB 2016). To complement the disaggregated export data, tariff data (both MFN and LDC-specific preferential tariffs) by country and product level were considered by using the WTO's Tariff Analysis Online facility (WTO 2017b). In addition, country-level data for macroeconomic variables, specifically GDP per capita (in US$), labour force and exchange rate ratio, were taken from the WDI database.

Products were considered to have received LDC-specific tariff preferences if the difference between MFN and LDC-specific preferential tariff rates was found to be not zero (some MFN tariff rates are at zero and hence no question of preference erosion arises). Considering the prevailing supply (or production) capacity of the RMG sector, products outside HS code 61 and 62 were assumed to have limited supply capacity given Bangladesh's present state of comparative advantage and resources (in producing manufactured products beyond RMG). To capture the mixed effects of Bangladesh's present supply capacity in RMG and non-RMG products, interaction dummies were used for preferential market access within and outside the EU and products that received LDC-specific tariff preferences.

The regression model used in this study is given as follows (results are presented in column 6 of Annex Table 4.a.1):

$$Exp_{val,i} = \alpha \left(GDP_j\right)^{\beta_1} \left(LF_j\right)^{\beta_2} \left(distance_{i,j}\right)^{\beta_3} \left(e^{\beta_4 \times LDC_{pref.\,rate\,i,j}}\right)$$
$$\left(Exchange\,rate\,ratio_{i,j}\right)^{\beta_5}$$
$$\left(e^{\beta_{6-7} \times \left(EU_{dummy,\,j=EU(28)} \times Prod_{pref.\,dummy}\right) + \beta_{8-10} \times \left(Prod_{pref.\,dummy} \times Prod_{capa.\,dummy}\right)}\right) + \varepsilon$$

(iii)

GDP_j – GDP per capita of partner countries

LF_j – labour force of partner countries

$distance_{i,j}$ = distance between capital of Bangladesh and respective importing countries

$LDC_{pref.\,rate\,i,j}$ – preferential LDC rates

$Exchange\,rate\,ratio_{i,j}$ – exchange rate ratio $\left(\dfrac{Bangladesh}{partner}\right)$

$EU_{dummy,\,j=EU(28)} \times Prod_{pref.\,dummy}$ – interaction dummy between EU and *products that received LDC-specific tariff preferences*

$Prod_{pref.\,dummy} \times Prod_{capa.\,dummy}$
– interaction dummy between products that received LDC-specific tariff preferences and products for which Bangladesh has higher supply capacity

Log transformation of equation (iii):

$$\ln\left(Exp_{val,i}\right) = \ln\alpha + \beta_1 \ln\left(GDP_j\right) + \beta_2 \ln\left(LF_j\right) + \beta_3 \ln\left(distance_{i,j}\right) +$$
$$\beta_4\left(LDC_{pref.\,rate\,i,j}\right) + \beta_5 \ln\left(Exchange\,rate\,ratio_{i,j}\right) +$$
$$\beta_{6-7}\left(EU_{dummy,\,j=EU(28)} \times Prod_{pref.\,dummy}\right) +$$
$$\beta_{8-10}\left(Prod_{pref.\,dummy} \times Prod_{capa.\,dummy}\right) + \varepsilon \qquad \text{(iv)}$$

The change in export revenue was calculated using the following steps after executing a (partial) first-order condition on log of export value with respect to LDC-specific tariff preferences (dummy):

$$\frac{\partial \ln\left(Exp_{val,i}\right)}{\partial LDC_{pref.\,rate\,i,j}} = \beta_4 \times \frac{\partial LDC_{pref.\,rate\,i,j}}{\partial LDC_{pref.\,rate\,i,j}}$$

$$\Rightarrow \frac{1}{Exp_{val,i}} \times \frac{\partial\left(Exp_{val,i}\right)}{\partial LDC_{pref.\,rate\,i,j}} = \beta_4$$

$$\Rightarrow \frac{\partial Exp_{val,i}}{\partial LDC_{pref.\,rate\,i,j}} = \beta_4 \times Exp_{val,i} \qquad \text{(v)}$$

Annex

Table 4.a.1 Regression results

Explanatory variable	Dependent variable: log of export value (in US$)					
	1	2	3	4	5	6
Log of GDP per capita of partner countries	0.071 (1.30)	0.239 (4.45)***	0.262 (4.85)***	0.249 (4.61)***	0.265 (4.90)***	0.251 (4.64)***
Log of labour force of partner countries	0.311 (10.48)***	0.434 (15.40)***	0.425 (15.06)***	0.433 (15.29)***	0.426 (15.11)***	0.433 (15.29)***
Log of distance between capitals	0.675 (5.87)***	0.314 (2.72)***	0.304 (2.63)***	0.340 (2.94)***	0.327 (2.82)***	0.346 (2.99)***
Preferential LDC rates	−0.027 (2.25)**	−0.016 (1.53)*	−0.021 (1.80)*	−0.019 (1.73)*	−0.021 (1.81)*	−0.019 (1.74)*
Log of exchange rate ratio (Bangladesh/partner)	0.062 (2.62)***	0.080 (3.45)***	0.093 (3.97)***	0.086 (3.67)***	0.091 (3.90)***	0.086 (3.66)***
EU dummy (1 = non-EU countries)	−0.646 (6.59)***	−0.600 (6.64)***	−0.458 (4.87)***	–	−0.486 (5.11)**	–
Products with higher supply capacity dummy (1 = lower capacity)	–	−2.035 (30.06)***	−1.917 (27.40)***	−1.863 (26.13)***	–	–
Products receive LDC preference dummy (1 = outside of preference basket)	–	–	−0.582 (6.01)***	–	–	–
Products receive preference × Non-EU partner (0 = products receive preference; 0 = EU; 1 = otherwise)	–	–	–	−0.617 (6.12)***	–	−0.616 (6.11)***
Products don't receive preference × EU partner (0 = product receive preference; 0 = EU; 1 = otherwise)	–	–	–	−1.059 (6.51)***	–	−0.076 (0.37)*
Products don't receive preference × Non-EU partner (0 products receive preference; 0 = EU; 1 = otherwise)	–	–	–	−0.927 (7.87)***	–	–

	(1)	(2)	(3)	(4)	(5)	(6)
Products receive preference × Products with lower supply capacity (0 = products receive preference; 0 = higher supply capacity; 1 = otherwise)	—	—	—	—	−1.847 (23.88)***	−1.839 (23.78)***
Products don't receive preference × Products with higher supply capacity (0 = products receive preference; 0 = higher supply capacity; 1 = otherwise)	—	—	—	—	−0.279 (1.82)	−0.824 (5.33)***
Products don't receive preference × Products with lower supply capacity (0 = products receive preference; 0 = higher supply capacity; 1 = otherwise)	—	—	—	—	−2.558 (23.29)***	−2.838 (18.99)***
Constants	−0.585 (0.50)	−0.334 (0.29)	−0.366 (0.32)	−0.618 (0.54)	−0.629 (0.55)	−0.706 (0.62)
R^2	0.03	0.14	0.14	0.14	0.14	0.14
N	7,427	7,427	7,427	7,427	7,427	7,427

Source: authors' estimations.

Note
Values in parenthesis are standard errors.
* $p<0.1$;
** $p<0.05$;
*** $p<0.01$.

Table 4.a.2 Likelihood of export preference erosion in EU and selected non-EU countries

Country	Share of LDC-specific tariff preferential export basket (%)	Increase in aggregate tariff rate (%)
Australia	98.6	1.8
Canada	95.7	7.3
Chile	100.0	4.5
China	94.7	3.1
India	76.0	2.4
Japan	90.8	3.8
New Zealand	95.7	8.4
Norway	90.0	8.4
Russia	12.9	1.0
South Korea	98.4	3.3
Switzerland	0.0	0.0
Turkey	70.7	3.6
Selected non-EU countries	80.6	3.9
Austria	99.1	12.5
Belgium	96.2	5.5
Bulgaria	80.3	19.5
Croatia	99.8	10.8
Cyprus	97.8	36.8
Czech Republic	99.7	14.2
Denmark	99.5	6.8
Estonia	97.0	66.2
Finland	99.9	14.2
France	99.8	4.3
Germany	99.7	3.6
Greece	96.8	12.4
Hungary	96.8	31.4
Ireland	99.8	13.9
Italy	96.2	3.7
Latvia	97.7	57.3
Lithuania	35.0	28.8
Luxemburg	100.0	299.5
Malta	99.7	67.1
Netherlands	99.2	4.9
Poland	99.0	6.3
Portugal	94.9	16.5
Romania	83.4	12.1
Slovakia	99.9	22.9
Slovenia	89.7	18.1
Spain	98.4	4.5
Sweden	99.9	5.3
United Kingdom	99.4	3.2
EU (28 countries)	97.8	8.7

Source: authors' estimations.

Notes

1 During the 2012 CDP review, Equatorial Guinea was found eligible for graduation for the second time. The UNGA added six months to the three-year preparatory process leading to the country's graduation and invited it to prepare a national smooth-transition strategy, which was to be done with the support of the UN system and in cooperation with its bilateral and multilateral development and trading partners (UNCTAD 2016).

2 A prolonged military conflict is likely to have adverse implications for the country's graduation according to all the three graduation criteria.

3 Detailed methodology and assumptions are presented in Annexes 4.1 and 4.2 respectively.

4 World merchandise trade volume was expected to grow at only 2.4 per cent and world real GDP at 2.7 per cent in 2017 (WTO 2017a). For the second consecutive year, since 2001, the growth rate of global trade was below that of global GDP (WTO 2016, 2017a). Notably, world merchandise trade volume rose about twice as fast as world real GDP during the peak period of the 1990s (WTO 2016).

5 The log of labour force as a proxy of labour supply in partner countries and the distance between trading partners do not align with the traditional assumptions of gravity regression models. Bangladesh's increasing integration with the global economy may neutralise the assumption of distance as a barrier to trade. On the other hand, since Bangladesh mostly exports lower value added products, partner countries' labour supply may not have a significant substitution effect.

6 Since 1990, MMR has come down significantly over the last two decades (from 569 in 1990 to 176 in 2015 per 100,000 live births) for Bangladesh. As a matter of fact, the country has reduced MMR by 4.8 per cent on average, annually between 1990 and 2015.

7 Given their small populations, which at the time of graduation varied between 0.2 million and 1.5 million, the four countries had relatively large ODA receipts per capita, averaging US$163 for the Maldives, US$181 for Botswana, US$387 for Cape Verde and US$437 for Samoa (at 2013 prices) in the decade prior to their graduation. These figures are between 3.3 and 9.0 times that for LDCs as a group for the 2005–14 period (UNCTAD 2016).

8 For GNI per capita of more than US$1,905, a country is only eligible for IBRD (World Bank 2017b).

9 The commitment fee of 0.25 per cent and management fee of 0.025 per cent would make it somewhat more costly.

10 India has provided US$1 billion, 2 billion and 5 billion under its three lines of credit at concessional lending rates varying between 1 per cent and 1.75 per cent per year with a repayment period of 20 years and grace period of five years.

11 The assumption is that interest rates would be lower or preferential. However, terms of loan also depend on the political situation of a country.

12 Bangladesh's scores for macroeconomic management and implementing policies for social inclusion were 3.8 and 3.5 respectively. These were higher than the average scores of 3.3 and 3.2 when compared to the 15 LDCs that are expected to graduate by 2024.

13 Bangladesh's scores for implementing structural policies and public sector management and institutions were respectively 3.0 and 2.9, which were lower than the average scores of 3.1 (for both these indicators) when compared to the 15 LDCs expected to graduate by 2024 (World Bank 2017c).

14 Forty countries were selected for which data was available.

15 By using the coefficient value ($e \uparrow (\beta \downarrow 4) - 1$) represented in column 6 of Annex Table 4.a.1.

16 GSP is a preferential tariff system which offers exemption of tariffs to developing countries to export to the US from the more general rules of the WTO. Similarly, GSP is a scheme whereby the EU members offer partial or full removal of tariffs on two-thirds of products originating from developing countries. GSP plus is an enhanced preference scheme that provides full removal of tariffs on essentially the same product categories.

17 Assuming that the basket of exports and MFN rates remain the same.

18 In an earlier study using the Global Trade Analysis Project model, Parra (2008) showed that withdrawal of the GSP plus scheme was expected to negatively affect Sri Lanka in the following ways: a 2 per cent fall in GDP, a decrease in total exports by 0.67 per cent, a fall in household expenditure by 2.04 per cent, a decline in welfare by nearly US$88 million and an increase in the incidence of poverty resulting from a decrease in wages in the apparels sector.

19 'Best endeavours' is a commonly known term in commercial contracts, which places the obligation upon the party given such an undertaking to use all possible efforts necessary to fulfil the commitment.

20 The eligibility period was first extended until December 2015 in Doha in 2001 and then for another 17 years until December 2032 in Nairobi at the WTO's Tenth Ministerial Conference in 2015.

21 The extent of this loss is difficult to quantify because negotiations have not been completed.

22 The likelihood of Bangladesh meeting the criterion is high.

23 ODA was equivalent to 14 per cent of post-graduation GNI, albeit somewhat below the 18 per cent of the pre-graduation period (OECD.Stat 2016).

References

Ahmed, A. U. and Arends-Kuenning, M., 2006. Do crowded classrooms crowd out learning? Evidence from the food for education program in Bangladesh. *World Development*, 34 (4), 665–684.

Ahmed, A. U. and Del Ninno, C., 2002. *The food for education program in Bangladesh: An evaluation of its impact on educational attainment and food security*. Discussion Paper 138. Washington, DC: Food Consumption and Nutrition Division of the International Food Policy Research Institute. Available from: http://ageconsearch.umn.edu/bitstream/15998/1/dp02138b.pdf [Accessed 12 February 2017].

Ahmed, N., 2009. Sustaining ready-made garment exports from Bangladesh. *Journal of Contemporary Asia*, 39(4), 597–618.

Aiello, F. and Cardamone, P., 2007. *Analysing the impact of the EBA initiative using a gravity model*. Working Paper 10/7. Rome: Italian Ministry of Education, University and Research. Available from: www.ecostat.unical.it/anania/PUE&PIEC/WPs/WP%2010-7%20Aiello%20e%20Cardamone.pdf [Accessed 19 March 2017].

Alesina, A., et al., 1996. Political instability and economic growth. *Journal of Economic growth*, 1 (2), 189–211.

Audiguier, C., 2012. *The impact of the global financial crisis on the least developed countries*. Development Policies, Working Paper 50. Clermont-Ferrand: Fondation pour les études et recherches sur le développement international. Available from: http://dev.eudevdays.eu/sites/default/files/Ferdi-DT50-C.Audigier_WEB_0.pdf [Accessed 17 February 2017].

Bakht, Z. and Basher, A., 2015. *Strategy for development of the SME sector in Bangladesh*. Dhaka: Bangladesh Institute of Development Studies. Available from: www.plancomm.gov.bd/wp-content/uploads/2015/02/2_Strategy-for-Development-of-SME-in-Bangladesh.pdf [Accessed 11 March 2017].

Baldwin, R. and Taglioni, D., 2006. *Gravity for dummies and dummies for gravity equations.* Working Paper 12516. Cambridge: National Bureau of Economic Research. Available from: http://graduateinstitute.ch/files/live/sites/iheid/files/sites/ctei/shared/CTEI/Baldwin/Publications/Chapters/Trade%20Effects%20Euro/Gravity%20Dummies.pdf [Accessed 12 February 2017].

Bandara, J. S. and Naranpanawa, A., 2015. Garment industry in Sri Lanka and the removal of GSP plus by EU. *World Economy*, 38 (9), 1438–1461.

Bangladesh Bank, 2017. *Bangladesh Bank open data initiative* [dataset]. Dhaka: Bangladesh Bank. Available from: www.bb.org.bd/econdata/index.php [Accessed 18 February 2017].

Bangladesh Planning Commission, 2015. *Seventh Five Year Plan FY2016 – FY2020.* Five Year Plan. Dhaka: General Economics Division, Planning Commission, Government of Bangladesh. Available from: www.plancomm.gov.bd/wp-content/uploads/2015/10/7th_FYP_18_02_2016.pdf [Accessed 7 March 2017].

BBS, 1990. *Statistical yearbook of Bangladesh 1989.* Dhaka: Bangladesh Bureau of Statistics.

BBS, 1996. *Statistical yearbook of Bangladesh 1995.* Dhaka: Bangladesh Bureau of Statistics.

BBS, 2005. *Statistical yearbook of Bangladesh 2004.* Dhaka: Bangladesh Bureau of Statistics.

BBS, 2017. *Statistical yearbook of Bangladesh 2016.* Dhaka: Bangladesh Bureau of Statistics. Available from: http://bbs.portal.gov.bd/sites/default/files/files/bbs.portal.gov.bd/page/b2db8758_8497_412c_a9ec_6bb299f8b3ab/StatisticalYearBookFinal2016.pdf [Accessed 18 October 2017].

Bhattacharya, D. and Khan, T. I., 2014. The challenges of structural transformation and progress towards the MDGs in LDCs. In: LDC IV Monitor, *Istanbul programme of action for the LDCs (2011–2020): Monitoring deliverables, tracking progress – analytical perspectives.* London: Commonwealth Secretariat, 1–37.

Bianco, D. A., et al., 2016. Tariffs and non-tariff frictions in the world wine trade. *European Review of Agricultural Economics*, 43 (1), 31–57.

BMET, 2017. *Statistical reports* [dataset]. Dhaka: Bureau of Manpower, Employment and Training. Available from: www.bmet.gov.bd/BMET/stattisticalDataAction [Accessed 1 October 2017].

Brouwer, R., et al., 2007. Socioeconomic vulnerability and adaptation to environmental risk: A case study of climate change and flooding in Bangladesh. *Risk Analysis*, 27 (2), 313–326.

Cariolle, J., Goujon, M. and Guillaumont, P., 2016. Has structural economic vulnerability decreased in Least Developed Countries? Lessons drawn from retrospective indices. *Journal of Development Studies*, 52 (5), 591–606.

CDP and UN DESA, 2015. *Handbook on the least developed country category: Inclusion, graduation and special support measures.* 2nd edn. New York: Committee for Development Policy and United Nations Department of Economic and Social Affairs.

Chowdhury, A. M. R., et al., 2013. The Bangladesh paradox: Exceptional health achievement despite economic poverty. *Lancet*, 382 (9906), 1734–1745.

Chowdhury, A. M. R., Nath, S. R. and Choudhury, R. K., 2002. Enrolment at primary level: Gender difference disappears in Bangladesh. *International Journal of Educational Development*, 22 (2), 191–203.

CIESIN, 2017. *Data profiles.* New York: Center for International Earth Science Information Network. Available from: http://ciesin.columbia.edu/ [Accessed 12 March 2017].

Cortez, A. L., Kinniburgh, I. and Mollerus, R., 2014. *Accelerating development in the least developed countries through international support measures: Findings from country case studies.* CDP Background Paper 22. New York: United Nations Department of Economic and Social Affairs.

CPD, 2017. *State of the Bangladesh economy in FY2016–17: First reading*. Dhaka: Centre for Policy Dialogue. Available from: http://cpd.org.bd/wp-content/uploads/2017/01/state-of-the-bangladesh-economy-in-fy2016-17-first-reading.pdf [Accessed 17 September 2017].

CRED, 2017. *Database*. Brussels: Centre for Research on the Epidemiology of Disasters. Available from: www.emdat.be/database [Accessed 12 March 2017].

Davies, E. and Nilsson, L., 2013. *A comparative analysis of EU and US trade preferences for the LDCs and the AGOA beneficiaries*. Chief Economist Note. Ref. Ares (2013) 157432–07/02/2013. Brussels: European Commission. Available from: www.researchgate.net/profile/Lars_Nilsson5/publication/256297981_A_comparative_analysis_of_EU_and_US_trade_preferences_for_the_LDCs_and_the_AGOA_beneficiaries/links/00b7d5224358b77da6000000/A-comparative-analysis-of-EU-and-US-trade-preferences-for-the-LDCs-and-the-AGOA-beneficiaries.pdf [Accessed 12 July 2017].

Davies, S., 2016. *Bangladesh: Four graduations and a new perspective plan?* Unpublished.

Dawson, P. J., 2006. The export–income relationship and trade liberalisation in Bangladesh. *Journal of Policy Modeling*, 28 (8), 889–896.

De Bruyn, T. and Kuddus, U., 2005. *Dynamics of remittance utilization in Bangladesh*. IOM Migration Research Series 18. Geneva: International Organization for Migration. Available from: http://publications.iom.int/system/files/pdf/mrs_18.pdf [Accessed 12 July 2017].

Economic Relations Division, 2016a. *Mid-term review of the implementation of the Istanbul programme of action for the LDCs for the decade 2011–2020*. Dhaka: Ministry of Finance, Government of Bangladesh. Available from: http://unohrlls.org/custom-content/uploads/2016/03/Bangladesh-National-Report.pdf [Accessed 24 August 2017].

Economic Relations Division, 2016b. *Aging of project aid pipelines as of 30 June 2016* [online]. Dhaka: Ministry of Finance, Government of Bangladesh. Available from: http://erd.portal.gov.bd/sites/default/files/files/erd.portal.gov.bd/page/5b21cbd3_5877_4b24_889d_a03301bb974c/Tbl-3.11_1516%20%282%29.pdf [Accessed 7 January 2017].

Elliott, K., 2016. *How much 'Mega' in the mega-regional TPP and TTIP: Implications for developing countries*. Center for Global Development Policy Paper 079. Washington, DC: Center for Global Development. Available from: www.cgdev.org/sites/default/files/CGD-Policy-Paper-79-Elliott-Mega-Regional-TPP-TTIP_0.pdf [Accessed 21 September 2017].

EPB, 2016. *Statistic data* [dataset]. Dhaka: Export Promotion Bureau, Ministry of Commerce, Government of Bangladesh. Available from: http://epb.portal.gov.bd/site/files/9efa4995-2501-4c9e-8ca6-8b8f7208c3a0/Statistic [Accessed 14 January 2017].

EPB, 2017. *Statistic data* [dataset]. Dhaka: Export Promotion Bureau, Ministry of Commerce, Government of Bangladesh. Available from: http://epb.portal.gov.bd/site/files/51916ae6-a9a3-462e-a6bd-9ef074d835af/Statistic-Data-2016-2017 [Accessed 7 December 2017].

European Commission, 2015. Commission delegated regulation (EU) 2015/602 of 9 February 2015 amending regulation (EU) No 978/2012 of the European parliament and the council as regards the vulnerability threshold defined in point 1(b) of Annex VII to that regulation. *Official Journal of the European Union*, 8–9.

European Commission, 2018. Report on the Generalised Scheme of Preferences covering the period 2016–2017. COM (2018) 36 final. Report from the Commission to the European Parliament and the Council. Available from: http://trade.ec.europa.eu/doclib/docs/2018/january/tradoc_156536.pdf [Accessed 12 February 2018].

Excel Clout, n.d. *Historical exchange rates in Excel* [dataset]. Available from: www.excel-clout.com/historical-exchange-rates-in-excel [Accessed 16 March 2017].

FAOSTAT, 2017. *Suite of food security indicators*. Rome: Food and Agriculture Organization Corporate Statistical Database. Available from: www.fao.org/faostat/en/#data/FS [Accessed 12 March 2017].

Filippini, C. and Molini, V., 2003. The determinants of East Asian trade flows: A gravity equation approach. *Journal of Asian Economics*, 14 (5), 695–711.

Haque, A. K. E. and Bari, E., 2015. *Garments workers in Bangladesh: Social impact of the garments industry*. Dhaka: Asian Center for Development. Available from: www.researchgate.net/publication/302963415_GARMENT_WORKERS_IN_BANGLADESH_SOCIAL_IMPACT_OF_THE_GARMENT_INDUSTRY [Accessed 11 July 2017].

Hatab, A. A., Romstad, E. and Huo, X., 2010. Determinants of Egyptian agricultural exports: A gravity model approach. *Modern Economy*, 1 (3), 134–143.

Hatemi-J, A. and Uddin, G. S., 2014. On the causal nexus of remittances and poverty reduction in Bangladesh. *Applied Economics*, 46 (4), 374–382.

IMF, 2015. *Press release: IMF's executive board completes review of SDR basket, includes Chinese Renminbi* [online]. Press Release No. 15/540. Washington, DC: International Monetary Fund. Available from: www.imf.org/external/np/sec/pr/2015/pr15540.htm [Accessed 16 March 2017].

IMF, 2016. *IMF launches new SDR basket including Chinese Renminbi, determines new currency amounts* [online]. Press Release No. 16/440. Washington, DC: International Monetary Fund. Available from: www.imf.org/en/News/Articles/2016/09/30/AM16-PR16440-IMF-Launches-New-SDR-Basket-Including-Chinese-Renminbi [Accessed 16 March 2017].

ITC, 2017. *Trade statistics* [dataset]. Geneva: International Trade Centre. Available from: www.trademap.org/Index.aspx [Accessed 15 March 2017].

Jungbluth, C., Aichele, R. and Felbermayr, G., 2016. *Asia's rise in the new world trade order: The effects of mega-regional trade agreements on Asian countries*. Global Economic Dynamics Study Series Part 2. Gütersloh: Bertelsmann Stiftung.

Karim, M. F. and Mimura, N., 2008. Impacts of climate change and sea-level rise on cyclonic storm surge floods in Bangladesh. *Global Environmental Change*, 18 (3), 490–500.

Kawamura, H., 2014. *The likelihood of 24 least developed countries graduating from the LDC category by 2020: An achievable goal?* CDP Background Paper 20. New York: United Nations Department of Economic and Social Affairs.

Lakatos, C., *et al.*, 2016. Potential macroeconomic implications of the Trans-Pacific Partnership. *In*: World Bank, ed. *Global economic prospects, January 2016: Spillovers amid weak growth*. Washington, DC: World Bank, 219–236. Available from: www.worldbank.org/content/dam/Worldbank/GEP/GEP2016a/Global-Economic-Prospects-January-2016-Spillovers-amid-weak-growth.pdf [Accessed 15 April 2017].

Love, J. and Chandra, R., 2005. Testing export-led growth in Bangladesh in a multivariate VAR framework. *Journal of Asian Economics*, 15 (6), 1155–1168.

Mahmud, W., Ahmed, S. and Mahajan, S., 2008. Economic reforms, growth, and governance: The political economy aspects of Bangladesh's development surprise. *In*: D. Brady and M. Spence, eds. *Leadership and growth*. Washington, DC: Commission on Growth and Development, World Bank, 227–254.

Melo, J. D. and Wagner, L., 2016. Aid for trade and the trade facilitation agreement: What they can do for LDCs. *Journal of World Trade*, 50 (6), 935–969.

Nguyen, H. T., 2013. *Determinants of Vietnam's exports: A gravity model approach*. Thesis (Masters). Assumption University.

Nicita, A. and Seiermann, J., 2016. *G20 policies and export performance of least developed countries*. Policy Issues in International Trade and Commodities Research Study Series

75. New York: United Nations. Available from: http://unctad.org/en/PublicationsLibrary/itcdtab77_en.pdf [Accessed 12 February 2017].

OECD.Stat, 2016. *Creditor reporting system (CRS)* [dataset]. Paris: Organisation for Economic Co-operation and Development. Available from: https://stats.oecd.org/Index. aspx?DataSetCode=CRS1 [Accessed 11 February 2017].

Parra, M. M., 2008. *Removing Sri Lanka's preferences in the European Union: A general equilibrium exercise.* Paper prepared for the International Crisis Group. Unpublished. Brighton: Sussex University.

Rahman, M. and Bari, E., 2016. *Escaping the middle-income trap: Perspectives from Bangladesh.* Dhaka: Friedrich-Ebert-Stiftung, Bangladesh Office. Available from: http://library.fes.de/pdf-files/bueros/bangladesch/12938.pdf [Accessed 4 June 2017].

Rahman, M. M. and Ara, L. A., 2015. TPP, TTIP and RCEP: Implications for South Asian economies. *South Asia Economic Journal*, 16 (1), 27–45.

Rahman, S., 2010. Six decades of agricultural land use change in Bangladesh: Effects on crop diversity, productivity, food availability and the environment, 1948–2006. *Singapore Journal of Tropical Geography*, 31 (2), 254–269.

Rai, N., Huq, S. and Huq, M. J., 2014. Climate resilient planning in Bangladesh: A review of progress and early experiences of moving from planning to implementation. *Development in Practice*, 24 (4), 527–543.

Ratha, D., *et al.*, 2016. *Migration and remittances: Recent developments and outlook.* Migration and Development Brief 26. Washington, DC: World Bank. Available from: http://pubdocs.worldbank.org/en/661301460400427908/MigrationandDevelopmentBrief26. pdf [Accessed 19 April 2017].

Rollo, J., *et al.*, 2013. *Potential effects of the proposed transatlantic trade and investment partnership on selected developing countries.* A report by CARIS, University of Sussex for the Department for International Development. Brighton: Centre for the Analysis of Regional Integration at Sussex. Available from: http://tradesift.com/Reports/Potential%20 Effects%20of%20the%20Proposed%20Transatlantic%20Trade%20and%20Investment%20Partnership%20on%20Selected%20Developing%20Countries_DFID_ Final%20Report_July2013.pdf [Accessed 19 February 2017].

Sab, M. R., 2014. *Economic impact of selected conflicts in the Middle East: What can we learn from the past?* IMF WP/14/100. Washington, DC: International Monetary Fund. Available from: www.imf.org/external/pubs/ft/wp/2014/wp14100.pdf [Accessed 13 March 2017].

UN DESA, 2017a. *Equatorial Guinea graduates from the LDC category* [online]. Available from: www.un.org/development/desa/dpad/publication/equatorial-guinea-graduates-from-the-ldc-category/ [Accessed 20 June 2017].

UN DESA, 2017b. *Time frame of the eligibility procedure* [online]. Available from: www. un.org/development/desa/dpad/least-developed-country-category/ldc-graduation.html [Accessed 24 February 2017].

UNCTAD, 2013. *Growth with employment for inclusive and sustainable development.* The Least Developed Countries Report 2013. New York: United Nations Conference on Trade and Development. Available from: http://unctad.org/en/PublicationsLibrary/ ldc2013_en.pdf [Accessed 21 April 2017].

UNCTAD, 2014. *Growth with structural transformation: A post-2015 development agenda.* The Least Developed Countries Report 2014. New York: United Nations Conference on Trade and Development. Available from: http://unctad.org/en/PublicationsLibrary/ ldc2014_en.pdf [Accessed 28 February 2017].

UNCTAD, 2015. *Transforming rural economies.* The Least Developed Countries Report 2015. New York: United Nations Conference on Trade and Development. Available from: http://unctad.org/en/PublicationsLibrary/ldc2015_en.pdf [Accessed 28 February 2017].

UNCTAD, 2016. *The path to graduation and beyond: Making the most of the process.* The Least Developed Countries Report 2016. New York: United Nations Conference on Trade and Development. Available from: http://unctad.org/en/PublicationsLibrary/ldc2016_en.pdf [Accessed 19 March 2017].

UNCTAD, 2017. *UNCTADstat* [dataset]. New York: United Nations Conference on Trade and Development. Available from: http://unctadstat.unctad.org [Accessed 16 March 2017].

UNCTADstat, 2017. *Merchandise: Product concentration and diversification indices of exports and imports, annual, 1995–2016.* New York: United Nations Conference on Trade and Development. Available from: http://unctadstat.unctad.org/wds/Table Viewer/tableView.aspx?ReportId=120 [Accessed 12 March 2017].

UNESCO, 2017. *Education: Gross enrolment ratio by level of education* [dataset]. Available from: http://data.uis.unesco.org/index.aspx?queryid=142 [Accessed 12 March 2017].

United Nations, 2005. *Smooth transition strategy for countries graduating from the list of least developed countries.* A/RES/59/209. New York: United Nations.

United Nations, 2011. *Draft Istanbul declaration: Renewed and strengthened global partnership for the development of least developed countries.* A/CONF.219/L.1. New York: United Nations. Available from: https://digitallibrary.un.org/record/792251/files/A_CONF.219_L.1-EN.pdf [Accessed 16 March 2017].

United Nations, 2017. *UN target for ODA to LDCs* [online]. Available from: http://iif.un.org/content/un-target-oda-ldcs-ipoa [Accessed 16 March 2017].

UN-OHRLLS, 2017. *Press release* [online]. New York: United Nations Office of the High Representative for the Least Developed Countries, Landlocked Developing Countries and Small Island Developing States. Available from: http://unohrlls.org/custom-content/uploads/2016/12/FINAL-Press-Release-23-December-2016-Technology-Bank-for-Least-Developed-Countries-established-by-UN-General-Assembly.pdf [Accessed 14 January 2017].

UNSC, 2017. *Bangladesh: data availability.* New York: United Nations Statistical Commission. Available from: https://unstats.un.org/unsd/snaama/cavailability.asp [Accessed 12 March 2017].

Vanhnalat, B., *et al.*, 2015. Assessment the effect of free trade agreements on exports of Lao PDR. *International Journal of Economics and Financial Issues,* 5 (2), 365–376.

WHO, 2015. *Trends in maternal mortality: 1990 to 2015.* Geneva: World Health Organization. Available from: www.who.int/reproductivehealth/publications/monitoring/maternal-mortality-2015/en/ [Accessed 16 March 2017].

World Bank, n.d.a. *The World Bank Atlas method: detailed methodology* [online]. Washington, DC: World Bank. Available from: https://datahelpdesk.worldbank.org/knowledge-base/articles/378832-the-world-bank-atlas-method-detailed-methodology [Accessed 20 January 2017].

World Bank, n.d.b. *What is the SDR deflator?* [online]. Washington, DC: World Bank. Available from: https://datahelpdesk.worldbank.org/knowledgebase/articles/378829-what-is-the-sdr-deflator [Accessed 16 March 2017].

World Bank, 2005. *Bangladesh: Social safety nets in Bangladesh: An assessment.* Washington, DC: World Bank. Available from: http://documents.worldbank.org/curated/en/680721468199765276/Bangladesh-Social-safety-nets-in-Bangladesh-an-assessment [Accessed 12 March 2017].

World Bank, 2017a. *World development indicators* [dataset]. Washington, DC: World Bank. Available from: http://data.worldbank.org/data-catalog/world-development-indicators [Accessed 16 March 2017].

World Bank, 2017b. *World Bank country and lending groups* [dataset]. Washington, DC: World Bank. Available from: https://datahelpdesk.worldbank.org/knowledgebase/articles/906519 [Accessed 14 August 2017].

World Bank, 2017c. *Country policy and institutional assessment* [dataset]. Washington, DC: World Bank. Available from: http://databank.worldbank.org/data/reports.aspx?source=country-policy-and-institutional-assessment [Accessed 20 February 2017].

WTO, 2016. *Trade in 2016 to grow at slowest pace since the financial crisis.* Trade Statistics and Outlook. Press/779. Geneva: World Trade Organization.

WTO, 2017a. *Trade recovery expected in 2017 and 2018, amid policy uncertainty.* Trade Statistics and Outlook. Press/791. Geneva: World Trade Organization.

WTO, 2017b. *Tariff analysis online* [dataset]. Geneva: World Trade Organization. Available from: https://tao.wto.org [Accessed 16 March 2017].

Zohir, S., 2004. NGO sector in Bangladesh: An overview. *Economic and Political Weekly*, 39 (36), 4109–4113.

5 Bangladesh's pursuit of the 2030 Agenda

Will it facilitate smooth transition after LDC graduation?

Fahmida Khatun, Shahida Pervin and Md. Masudur Rahman

Introduction

Bangladesh will cross a number of milestones during its implementation of the 2030 Agenda for Sustainable Development, which outlines the Sustainable Development Goals (SDGs), over the 2016–30 period. The first five years of the SDGs coincide with the last five years of implementation of the Istanbul Programme of Action (IPoA) for the least developed countries (LDCs) for the 2011–20 period, which aims to halve the number of LDCs by 2020. Bangladesh has become eligible for graduation at the 2018 triennial review of the Committee for Development Policy (CDP) of the United Nations Economic and Social Council (UN ECOSOC) given its progress in gross national income (GNI) per capita and the Human Assets Index (HAI) and the Economic Vulnerability Index (EVI). Once monitoring of Bangladesh's progress and all relevant procedures are completed, the country will achieve the status of a developing country in 2024.

Bangladesh has performed very well in achieving several Millennium Development Goals (MDGs) (Bangladesh Planning Commission 2015). The country has achieved significant success in a number of MDG targets including reducing poverty head count and poverty gap ratio, reducing the prevalence of underweight children, attaining gender parity at primary and secondary education, and under-five mortality rate reduction. Besides, progress has also been made in areas such as increasing enrolment at primary schools, lowering the infant mortality rate and maternal mortality ratio, improving immunisation coverage and reducing the incidence of communicable diseases. Though concerns remain in a number of areas including poverty reduction and employment generation, the country has in fact set an example as to how global commitments can be achieved at the national level. This has been possible due to the fact that Bangladesh had already put various policies in place, which had objectives similar to that of the MDGs. As a result, many of the goals contained in the MDGs would have been achieved even in the absence of any MDG type global goals. Of course, the urge for implementation of the MDGs had reinforced the persuasion of the goals and targets that Bangladesh had achieved during the MDG period.

While implementing various global agendas, Bangladesh has to be mindful about possible implications of pursuing one agenda for the achievement of other agendas. Specifically, what will be the impact of the Government of Bangladesh's (GoB) pursuit of the SDGs on the process of LDC graduation? Will efforts towards SDG implementation contribute to graduation? How should the graduation be made sustainable?

It has been emphasised that LDCs need to graduate with momentum in order to avoid the pitfalls of the post-graduation phase. Development of productive capacities and structural transformation have been identified as key factors for graduation (UNCTAD 2016). Bangladesh's implementation of the SDGs may help boost the momentum of graduation. On the face of it, efforts towards SDG implementation may facilitate graduation since several objectives of the IPoA and the SDGs have commonalities (UN-OHRLLS 2016a). Many of the SDGs are also similar to Bangladesh's objectives for the medium term outlined in its Seventh Five Year Plan (7FYP) for the 2016–20 period. Thus, as Bangladesh works towards fulfilling its objectives through national policies, efforts may also help achieve several SDGs.

This study is the first of its kind that undertakes the task of identifying the connections among these global agendas and national plans and offers policy recommendations. The motivation for this study originates from the idea that given the similarities among global agendas such as the SDGs and the IPoA as well as national development plans such as 7FYP, policymakers need to be apprised of the extent and nature of their connections. This will help Bangladesh's policymakers implement or adopt relevant measures in a more informed manner. The study also has significance for other countries who want to explore the relevance of global goals in their country context. Moreover, despite the study's focus on Bangladesh, it has larger value at the global level given that the analyses presented in this chapter are done in view of various global milestones.

The chapter is organised in the following manner. The rest of this introduction comprises objectives and research questions, methodology and sources of data and information, and a literature review of similar studies. The next section applies network analysis to understand the connections between the SDGs and LDC graduation criteria. The section also shows how SDG targets are reflected in Bangladesh's national policies. The following section presents an empirical exercise to demonstrate whether or not the SDGs and LDC graduation criteria are mutually reinforcing. Concluding remarks and policy recommendations are provided in the final section.

Objectives and research questions

The broad objective of this chapter is to examine whether Bangladesh's pursuit of the SDGs can facilitate smooth transition after LDC graduation. In doing so, the chapter reviews the linkages between the SDGs and LDC graduation criteria as well as the IPoA. Most importantly, it examines how Bangladesh's national policies are informed by the SDGs and LDC graduation process. The specific research questions are:

- How are the SDGs and LDC graduation criteria linked?
- What are the linkages between the SDGs and IPoA priority areas?
- How aligned are Bangladesh's national policies with the SDGs?
- Based on findings, what policy recommendations can be made as regards the alignment of Bangladesh's national policies with the SDGs to facilitate smooth transition after LDC graduation?

Methodology and sources of data and information

Three methods were adopted to answer the research questions. First, detailed matching exercises are undertaken to examine which SDG targets are aligned with the LDC graduation criteria and IPoA. How those targets are reflected in Bangladesh's national policies, such as 7FYP and other national and sectoral policies, is also explored. Second, network analysis is conducted to map the linkages between the SDGs and LDC graduation criteria. More specifically, SDG targets are examined vis-à-vis the criteria to understand which targets are similar to the criteria. Indicators under each criterion are mapped as a network of linkages with the SDG targets. Mapping of the network is done based on information provided in Annex Tables 5.a.1, 5.a.2 and 5.a.3. Network analysis also helps understand connections between the SDGs and IPoA as well as the SDGs and Bangladesh's national policies. Third, an exercise is undertaken to determine the directions and strengths of relationships between the indicators of SDG targets and LDC graduation criteria identified in the network analysis. Granger causality and pairwise correlation tests were selected to understand such relationships. Together, these methods assist in deriving policy recommendations regarding the alignment of Bangladesh's national policies with the SDGs.

Analyses are based on data and information collated from a number of sources. Data for indicators under the LDC graduation criteria are from the database of the Foundation for International Development Study and Research (FERDI 2016). Data for SDG indicators are from the UN Statistics Division (UNSD 2017), the World Development Indicator's database (World Bank 2017), the GoB's Ministry of Finance (MoF 2017), the Ministry's Economic Relations Division (Economic Relations Division 2016) and several reports of different years, for example Statistical Year Book, Report of Vital Statistics, Labour and Employment Survey Report published by the Bangladesh Bureau of Statistics.

Literature review

Research on linkages between smooth transition after LDC graduation and implementation of the SDGs is few and far between. *State of the Least Developed*

Countries 2016, the latest flagship report of the UN Office of the High Representative for the Least Developed Countries, Landlocked Developing Countries and Small Island Developing States, includes a chapter on coherence and synergy between the SDGs and IPoA. The report compares the goals and targets of both global agendas to understand the extent to which the 2030 Agenda took into consideration the issues raised in the IPoA. Based on a mapping exercise, the report concludes that the SDGs and IPoA are largely mutually reinforcing in their support of LDC graduation (UN-OHRLLS 2016a). Rahman *et al.* (2016) reiterates that the realisation of the work plan under the IPoA would be easier through the implementation of the SDGs. The study refers to the need for synergies and coherence of the objectives in those two sets of global goals.

Focusing on the SDGs, some studies have come up with specific measures to support LDC graduation. For example, one study proposed four guiding principles that must underpin the SDG framework to effectively contribute to sustainable development in LDCs. These include respecting previous international commitments on development, being mindful about the objective to 'leave no one behind', supporting productive capacity-building and structural transformation of LDCs, and creation of a coherent framework for LDCs to pursue sustainable development (UN-OHRLLS 2016b). Rahman *et al.* (2016) also emphasised coherence, synergies and coordination between the SDGs and the IPoA implementation.

In achievement of the SDGs, emphasis has been put on national level policies. Allen *et al.* (2017) feel that the success or failure of the SDGs, to a large extent, will rely upon their implementation at the national level. They suggested national scenario modelling as a tool for governments in formulating their national SDG strategies.

Some countries have taken alignment exercises between SDGs and objectives of their national policies. These are useful for the governments to take initiatives towards achieving the SDGs. The GoB, for instance, identified the SDGs which are in the categories of 'fully aligned', 'partially aligned' and 'not aligned' with the objectives of 7FYP of Bangladesh (Bangladesh Planning Commission 2016). Among the SDG targets, 36 targets from 11 SDGs are fully aligned, 29 targets from 12 SDGs are partially aligned and another 29 targets from nine SDGs are not aligned with the objectives of the 7FYP.

The United Nations Development Programme (UNDP) conducted a rapid integrated assessment[1] of Cambodia's National Strategic Development Plan and relevant sectoral plans and strategies, which shows that in Cambodia 85 SDG targets are aligned with national strategies, 17 are partially aligned, seven are not aligned and four are not applicable for the country.

None of these exercises, however, had the objective to examine whether and how implementation of the SDGs can help improve prospects for smooth transition from the LDC category.

The use of network analysis in discussing the SDGs is also new. Social network analysis is a method for investigating social structures through the use of networks and graphs (Otte and Rousseau 2002). It is preferred by researchers since it represents the complexity of large networks in technically accurate and visually attractive ways (Bastian *et al.* 2009). Using this method to show how some of the thematic areas of the SDGs are well connected with each other, Le Blanc (2015) suggested that the implementation of one SDG may help implement other connected SDGs.

Exploring linkages

SDGs and LDC graduation

Here, a detailed matching exercise separately compares the three LDC graduation criteria with SDG targets in order to better understand the similarities and connections among them. Annex Tables 5.a.1, 5.a.2 and 5.a.3 provide full details about the mapping of linkages. The relationships among the graduation criteria and SDGs are represented as networks in Figures 5.1 and 5.2.

On the one hand, there are 169 targets under 17 SDGs that consider the economic, social and environmental pillars of sustainability. On the other hand, there are three LDC graduation criteria – GNI per capita points to a country's income status and is widely referred to as the 'income criterion', the HAI measures the level of human development capturing health and education, and the EVI indicates a country's structural vulnerabilities to exogenous economic and environmental shocks. The World Bank bases a country's income status on GNI per capita, which is calculated using its Atlas method (World Bank 2016). The HAI has four indicators: percentage of population undernourished, under-five mortality rate, gross secondary school enrolment ratio and adult literacy rate. The EVI has eight indicators: population; remoteness; share of population in low elevated coastal zones; merchandise export concentration; share of agriculture, forestry and fishing in gross domestic product (GDP); victims of natural disasters; instability of agricultural production; and instability of exports. During the research for this chapter, every target under each SDG was scrutinised against every indicator under each LDC graduation criterion.

SDG target 8.1 refers to sustaining per capita economic growth in accordance with national circumstances and, in particular, at least 7 per cent GDP growth per annum in LDCs. The sole indicator for this target is annual growth rate of real GDP per capita (SDG indicator 8.1.1). This target is similar to the income criterion. Also similar is SDG target 10.1, which explicitly refers to progressively achieving and sustaining income growth of the bottom 40 per cent of the population at a higher rate than the national average. The income criterion can also be linked to several other SDGs since increased per capita income can be achieved by pursuing other objectives. For example, the objectives of employment generation, productivity enhancement or infrastructure development can lead to higher incomes for individuals and income status of a country. Moreover, good health and well-being (SDG 3), quality education (SDG 4) and industry, innovation and infrastructure (SDG 9) can influence GNI per capita. Therefore, in this chapter GNI per capita is linked with a

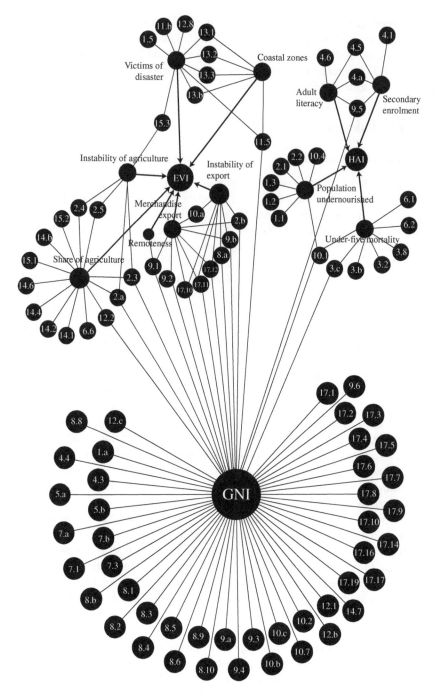

Figure 5.1 Network of LDC graduation criteria and SDG targets.

Sources: prepared by the authors based on Annex Tables 5.a.1, 5.a.2 and 5.a.3.

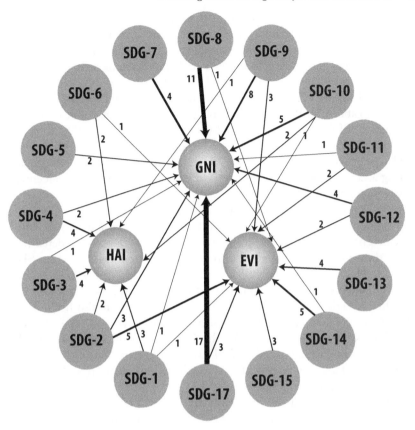

Figure 5.2 Number of SDG targets under each graduation criterion.
Source: prepared by the authors based on Table 5.1.

number of SDGs beyond SDG targets 8.1 and 10.1, which are considered to have direct linkages.

The SDGs that have clear connections with increasing GNI per capita are categorised into 20 broad areas (Annex Table 5.a.1) by the authors of this chapter for convenience. Out of 169 SDG targets, 60 targets under 13 SDGs have clear potential linkages with GNI per capita (Table 5.1). The other SDGs, specifically SDG 6 (water and sanitation), SDG 13 (climate change), SDG 15 (ecosystem, land degradation and biodiversity loss) and SDG 16 (peaceful and inclusive society, justice for all, effective, accountable and inclusive institutions), have not been linked to the income criterion since the authors contend that they have unclear relationships with GNI per capita.

Indicators under the HAI mainly measure human development, specifically health and education. In addition to direct connections between HAI indicators and SDG targets, indicators can be connected with poverty, hunger and social protection, which are basic needs that must be addressed in the human development process. Indicators under any graduation criterion may have linkages with SDG targets that have similar objectives. For example, the indicators 'percentage of population undernourished' and 'under-five mortality rate' under the HAI criterion have linkages with SDG target 10.1. A total of 17 targets under six SDGs have connections with the HAI that relate to health and education (Table 5.1). While SDGs 3 and 4 have explicit indicators on human development, SDG 1 (poverty), SDG 2 (hunger and nutrition), SDG 6 (access to safe water and sanitation) and SDG 10 (inequality) have clear linkages with the HAI. For example, SDG target 2.1, which refers to ending hunger and ensuring access to nutritious food, has a linkage with the indicator 'percentage of population undernourished'.

EVI indicators are mainly related to natural disasters, climate change, export concentration and instability, agricultural output and instability, population and remoteness. Population and remoteness indicators are not considered here because they do not change significantly in the short and medium terms. SDG target 2.3, which refers to doubling agricultural productivity, has linkages with the EVI indicators 'share of agriculture, forestry and fisheries in GDP' and 'instability of agricultural production'. The income criterion also has linkages with SDG target 2.3. The network of such linkages is visually represented in Figure 5.1. Notably, indicators under the EVI are not directly linked to the SDGs, but rather 31 targets under 12 SDGs are indirectly linked with the EVI (Table 5.1). Thus, it is expected that implementation of these SDGs will support progress on the EVI as well.

In order to understand the strength of the linkages between the SDGs and LDC graduation criteria, the number of SDG targets that are connected to each criterion is considered to be a proxy indicator of strength of linkages. Table 5.1 shows how many targets under each SDG were found to have connections with each criterion.

The findings from Table 5.1 are then presented as networks in Figure 5.1. As depicted in the figure, a few SDG targets have linkages with more than one graduation criterion. Also, some indicators under the LDC graduation criteria are linked with each other. Notably, two targets linked to the HAI criterion (3.c and 10.1) and 12 targets linked to the EVI criterion (2.3, 2.a, 2.b, 8.a, 9.1, 9.2, 9.b, 11.5, 12.2, 17.10, 17.11, 17.12) are also linked with GNI per capita (Figure 5.1 and Annex Tables 5.a.1, 5.a.2 and 5.a.3). The HAI and EVI criteria are not connected with each other through any indicators. Also, a straightforward relationship between SDG 16 and the LDC graduation criteria cannot be established. SDG 16, which calls for peace, justice and strong institutions without which no development initiative can be successful, is perceived to be the backbone for achieving all other SDGs. SDG 17 is a cross-cutting goal that relates to all other SDGs and can also influence the fulfilment of the LDC graduation criteria.

The thickness of the connecting lines in Figure 5.2 indicates the number of SDG targets linked to an LDC graduation criterion. The thicker lines indicate

Table 5.1 Number of SDG targets under each LDC graduation criterion

SDG	Number of SDG targets linked to:		
	GNI per capita	HAI	EVI
SDG 1: No poverty – End poverty in all its forms everywhere	1	3	1
SDG 2: Zero hunger – End hunger, achieve *food security* and improved nutrition and promote sustainable agriculture	3	2	5
SDG 3: Good health and well-being – Ensure healthy lives and promote well-being for all at all ages	1	4	0
SDG 4: Quality education – Ensure inclusive and equitable quality education and promote lifelong learning opportunities for all	2	4	0
SDG 5: Gender equality – Achieve gender equality and *empower* all women and girls	2	0	0
SDG 6: Clean water and sanitation – Ensure *availability* and sustainable management of water and sanitation for all	0	2	1
SDG 7: Affordable and clean energy – Ensure access to affordable, reliable, sustainable and modern energy for all	4	0	0
SDG 8: Decent work and economic growth – Promote sustained, inclusive and sustainable economic growth, full and productive employment and decent work for all	11	0	1
SDG 9: Industry, innovation and infrastructure – Build resilient infrastructure, promote inclusive and sustainable industrialisation and foster innovation	8	0	3
SDG 10: Reduced inequalities – Reduce income *inequality* within and among countries	5	2	1
SDG 11: Sustainable cities and communities – Make cities and human settlements inclusive, safe, resilient and sustainable	1	0	2
SDG 12: Responsible consumption and production – Ensure sustainable consumption and production patterns	4	0	2
SDG 13: Climate action – Take urgent action to combat *climate change* and its impacts	0	0	4
SDG 14: Life below water – *Conserve* and sustainably use the oceans, seas and marine resources for sustainable development	1	0	5
SDG 15: Life on land – Protect, restore and promote sustainable use of terrestrial ecosystems, sustainably manage forests, combat *desertification*, and halt and reverse *land degradation* and halt *biodiversity* loss	0	0	3
SDG 16: Peace, justice and strong institutions – Promote peaceful and inclusive societies for *sustainable development*, provide access to justice for all and build effective, accountable and inclusive institutions at all levels	0	0	0
SDG 17: Partnerships for the goals – Strengthen the means of implementation and revitalise the Global Partnership for Sustainable Development	17	0	3
Total	60	17	31

Sources: authors' compilation based on United Nations (2015) and UN DESA (n.d.).

higher strength of linkages between two sets of global objectives – LDC graduation and the SDGs. The strongest link is between SDG 17 and GNI per capita since 17 targets under SDG 17 have links with the income criterion. SDGs 8 and 9 also have strong links with GNI per capita, as 11 targets under SDG 8 and eight targets under SDG 9 have links with the income criterion. Understandably, there are strong connections between the HAI and SDGs 3 and 4 as they are all related to health and education. SDGs 2, 13 and 14, which consider economic and environmental vulnerabilities, have strong connections with the EVI.

UNCTAD outlined a number of policies that a country needs to pursue to graduate with momentum from the LDC category, with the justification being that graduation should be seen as a long-term development process rather than a narrow objective in a statistical sense. It identified six broad areas for action and highlighted gender as a cross-cutting issue for continuing development beyond the graduation milestone: rural transformation; industrial policy; science, technology and innovation (STI) policy; development finance; macroeconomic policies; and employment generation (UNCTAD 2016). Commonalities between these seven areas and the SDGs are evident. A total of 50 SDG targets were found to be related with the seven key areas of UNCTAD's 'graduation-plus' strategies for graduation with momentum. The network of SDG targets and key areas is presented in Figure 5.3.

SDGs and IPoA

Here, a detailed matching exercise comparing the IPoA priority areas and SDGs indicates that all areas covered by the IPoA are also included in the SDGs (UN-OHRLLS 2016a). While the SDG framework includes goals, targets and indicators, the IPoA has goals, targets and actions. The priority areas of the IPoA include: productive capacity; agriculture, food security and rural development; trade; commodities; human and social development; multiple crises and other emerging challenges; mobilising financial resources for development and capacity-building; and good governance at all levels. The actions for implementing the IPoA goals and targets are categorised into three groups: joint actions by LDCs and developed countries, actions by LDCs and actions by development partners (United Nations 2011).

There are 47 goals and targets, 16 joint actions for LDCs and developed countries, 126 actions for LDCs and 109 actions for development partners under eight IPoA priority areas. Despite differences in terms of approach, coverage, targets and indicators, both the IPoA and SDGs have the common objective to eradicate poverty. This chapter identifies the SDG targets that can directly and indirectly contribute to progress in the eight priority areas of the IPoA. Linkages between SDG targets and IPoA goals, targets and selected actions are represented as a network in Figure 5.4, which shows that 83 SDG targets have connections with the IPoA.

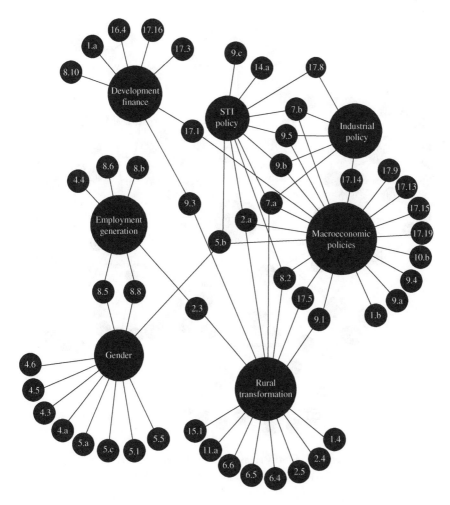

Figure 5.3 Network of key areas for graduation with momentum and SDG targets.
Sources: authors' elaboration based on United Nations (2015) and UNCTAD (2016).

SDGs and national policies

Here, networks illustrate the alignment of national policies, mainly Bangladesh's 7FYP, with the SDGs. They help understand whether pursuit of the
SDGs by the GoB through national plans and policies has any connections to
LDC graduation and smooth transition. Following a study conducted by Bhattacharya *et al.* (2016), selected SDG targets under the three LDC graduation criteria, key areas for graduation with momentum and the IPoA are also
considered. To understand how they are reflected in 7FYP, the selected SDG

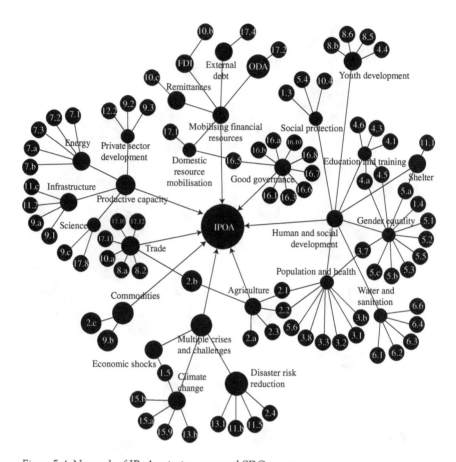

Figure 5.4 Network of IPoA priority areas and SDG targets.

Sources: authors' elaboration based on United Nations (2015) and UN-OHRLLS (2016a).

targets are categorised into following five groups: (i) fully overlapping, (ii) partially overlapping, (iii) overlapping in essence, (iv) SDG is global in nature and (v) no target in 7FYP. A number of other relevant national and sectoral policies were also reviewed to check whether SDG targets, not reflected in 7FYP, are reflected in those policies.

The 'fully overlapping' category includes six SDG targets that match completely with national policies. For example, SDG target 3.2 calls for ending preventable deaths of newborns and children under five years of age by 2030, while 7FYP says that the under-five mortality rate has to be reduced to 37 per 1,000 live births. The 'partially overlapping' category includes 40 SDG targets that partly relate to national policies. For example, SDG target 1.1 says eradicate extreme poverty for all people everywhere by 2030, currently measured as people living on less than US$1.25 a day, while 7FYP says reduce extreme poverty by about 4 percentage points to 8.9 per cent by 2020. The 'overlapping in essence' category includes 37 SDG targets that do not match directly with national policies but overlap in essence. For instance, SDG target 1.a is to ensure significant mobilisation of resources from a variety of sources, including through enhanced development cooperation, in order to provide adequate and predictable means for developing countries, in particular LDCs, to implement programmes and policies to end poverty in all its dimensions, while 7FYP calls for total revenue to be raised from 10.7 per cent of GDP to 16.1 per cent by 2020. The 'global in nature' category covers universal targets and global initiatives to implement those targets. Bangladesh alone can do little in these cases, so such targets have not been searched for in 7FYP.

The 'no target in 7FYP' category includes 21 SDG targets, which have been searched for in other national and sectoral policies (Annex Table 5.a.5). Policies including the National Women Development Policy (2011), National Social Security Strategy of Bangladesh (2015), National Food Policy Plan of Action (2008–15), National Agricultural Policy (2013), National Skills Development Policy (2011), National Industrial Policy (2016), Perspective Plan of Bangladesh (2010–21) and National Sustainable Development Strategy (2010–21) were reviewed. Among the 21 SDG targets not found in 7FYP, 12 specific policies are overlapping in essence. For example, SDG target 8.10 is to strengthen the capacity of domestic financial institutions to encourage and expand access to banking, insurance and financial services for all, while the Perspective Plan of Bangladesh (2010–21) refers to various strategies including access to finance by rural people (Bangladesh Planning Commission 2012). In another example, SDG target 14.6 is to prohibit certain forms of fisheries subsidies which contribute to overcapacity and overfishing by 2020, while the National Sustainable Development Strategy (2010–2021) emphasises sustainable exploitation of marine resources (Bangladesh Planning Commission 2013).

There are no similarities in the other national and sectoral policies for the remaining nine SDG targets, specifically SDG targets 2.5 (genetic diversity of flora and fauna), 10.7 (migration and mobility of people), 11.a (national and regional development planning), 11.b (number of cities and human settlements), 16.1 (violence and related death rates), 16.4 (reduction of illicit financial and arms flows, recovery and return of stolen assets and combating organised crime), 16.7 (responsive, inclusive, participatory and representative decision-making), 16.a (national institutions for building capacity to prevent violence and combat terrorism and crime) and 16.b (non-discriminatory laws and policies). Given the importance of each of these targets, the GoB must set policies to attain them.

SDG targets in different policies and plans and under different criteria are not always mutually exclusive – there are connections between and among them. In total, 94 SDG targets under the LDC graduation criteria, 50 in the key areas for graduation with momentum and 83 in the IPoA are considered in the whole analysis of this chapter. Figures 5.5, 5.6, 5.7, 5.8 and 5.9 present linkages

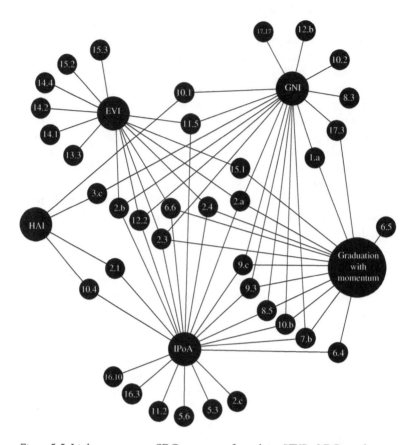

Figure 5.5 Linkages among SDG targets reflected in 7FYP, LDC graduation criteria, graduation with momentum and the IPoA – *fully overlapping*.

Sources: authors' elaboration based on United Nations (2015), UNCTAD (2016), UN DESA (n.d.), UN-OHRLLS (2016a) and Annex Table 5.a.4.

targets reflected in 7FYP, LDC graduation criteria, graduation with momentum and the IPoA. Annex Tables 5.a.4 and 5.a.5 provide the detailed matrix of alignment of SDG targets with 7FYP and other national and sectoral policies.

Summary and findings on SDG linkages

Using network analysis techniques, this chapter has shown how LDC graduation criteria are linked to several SDG targets and to national policies. Major findings of the network analysis are the following:

- The first LDC graduation criterion GNI has connection with 17 targets of SDG 17, 11 targets of SDG 8, eight targets of SDG 9, five targets of SDG

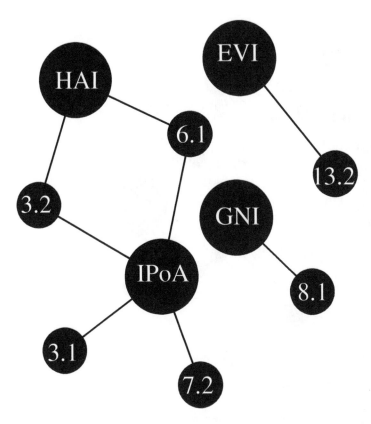

Figure 5.6 Linkages among SDG targets reflected in 7FYP, LDC graduation criteria, graduation with momentum and the IPoA – *partially overlapping*.

Sources: authors' elaboration based on United Nations (2015), UNCTAD (2016), UN DESA (n.d.), UN-OHRLLS (2016a) and Annex Table 5.a.4.

10, four targets from each of SDG 7 and SDG 12, three targets of SDG 2, two targets from each of SDG 4 and SDG 5 and one target from each of SDG 1, SDG 3, SDG11 and SDG 14 (Figures 5.1 and 5.2).

- GNI has stronger connections with inclusive and sustainable economic growth (SDG 8), industry, innovation and infrastructure (SDG 9), reducing inequality among the countries (SDG 10) and partnerships (SDG 17). (Figures 5.1 and 5.2).

- HAI is connected with SDG 3 and SDG 4 through four targets from each goal; with SDG 1 through three targets; and with SDG 2, SDG 6 and SDG 10 through two targets from each goal. It shows that, good health and well-being (SDG 3) and quality education (SDG 4) have stronger connections with LDC graduation criterion HAI (Figures 5.1 and 5.2).

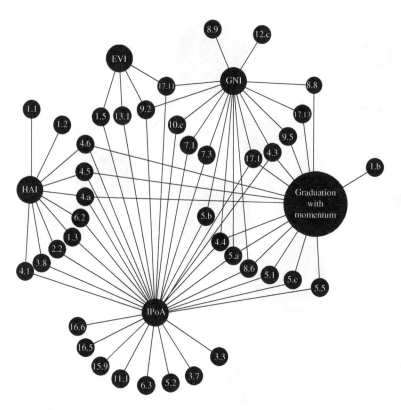

Figure 5.7 Linkages among SDG targets reflected in 7FYP, LDC graduation criteria, graduation with momentum and the IPoA – *overlapping in essence.*

Sources: authors' elaboration based on United Nations (2015), UNCTAD (2016), UN DESA (n.d.), UN-OHRLLS (2016a) and Annex Table 5.a.4.

- EVI is connected with five targets from each of SDG 2 and SDG 14, with four targets of SDG 13, three targets from each of SDG 9, SDG 15 and SDG 17, two targets from each of SDG 11 and SDG 12, one target from each of SDG 1, SDG 6, SDG 8 and SDG 10. It shows zero hunger (SDG 2), industry, innovation and infrastructure (SDG 9), climate action (SDG 13), life below water (SDG 14), life on land (SDG 15) and partnership (SDG 17) have strong connections with the EVI criterion (Figures 5.1 and 5.2).
- Out of 17 SDGs, 16 goals have direct and indirect similarity with the graduation criteria (Figure 5.2).
- A total of 50 SDG targets are related with the seven key areas of UNCTAD's 'graduation-plus' strategies for graduation with momentum (Figure 5.3).

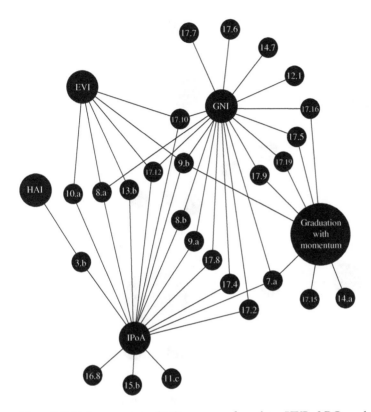

Figure 5.8 Linkages among SDG targets reflected in 7FYP, LDC graduation criteria, graduation with momentum and the IPoA – *no target in 7FYP.*

Sources: authors' elaboration based on United Nations (2015), UNCTAD (2016), UN DESA (n.d.), UN-OHRLLS (2016a) and Annex Table 5.a.4.

- A detailed matching exercise comparing the IPoA priority areas and SDGs indicates that 83 SDG targets have potential linkages with goals, targets and selected actions of eight priority areas of the IPoA (Figure 5.4).
- In case of matching with national policies, six SDG targets match completely with national policies and fall in the 'fully overlapping' category, 40 SDG targets are 'partially overlapping', 37 targets do not match directly with national policies but are 'overlapping in essence', 21 SDG targets are in the 'no target in 7FYP' category and another 26 targets are in the 'global in nature' category whose implementation requires global initiatives (Figures 5.5–5.9).

Granger causality and correlation analysis

Network analysis in the previous section provides visual representations of SDGs' linkages with LDC graduation criteria, but it is unclear whether they

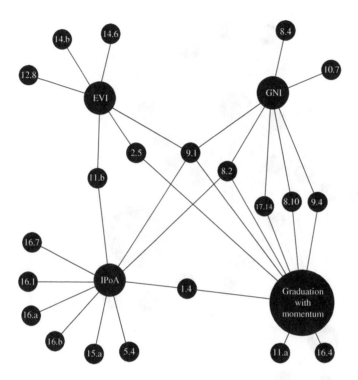

Figure 5.9 Linkages among SDG targets reflected in 7FYP, LDC graduation criteria, graduation with momentum and the IPoA – *global in nature*.

Sources: authors' elaboration based on United Nations (2015), UNCTAD (2016), UN DESA (n.d.), UN-OHRLLS (2016a) and Annex Table 5.a.4.

are mutually reinforcing or hinder each other's objectives. If they are mutually reinforcing, then pursuit of one set of commitments may help achieve the other set of commitments. If they are not, pursuit of the SDGs could deter the fulfilment of LDC graduation or vice versa, particularly when there are resource constraints and policymakers thus have to choose only certain commitments based on their priorities. Also, network analysis does not say anything about the strength of linkages. Empirical analysis has the potential to improve understanding of the directions and strengths of linkages between the SDGs and LDC graduation criteria if comprehensive data for various indicators are available.

This section presents the results of Granger causality and pairwise correlation tests between a number of SDG indicators and LDC graduation criteria for which data are available for the 1990–2015 period for Bangladesh. This period was selected in consideration of the 1990 baseline year of the MDGs and the consistency of data for all indicators. Due to paucity of data for some variables for the entire period, observations for some variables were interpolated using the time variable. The bivariate Granger causality test shows whether the effect of selected variables is from an SDG indicator to an LDC graduation criterion or vice versa, the effect is both ways or there is no effect. The pairwise correlation test shows the strength of the connection between the variables. The findings of the analysis have been supported with relevant literature and compared with other countries.

Since time series data were used, the Augmented Dickey–Fuller (ADF) and Phillips–Perron tests were first performed to investigate the stationarity of variables. If the Phillips–Perron test and any of the three criteria of the ADF test – ADF with trend, ADF with drift and ADF with no constant – are significant, a variable is determined to be stationary. Results of the tests are presented in Annex Table 5.a.6.

Next, the Granger causality test was performed to determine the directions of the relationships between the SDG indicators and LDC graduation criteria. The pairwise correlation test was performed for each selected SDG indicator separately with the GNI per capita graduation criterion in order to determine whether there is positive correlation and one-sided Granger causality, positive correlation and two-sided Granger causality (synergy), negative correlation and one-sided Granger causality or negative correlation and two-sided Granger causality (trade-off). For Granger causality, lag was selected using the final prediction error criterion, Akaike's information criterion, the Hannan–Quinn information criterion and Schwarz's Bayesian information criterion. Lag was decided according to the results of at least two of these criteria.

Results of empirical analysis

GNI per capita and SDG indicators

Among the 82 indicators under the SDG targets that were selected in the network analysis for the GNI per capita criterion of LDC graduation (Annex Table 5.a.1), data for only 17 indicators are available for the full 1990–2015 period. Of these 17 indicators, 13 are aligned with the IPoA (Annex Table 5.a.7).[2] Hence, the selected SDG indicators cover both LDC graduation and smooth transition criteria. Among them, annual growth rate of real GDP per capita (SDG indicator 8.1.1) is directly related with GNI per capita, so it was not included in the estimation. Therefore, 16 indicators were included in the empirical analysis. Among them, eight were found to have significant causal relationships with GNI per capita: SDG indicators 2.a.2 (disbursement of project aid to agriculture sector, in United States dollar (US$) million, 8.2.1 (annual growth rate of real GDP per employed person in Bangladeshi taka (BDT)), 9.1.2 (total air passenger movement (number in thousands)), 9.2.1 (industry, value added (per cent of GDP)), 9.2.2 (manufacturing employment as a proportion of total employment), 17.1.1 (total government revenue as a proportion of GDP), 17.1.2 (proportion of domestic budget funded by domestic taxes) and 17.3.2 (volume of remittances in US$ as a proportion of total GDP). The remaining eight SDG indicators do not have significant causal relationships, so they were dropped from further analysis: SDG indicators 7.1.1 (proportion of population with access to electricity), 9.1.2 (number of passengers carried by Bangladesh Railway), 9.1.2 (water transport operation under Bangladesh Inland Water Transport Authority [number of passengers (in thousands)]), 10.b.1 (net official development assistance (ODA) received (constant 2013 US$)), 12.2.1 (material footprint, material footprint per capita, and material footprint per capita GDP), 17.3.1 (foreign direct investment (FDI) as per cent of budget), 17.3.1 (ODA as per cent of budget) and 17.4.1 (debt service as a proportion of exports of goods and services). The following discussion is based on the results of the empirical analysis.

GNI per capita and remittances

GNI per capita was found to have a negative effect on 'personal remittances received as percentage of GDP'. Evidence from various countries indicates that remittance flow is not necessarily associated with higher GNI per capita. For example, while 'personal remittances received as percentage of GDP' was 7.9 per cent for Bangladesh in 2015, figures were below 1 per cent for most developed countries – the United States received 0.04 per cent, Switzerland received 0.38 per cent and Japan received 0.08 per cent (World Bank 2017). Lower remittance flows to home countries may happen for various reasons. For instance, appreciation of domestic currency due to a high volume of remittances may discourage migrants from sending remittances to their home countries and encourage them to spend in their host countries. From recipients' points of view, they may need a lower amount of remittances if per capita income increases. As Bangladesh is an LDC with high potential for further economic growth, the role of remittances in its economy is significant. Siddique *et al.* (2012) used time series data for the period 1976–2006 to examine the role of remittances in Bangladesh. They found that remittances have an important role in promoting economic growth in Bangladesh. Uddin and Sjö (2013) demonstrated that the role of remittance differs in the long-run and short-run in Bangladesh. Using data for the period 1976–2011, they find that the inflow of remittances and expansion of the financial sector promote GDP growth in the long-run while remittances act as a shock absorber to income changes in the short-run.

GNI per capita and aid to agriculture sector

SDG indicator 'disbursement of project aid to agriculture sector' was found to have a two-way positive causal relationship, which was the expected result and can be explained logically. If aid to the agriculture sector is properly invested, agricultural output is expected to increase and, in turn, per capita income of a country should increase. When the contribution of aid to the sector results in a positive outcome, the possibility of receiving more aid improves. Although the impact of aid on economies and various sectors is a well-researched area, literature on agriculture sector aid is scant, particularly in Bangladesh's context. Results similar to those in this chapter are found in Kaya *et al.* (2012), classifying foreign aid into four sub-categories – agricultural aid, social infrastructure aid, investment aid and non-investment aid. They found that in developing countries, aid to the agriculture sector had influenced their economic growth positively and significantly, and affected their growth in the short-run. Alabi (2014), using data for the 2002–10 period from 47 Sub-Saharan African countries, found that foreign aid to the agriculture sector contributed towards higher agricultural productivity as well as higher agricultural GDP. Norton *et al.* (1992) found that since 1970, impact of foreign aid on the agriculture sector had been better in Asia compared to Sub-Saharan Africa.

GNI per capita and air travel

SDG indicator 9.1.2 (total air passenger movement (number in thousands)) was found to influence the GNI per capita graduation criterion positively. The aviation sector forms a large part of the transportation network across the world. This also contributes towards enhanced business and tourism in emerging economies like Bangladesh. As a country develops, its population increasingly chooses air travel to save travel time and broaden global connections. Passenger movement through all of Bangladesh's domestic and international airports increased by about 40.3 per cent over the 2010–15 period, which indicates that the country's population increasingly chose to travel by air. At FY2005–06 base constant price, the value added of air travel in FY2009–10 was BDT 7,812 million and with an increase of about 30.4 per cent it reached BDT 10,343 million in FY2014–15 (BBS 2016).

GNI per capita and employment

SDG indicator 8.2.1 (average per employee constant GDP) and SDG indicator 9.2.2 (manufacturing employment as a proportion of total employment) were found to influence GNI per capita positively. As workers' productivity increases, their incomes and thus their country's GNI per capita increase. Shifting the labour force from the agriculture sector to the manufacturing sector, which is increasingly important in Bangladesh, ultimately impacts GNI as well as GNI per capita. Van Stel *et al.* (2005), using a sample of 36 countries, observed that depending on per capita income of countries, economic growth is influenced by potential young entrepreneurs. According to Kritikos (2014), introduction of innovative technologies, products and services by entrepreneurs boost the economic growth of the country. Also, new job opportunities, increasing the productivity of firms and economies, and accelerating structural change by replacing established sclerotic firms, increase the economic growth. Keane and te Velde (2008) suggested that the textile and clothing sector generates incomes and jobs, and earns foreign currency in the short-run. In the long-run, the sector supports economic development in a sustainable manner.

GNI per capita and industrial sector

SDG indicator 9.2.1 (industry value added (per cent of GDP)) was found to influence GNI per capita positively, which was expected. Bangladesh has been experiencing structural adjustment where, as mentioned, the importance of the manufacturing sector compared to the agriculture sector is increasing. As a result, the manufacturing sector has become a major source of employment and economic growth. The sector's share of GDP was about 28.8 per cent in FY2015–16, which was almost double the 14.8 per cent contributed by the agriculture sector (BBS 2017). Su and Yao (2016) indicated that development of manufacturing encourages incentives of savings, contributes to technological accumulation, and enhances the utilisation of human capital and economic institutions in middle-income economies.

GNI per capita and tax revenue

SDG indicator 17.1.1 (total revenue as per cent of GDP) and SDG indicator 17.1.2 (proportion of domestic budget funded by domestic taxes) were found to be positively related to the GNI per capita graduation criterion. The positive relationship between GNI per capita and tax revenue implies that increased GNI per capita will generate more tax revenue. This conclusion has been drawn in the literature, with factors such as per capita GDP, share of agriculture in GDP, trade openness and foreign aid having been found to significantly affect tax revenue performance in developing countries (Gupta 2007). Lalarukh and Chowdhury (2013) showed that the value added tax had a positive impact on Bangladesh's GDP between FY1991–92 and FY2011–12. Bose *et al.* (2007) found that the share of government capital expenditure in GDP and economic growth are positively and significantly correlated. Increased government expenditure must be supported by increased tax collection or government borrowing, which may require higher taxation in the future. Since the GoB is striving to improve the tax revenue–GDP ratio from a mere 9.9 per cent in FY2015–16, the relationship between GNI per capita and tax revenue carries particular significance.

The above discussion based on the empirical analysis indicates that the relationships between the SDGs and LDC graduation criteria are either mutually reinforcing or supportive in one direction. Figure 5.10 presents the empirical results of pairwise correlation and Granger causality of different variables with GNI per capita. The arrows in the diagram indicate the causal direction of relationships and the numbers inside the arrows indicate the correlation between the variables.

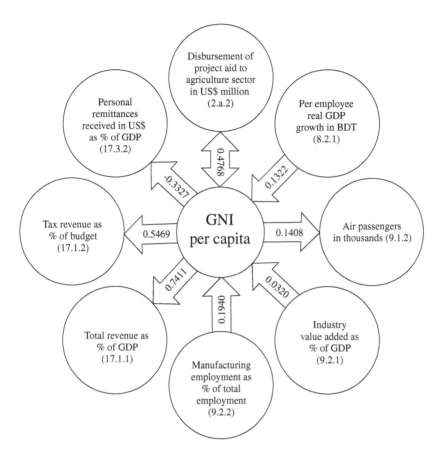

Figure 5.10 Causal directions between and correlation of the GNI per capita criterion and SDG indicators.

Source: authors' elaboration based on empirical estimations.

The HAI and SDG indicators

According to the mapping of the HAI graduation criterion, there are 26 indicators under relevant 17 SDG targets. Among these indicators, data are only available for four, namely those on undernourishment (SDG indicator 2.1.1), under-five mortality rate (SDG indicator 3.2.1), access to safe water (SDG indicator 6.1.1) and access to safe sanitation (SDG indicator 6.2.1). Of these four indicators, undernourishment and under-five mortality rate are also included in the HAI. There is no point in conducting causality and correlation tests with similar variables, so these two indicators have been dropped from the estimation. For the other two SDG indicators, it was found that there is positive correlation between the HAI and 'proportion of population using safely managed drinking water services' (SDG indicator 6.1.1), and between the HAI and 'proportion of population using improved sanitation facilities' (SDG indicator 6.2.1) with bidirectional causality. These results indicate that if Bangladesh dedicates efforts towards implementing the relevant SDG targets, the HAI graduation criterion will be achieved simultaneously. Focus on the SDGs is justified since they are more comprehensive than the HAI, but SDG targets that are connected with the HAI criterion should be prioritised because Bangladesh is expecting to graduate from the LDC category well before the end of the SDG period.

The EVI and SDG indicators

The EVI graduation criterion necessitates addressing exogenous economic and environmental shocks. Even though some SDGs and associated targets could be matched with the EVI (Figures 5.1 and 5.2), more disaggregated matching shows that the indicators in the EVI cannot be matched with SDG indicators. Hence, no meaningful correlation was found between the relevant SDG indicators and EVI criterion. At the time of writing, Bangladesh had already met the EVI graduation criterion, so utmost attention should be paid to maintaining continuous progress in this regard and preventing any situation that may cause the country to fall back below the threshold.

Summary of findings of empirical exercise

The empirical exercise, conducted to understand linkages between LDC graduation criteria and a selected number of SDG indicators, provides the following findings:

- There is significant causality and correlation between eight SDG indicators and GNI per capita graduation criteria. SDG indicator 2.a.2 on 'disbursement of project aid to agriculture sector' has a two-way causal relationship.
- Three indicators such as 'total airports passenger movement' (SDG indicator 9.1.2), 'total revenue as per cent of GDP' (SDG indicator 17.1.1) and 'proportion of domestic budget funded by domestic taxes' (SDG indicator 17.1.2) are positively related to the GNI per capita graduation criterion.
- 'Average per employee constant GDP' (SDG indicator 8.2.1), 'industry value added' (SDG indicator 9.2.1) and 'manufacturing employment as a proportion of total employment' (SDG indicator 9.2.2) influence GNI per capita positively.

Conclusions and recommendations

The network analysis undertaken in this chapter demonstrates that the SDGs are linked to the LDC graduation criteria, the IPoA and Bangladesh's national and sectoral policies. Overall, the SDGs support the LDC graduation process while LDC graduation helps in achieving the SDGs.

Two key recommendations for Bangladesh can be drawn from the network analysis.

First, Bangladesh should pursue global and national objectives simultaneously due to the various linkages between and among many of their indicators. While the achievement of a few objectives in one framework may help achieve some in another framework, equal efforts should be put into all global and national commitments.

Second, Bangladesh must pay attention to SDG targets that are not reflected in its national and sectoral policies for smooth transition after LDC graduation. Relevant targets include: maintain the genetic diversity of seeds, cultivated plants and farmed and domesticated animals and their related wild species (SDG 2.5); facilitate orderly, safe, regular and responsible migration and mobility of people (SDG 10.7); support positive economic, social and environmental links between urban, peri-urban and rural areas (SDG 11.a); substantially increase the number of cities and human settlements adopting and implementing integrated policies and plans towards inclusion, resource efficiency, mitigation and adaptation to climate change (SDG 11.b); significantly reduce all forms of violence and related death rates everywhere (SDG 16.1); significantly reduce illicit financial and arms flows, strengthen the recovery and return of stolen assets and combat all forms of organised crime (SDG 16.4); ensure responsive, inclusive, participatory and representative decision-making at all levels (SDG 16.7); strengthen relevant national institutions, including through international cooperation, for building capacity at all levels, particularly in developing countries, to prevent violence and combat terrorism and crime (SDG 16.a); and promote and enforce non-discriminatory laws and policies for sustainable development (SDG 16.b).

The empirical analysis provides details about the causal relationships between some of the SDG indicators and a few indicators under the LDC graduation criteria. Five recommendations can be derived from the results.

First, the relationship between GNI per capita and remittances reiterates the importance of remittances in Bangladesh's economy. Bangladesh should put continuous efforts into increasing the inflow of remittances. Specifically, it needs to develop the skills of potential migrants, facilitate and support the migration process, make better arrangements with host countries so that migrants receive better compensation packages and treatment, facilitate better use of migrants' earnings and support the foreign exchange market.

Second, 'disbursement of project aid to the agriculture sector' (SDG indicator 2.a.2) was found to have a two-way positive causal relationship with GNI per capita. Therefore, proper utilisation of aid to the agriculture sector is crucial. Such aid should be channelled towards employment generation and productivity enhancement within the sector.

Third, as Bangladesh's economy moves forward, the performance of the aviation sector has to be improved. The positive causal relationship between GNI per capita and movement of air passengers (SDG indicator 9.1.2) highlights the urgency of improving the aviation sector in the country. Apart from the development of modern and bigger airports, shortcomings in luggage handling, security and management need to be addressed.

Fourth, this chapter's results reinforce the importance of the industrial sector's value addition and employment generation (SDG indicators 9.2.1 and 9.2.2, respectively). With its relatively high productivity, the industrial sector plays a key role in increasing incomes in Bangladesh. Given its importance to Bangladesh's economy, the sector needs supportive measures, including fiscal policies and technical support, to boost employment generation and productivity.

Fifth, the significance of higher tax revenue generation is well understood in Bangladesh given that the country has a relatively low tax revenue–GDP ratio. Results of the study imply that efforts should be geared towards increasing GNI per capita, which will subsequently increase tax revenue. These efforts should be coupled with other measures including broadening the tax base, curtailing tax evasion, strengthening institutions and ensuring good governance.

Finally, the study finds synergy between the HAI and SDG indicators. The HAI graduation criterion will be achieved along with the SDG implementation, if Bangladesh attempts to implement the human development-related SDG targets. As the SDGs are more comprehensive than the HAI, more focus on the SDGs is justified. However, since Bangladesh desires to graduate from the LDC category before 2030, SDG targets that are linked to the HAI criterion should be given priority.

Annex

Table 5.a.1 Mapping of GNI per capita graduation criterion and SDG targets with potential influencing channels

Broad channel	Relevant SDG target	
GDP/income	8.1	Sustain per capita economic growth, at least 7 per cent GDP growth in the LDCs
	10.1	Progressively achieve and sustain income growth of the bottom 40 per cent of the population at a rate higher than the national average
Productivity	2.3	Double the agricultural productivity and incomes of small-scale food producers
	2.a	Increase investment in rural infrastructure, agricultural research and extension services, technology development and plant and livestock gene banks in order to enhance agricultural productive capacity
	8.2	Achieve higher levels of economic productivity through diversification, technological upgrading and innovation
Employment	4.4	Substantially increase the number of youth and adults who have relevant skills for employment, decent jobs and entrepreneurship
	8.3	Promote development-oriented policies that support productive activities, decent job creation, entrepreneurship, creativity and innovation
	8.5	Achieve full and productive employment and decent work for all and equal pay for work of equal value
	8.6	Substantially reduce the proportion of youth not in employment, education or training
	8.8	Protect labour rights and promote safe and secure working environments for all workers
	8.b	Develop and operationalize a global strategy for youth employment
Infrastructure and industrialisation	9.1	Develop quality, reliable, sustainable and resilient infrastructure
	9.2	Promote inclusive and sustainable industrialization, significantly raise industry's share of employment and GDP
	9.3	Increase access of small-scale industrial and other enterprises to financial services
	9.4	Upgrade infrastructure and retrofit industries to make them sustainable
	9.a	Facilitate sustainable and resilient infrastructure development through enhanced financial, technological and technical support

continued

Table 5.a.1 Continued

Broad channel	Relevant SDG target	
Research and development, technology and investment, capacity-building	9.5	Enhance scientific research and upgrade technological capabilities of industrial sectors
	9.b	Support domestic technology development, research and innovation for industrial diversification and value addition to commodities
	9.c	Significantly increase access to information and communications technology
	17.5	Adopt and implement investment promotion regimes for LDCs
	17.6	Enhance North–South, South–South and triangular regional and international cooperation on science, technology and innovation
	17.7	Promote development, transfer, dissemination and diffusion of environmentally sound technologies to developing countries
	17.8	Fully operationalize the technology bank and science, technology and innovation capacity-building mechanism for LDCs by 2017
	17.9	Enhance international support for implementing effective and targeted capacity-building in developing countries to implement the SDGs
	17.19	Build on existing initiatives to develop measurements of progress on sustainable development that complement GDP, and support statistical capacity-building in developing countries
Macroeconomic stability	17.13	Enhance global macroeconomic stability, including through policy coordination and policy coherence
Trade and exports	2.b	Correct and prevent trade restrictions and distortions in world agricultural markets
	8.a	Increase Aid for Trade support for developing countries, in particular LDCs
	17.10	Promote a universal, rules-based, open, non-discriminatory and equitable multilateral trading system under the World Trade Organization
	17.11	Significantly increase exports of developing countries, in particular with a view to doubling the LDCs' share of global exports by 2020
	17.12	Realize timely implementation of duty-free and quota-free market access on a lasting basis for all LDCs
Tourism and financial services	8.9	Devise and implement policies to promote sustainable tourism
	8.10	Strengthen the capacity of domestic financial institutions to encourage and expand access to banking, insurance and financial services for all
Shocks and disasters	11.5	Significantly reduce the number of deaths and the number of people affected and substantially decrease the direct economic losses relative to GDP caused by disasters

Category	Code	Description
Mobilisation of resources, development assistance and debt sustainability	1.a	Ensure significant mobilization of resources from a variety of sources in order to provide adequate and predictable means for developing countries, in particular LDCs, to implement programmes and policies to end poverty
	10.b	Encourage ODA and financial flows, including FDI
	17.1	Strengthen domestic resource mobilization to improve domestic capacity for tax and other revenue collection
	17.2	Developed countries to implement fully their official development assistance commitments
	17.3	Mobilize additional financial resources for developing countries from multiple sources
	17.4	Assist developing countries in attaining long-term debt sustainability through coordinated policies
Health	3.c	Substantially increase health financing and the recruitment, development, training and retention of the health workforce in developing countries, especially LDCs
Education	4.3	Ensure equal access for all women and men to affordable and quality technical, vocational and tertiary education, including university
Women and children	5.a	Undertake reforms to give women equal rights to economic resources
	5.b	Enhance the use of enabling technology to promote the empowerment of women
Energy and fuel subsidies	7.1	Ensure universal access to affordable, reliable and modern energy services
	7.3	Double the global rate of improvement in energy efficiency
	7.a	Enhance international cooperation to facilitate access to clean energy research and technology
	7.b	Expand infrastructure and upgrade technology for supplying modern and sustainable energy services for all in developing countries
	12.c	Rationalize inefficient fossil-fuel subsidies that encourage wasteful consumption by removing market distortions
Empowerment and inclusion	10.2	Empower and promote the social, economic and political inclusion of all
Migration and mobility	10.7	Facilitate orderly, safe, regular and responsible migration and mobility of people
	10.c	Reduce to less than 3 per cent the transaction costs of migrant remittances and eliminate remittance corridors with costs higher than 5 per cent
Sustainable consumption and production	8.4	Improve progressively global resource efficiency in consumption and production and endeavor to decouple economic growth from environmental degradation
	12.1	Implement the 10-Year Framework of Programmes on Sustainable Consumption and Production Patterns
	12.2	Achieve the sustainable management and efficient use of natural resources
	12.b	Develop and implement tools to monitor sustainable development impacts for sustainable tourism

continued

Table 5.a.1 Continued

Broad channel	Relevant SDG target	
Fishing, oceans, seas and marine resources	14.7	Increase economic benefits to small island developing States and LDCs from the sustainable use of marine resources
Policy coherence	17.14	Enhance policy coherence for sustainable development
Partnership	17.16	Enhance the Global Partnership for Sustainable Development, complemented by multi-stakeholder partnerships that mobilize and share knowledge, expertise, technology and financial resources, to support the achievement of the SDGs
	17.17	Encourage and promote effective public, public–private and civil society partnerships

Source: authors' compilation based on United Nations (2015).

Table 5.a.2 Mapping of HAI graduation criterion and SDG targets

HAI indicator	Relevant SDG target	
Percentage of population undernourished	1.1	Eradicate extreme poverty for all people everywhere
	1.2	Reduce at least by half the proportion of men, women and children of all ages living in poverty
	1.3	Implement nationally appropriate social protection systems and measures for all
	2.1	End hunger and ensure access by all people to safe, nutritious and sufficient food
	2.2	End all forms of malnutrition
	10.1	Progressively achieve and sustain income growth of the bottom 40 per cent of the population at a rate higher than the national average
	10.4	Adopt policies, especially fiscal, wage and social protection policies, and progressively achieve greater equality
Under-five mortality rate	3.2	End preventable deaths of newborns and children under 5 years of age
	3.8	Achieve universal health coverage, access to quality essential health-care services and access to safe, effective, quality and affordable essential medicines and vaccines for all
	3.b	Support research and development of vaccines and medicines
	3.c	Substantially increase health financing and the recruitment, development, training and retention of the health workforce in developing countries, especially LDCs
	6.1	Achieve universal and equitable access to safe and affordable drinking water for all
	6.2	Achieve access to adequate and equitable sanitation and hygiene for all
	10.1	Progressively achieve and sustain income growth of the bottom 40 per cent of the population at a rate higher than the national average
Adult literacy rate	4.5	Eliminate gender disparities in education and ensure equal access to all levels of education and vocational training for the vulnerable
	4.6	Ensure that all youth and a substantial proportion of adults, both men and women, achieve literacy and numeracy
	4.a	Build and upgrade education facilities that are child, disability and gender sensitive
Gross secondary school enrolment ratio	4.1	Ensure that all girls and boys complete free, equitable and quality primary and secondary education
	4.5	Eliminate gender disparities in education and ensure equal access to all levels of education and vocational training for the vulnerable
	4.a	Build and upgrade education facilities that are child, disability and gender sensitive

Sources: authors' compilation based on United Nations (2015) and UN DESA (n.d.).

Table 5.a.3 Mapping of EVI graduation criterion and SDG targets

EVI indicator	Relevant SDG target	
Share of population in low elevated coastal zones	11.5	Significantly reduce the number of deaths and the number of people affected and substantially decrease the direct economic losses relative to GDP caused by disasters
	13.1	Strengthen resilience and adaptive capacity to climate-related hazards and natural disasters in all countries
	13.2	Integrate climate change measures into national policies, strategies and planning
	13.3	Improve education, awareness-raising and human and institutional capacity on climate change mitigation, adaptation, impact reduction and early warning
	13.b	Promote mechanisms for raising capacity for effective climate change-related planning and management in LDCs and small island developing states
Merchandise export concentration	2.b	Correct and prevent trade restrictions and distortions in world agricultural markets
	9.1	Develop quality, reliable, sustainable and resilient infrastructure to support economic development and human well-being
	9.2	Promote inclusive and sustainable industrialization and significantly raise industry's share of employment and GDP
	9.b	Support domestic technology development, research and innovation for industrial diversification and value addition to commodities
	10.a	Implement the principle of special and differential treatment for developing countries, in particular LDCs, in accordance with World Trade Organization agreements
	17.10	Promote a universal, rules-based, open, non-discriminatory and equitable multilateral trading system under the World Trade Organization
	17.11	Significantly increase the exports of developing countries, in particular with a view to doubling the least developed countries' share of global exports by 2020
	17.12	Realize timely implementation of duty-free and quota-free market access on a lasting basis for all LDCs

Share of agriculture, forestry and fishing in GDP	2.3	Double the agricultural productivity and incomes of small-scale food producers
	2.4	Ensure sustainable food production systems and implement resilient agricultural practices that increase productivity and production
	2.5	Maintain the genetic diversity of seeds, cultivated plants and farmed and domesticated animals and their related wild species
	2.a	Increase investment in rural infrastructure, agricultural research and extension services, technology development and plant and livestock gene banks in order to enhance agricultural productive capacity
	6.6	Protect and restore water-related ecosystems, including mountains, forests, wetlands, rivers, aquifers and lakes
	12.2	Achieve the sustainable management and efficient use of natural resources
	14.1	Prevent and significantly reduce marine pollution of all kinds
	14.2	Sustainably manage and protect marine and coastal ecosystems
	14.4	Effectively regulate harvesting and end overfishing, illegal, unreported and unregulated fishing and destructive fishing practices and implement science-based management plans
	14.6	Prohibit certain forms of fisheries subsidies which contribute to overcapacity and overfishing
	14.b	Provide access for small-scale artisanal fishers to marine resources and markets
	15.1	Ensure the conservation, restoration and sustainable use of terrestrial and inland freshwater ecosystems and their services
	15.2	Promote the implementation of sustainable management of all types of forests, halt deforestation, restore degraded forests and substantially increase afforestation and reforestation globally
Victims of natural disasters	1.5	Build the resilience of the poor and those in vulnerable situations and reduce their exposure and vulnerability to climate-related extreme events
	11.5	Significantly reduce the number of deaths and the number of people affected and substantially decrease the direct economic losses relative to GDP caused by disasters
	11.b	Substantially increase the number of cities and human settlements adopting and implementing integrated policies and plans towards inclusion, resource efficiency, mitigation and adaptation to climate change
	12.8	Ensure that people everywhere have the relevant information and awareness for sustainable development and lifestyles in harmony with nature
	13.1	Strengthen resilience and adaptive capacity to climate-related hazards and natural disasters in all countries
	13.2	Integrate climate change measures into national policies, strategies and planning

continued

Table 5.a.3 Continued

EVI indicator	Relevant SDG target	
	13.3	Improve education, awareness-raising and human and institutional capacity on climate change mitigation, adaptation, impact reduction and early warning
	13.b	Promote mechanisms for raising capacity for effective climate change-related planning and management in LDCs and small island developing states
	15.3	Combat desertification, restore degraded land and soil and strive to achieve a land degradation-neutral world
Instability of agricultural production	2.3	Double the agricultural productivity and incomes of small-scale food producers
	2.4	Ensure sustainable food production systems and implement resilient agricultural practices that increase productivity and production
	2.5	Maintain the genetic diversity of seeds, cultivated plants and farmed and domesticated animals and their related wild species
	2.a	Increase investment in rural infrastructure, agricultural research and extension services, technology development and plant and livestock gene banks in order to enhance agricultural productive capacity
	15.3	Combat desertification, restore degraded land and soil and strive to achieve a land degradation-neutral world
Instability of exports of goods and services	2.b	Correct and prevent trade restrictions and distortions in world agricultural markets
	8.a	Increase Aid for Trade support for developing countries, in particular LDCs
	9.b	Support domestic technology development, research and innovation for industrial diversification and value addition to commodities
	10.a	Implement the principle of special and differential treatment for developing countries, in particular LDCs, in accordance with World Trade Organization agreements
	17.10	Promote a universal, rules-based, open, non-discriminatory and equitable multilateral trading system under the World Trade Organization
	17.11	Significantly increase exports of developing countries, in particular with a view to doubling the LDCs' share of global exports by 2020
	17.12	Realize timely implementation of duty-free and quota-free market access on a lasting basis for all LDCs

Sources: authors' compilation based on United Nations (2015) and UN DESA (n.d.).

Table 5.a.4 Alignment of 7FYP with SDG targets

Sl No.	SDG Targets	

Fully overlapping

1	3.1	Reduce the global maternal mortality ratio to less than 70 per 100,000 live births
2	3.2	End preventable deaths of newborns and children under Five years of age
3	6.1	Achieve universal and equitable access to safe and affordable drinking water for all
4	7.2	Increase substantially the share of renewable energy in the global energy mix
5	8.1	Sustain per capita economic growth, at least 7 per cent GDP growth in the LDCs
6	13.2	Integrate climate change measures into national policies, strategies and planning

Partially overlapping

1	1.1	Eradicate extreme poverty for all people everywhere
2	1.2	Reduce at least by half the proportion of men, women and children of all ages living in poverty
3	1.3	Implement nationally appropriate social protection systems and measures for all
4	1.5	Build the resilience of the poor and those in vulnerable situations and reduce their exposure and vulnerability to climate-related extreme events
5	1.b	Create sound policy frameworks at the national, regional and international levels, based on pro-poor and gender-sensitive development strategies, to support accelerated investment in poverty eradication actions
6	2.2	End all forms of malnutrition
7	3.3	End the epidemics of AIDS, tuberculosis, malaria and neglected tropical diseases and combat hepatitis, water-borne diseases and other communicable diseases
8	3.7	Ensure universal access to sexual and reproductive health-care services, including for family planning, information and education, and the integration of reproductive health into national strategies
9	3.8	Achieve universal health coverage access to quality essential health-care services and access to safe, effective, quality and affordable essential medicines and vaccines for all
10	4.1	Ensure that all girls and boys complete free, equitable and quality primary and secondary education
11	4.3	Ensure equal access for all women and men to affordable and quality technical, vocational and tertiary education, including university
12	4.4	Substantially increase the number of youth and adults who have relevant skills for employment, decent jobs and entrepreneurship
13	4.5	Eliminate gender disparities in education and ensure equal access to all levels of education and vocational training for the vulnerable
14	4.6	Ensure that all youth and a substantial proportion of adults, both men and women, achieve literacy and numeracy
15	4.a	Build and upgrade education facilities that are child, disability and gender sensitive
16	5.1	End all forms of discrimination against all women and girls everywhere
17	5.2	Eliminate all forms of violence against all women and girls in the public and private spheres, including trafficking and sexual and other types of exploitation

continued

Table 5.a.4 Continued

Sl No.		SDG Targets
18	5.5	Ensure women's full and effective participation and equal opportunities for leadership at all levels of decision-making in political, economic and public life
19	5.a	Undertake reforms to give women equal rights to economic resources
20	5.b	Enhance the use of enabling technology to promote the empowerment of women
21	5.c	Adopt and strengthen sound policies and enforceable legislation for the promotion of gender equality and the empowerment of all women and girls at all levels
22	6.2	Achieve access to adequate and equitable sanitation and hygiene for all
23	6.3	Improve water quality by reducing pollution, eliminating dumping and minimizing release of hazardous chemicals and materials, halving the proportion of untreated wastewater and increasing recycling and safe reuse globally
24	7.1	Ensure universal access to affordable, reliable and modern energy services
25	7.3	Double the global rate of improvement in energy efficiency
26	8.6	Substantially reduce the proportion of youth not in employment, education or training
27	8.8	Protect labour rights and promote safe and secure working environments for all workers
28	8.9	Devise and implement policies to promote sustainable tourism
29	9.2	Promote inclusive and sustainable industrialization, significantly raise industry's share of employment and GDP
30	9.5	Enhance scientific research, upgrade the technological capabilities of industrial sectors
31	10.c	Reduce to less than 3 per cent the transaction costs of migrant remittances and eliminate remittance corridors with costs higher than 5 per cent
32	11.1	Ensure access for all to adequate, safe and affordable housing and basic services and upgrade slums
33	12.c	Rationalize inefficient fossil-fuel subsidies that encourage wasteful consumption by removing market distortions
34	13.2	Strengthen resilience and adaptive capacity to climate-related hazards and natural disasters in all countries
35	15.9	Integrate ecosystem and biodiversity values into national and local planning, development processes, poverty reduction strategies and accounts
36	16.5	Substantially reduce corruption and bribery in all their forms by2020
37	16.6	Develop effective, accountable and transparent institutions at all levels
38	17.1	Strengthen domestic resource mobilization to improve domestic capacity for tax and other revenue collection
39	17.11	Significantly increase exports of developing countries, in particular with a view to doubling the LDCs' share of global exports by 2020
40	17.13	Enhance global macroeconomic stability, including through policy coordination and policy coherence

Overlapping in essence

1	1.a	Ensure significant mobilization of resources from a variety of sources in order to provide adequate and predictable means for developing countries, in particular LDCs, to implement programmes and policies to end poverty
2	2.1	End hunger and ensure access by all people to safe, nutritious and sufficient food
3	2.3	Double the agricultural productivity and incomes of small-scale food producers

Table 5.a.4 Continued

Sl No.	SDG Targets	
4	2.4	Ensure sustainable food production systems and implement resilient agricultural practices that increase productivity and production
5	2.a	Increase investment in rural infrastructure, agricultural research and extension services, technology development and plant and livestock gene banks in order to enhance agricultural productive capacity
6	2.b	Correct and prevent trade restrictions and distortions in world agricultural markets
7	2.c	Adopt measures to ensure the proper functioning of food commodity markets and their derivatives and facilitate timely access to market information, including on food reserves, in order to help limit extreme food price volatility
8	3.c	Substantially increase health financing and the recruitment, development, training and retention of the health workforce in developing countries, especially LDCs
9	5.3	Eliminate all harmful practices, such as child, early and forced marriage and female genital mutilation
10	5.6	Ensure universal access to sexual and reproductive health and reproductive rights as agreed in accordance with the Programme of Action of the International Conference on Population and Development and the Beijing Platform for Action and the outcome documents of their review conferences
11	6.4	Substantially increase water-use efficiency across all sectors and ensure sustainable withdrawals and supply of freshwater to address water scarcity and substantially reduce the number of people suffering from water scarcity
12	6.5	Implement integrated water resources management at all levels, including through transboundary cooperation as appropriate
13	6.6	Protect and restore water-related ecosystems, including mountains, forests, wetlands, rivers, aquifers and lakes
14	7.b	Expand infrastructure and upgrade technology for supplying modern and sustainable energy services for all in developing countries
15	8.3	Promote development-oriented policies that support productive activities, decent job creation, entrepreneurship, creativity and innovation
16	8.5	Achieve full and productive employment and decent work for all and equal pay for work of equal value
17	9.3	Increase access of small-scale industrial and other enterprises to financial services
18	9.c	Significantly increase access to information and communications technology
19	10.1	Progressively achieve and sustain income growth of the bottom 40 per cent of the population at a rate higher than the national average
20	10.2	Empower and promote the social, economic and political inclusion of all
21	10.4	Adopt policies, especially fiscal, wage and social protection policies, and progressively achieve greater equality
22	10.b	Encourage official development assistance and financial flows, including foreign direct investment
23	11.2	Provide access to safe, affordable, accessible and sustainable transport systems for all, improving road safety, notably by expanding public transport, with special attention to the needs of those in vulnerable situations, women, children, persons with disabilities and older persons

continued

Table 5.a.4 Continued

Sl No.	SDG Targets	
24	11.5	Significantly reduce the number of deaths and the number of people affected and substantially decrease the direct economic losses relative to GDP caused by disasters
25	12.2	Achieve the sustainable management and efficient use of natural resources
26	12.b	Develop and implement tools to monitor sustainable development impacts for sustainable tourism that creates jobs and promotes local culture and products
27	13.3	Improve education, awareness-raising and human and institutional capacity on climate change mitigation, adaptation, impact reduction and early warning
28	14.1	Prevent and significantly reduce marine pollution of all
29	14.2	Sustainably manage and protect marine and coastal ecosystems
30	14.4	Effectively regulate harvesting and end overfishing, illegal, unreported and unregulated fishing and destructive fishing practices and implement science-based management plans
31	15.1	Ensure the conservation, restoration and sustainable use of terrestrial and inland freshwater ecosystems and their services
32	15.2	Promote the implementation of sustainable management of all types of forests
33	15.3	Combat desertification, restore degraded land and soil and strive to achieve a land degradation-neutral world
34	16.3	Promote the rule of law at the national and international levels and ensure equal access to justice for all
35	16.10	Ensure public access to information and protect fundamental freedoms, in accordance with national legislation and international agreements
36	17.3	Mobilize additional financial resources for developing countries from multiple sources
37	17.17	Encourage and promote effective public, public-private and civil society partnerships

No target in 7FYP

1	1.4	Ensure that all men and women, in particular the poor and the vulnerable, have equal rights to economic resources, as well as access to basic services, ownership and control over land and other forms of property, inheritance, natural resources, appropriate new technology and financial services, including microfinance
2	2.5	Maintain the genetic diversity of seeds, cultivated plants and farmed and domesticated animals and their related wild species
3	5.4	Recognize and value unpaid care and domestic work through the provision of public services, infrastructure and social protection policies and the promotion of shared responsibility within the household and the family as nationally appropriate
4	8.2	Achieve higher levels of economic productivity through diversification, technological upgrading and innovation
5	8.4	Improve progressively global resource efficiency in consumption and production and endeavour to decouple economic growth from environmental degradation
6	8.10	Strengthen the capacity of domestic financial institutions to encourage and expand access to banking, insurance and financial services for all
7	9.1	Develop quality, reliable. sustainable and resilient infrastructure to support economic development and human well-being
8	9.4	Upgrade infrastructure and retrofit industries to make them sustainable

Table 5.a.4 Continued

Sl No.	SDG Targets	
9	10.7	Facilitate orderly, safe, regular and responsible migration, and mobility of people
10	11.a	Support positive economic, social and environmental links between urban, peri-urban and rural areas by strengthening national and regional development planning
11	11.b	Substantially increase the number of cities and human settlements adopting and implementing integrated policies and plans towards inclusion, resource efficiency, mitigation and adaptation to climate change
12	12.8	Ensure that people everywhere have the relevant information and awareness for sustainable development and lifestyles in harmony with nature
13	14.6	Prohibit certain forms of fisheries subsidies which contribute to overcapacity and overfishing by 2020
14	14.b	Provide access for small-scale artisanal fishers to marine resources and markets
15	15.a	Mobilize and significantly increase financial resources from all sources to conserve and sustainably use biodiversity and ecosystems
16	16.1	Significantly reduce all forms of violence and related death rates everywhere
17	16.4	Significantly reduce illicit financial and arms flows, strengthen the recovery and return of stolen assets and combat all forms of organized crime
18	16.7	Ensure responsive, inclusive, participatory and representative decision-making at all levels
19	16.a	Strengthen relevant national institutions, including through international cooperation, for building capacity at all levels, in particular in developing countries, to prevent violence and combat terrorism and crime
20	16.b	Promote and enforce non-discriminatory laws and policies for sustainable development
21	17.14	Enhance policy coherence for sustainable development
SDG is global in nature		
1	3.b	Support the research and development of vaccines and medicines
2	7.a	Enhance international cooperation to facilitate access to clean energy research and technology
3	8.a	Increase Aid for Trade support for developing countries, in particular LDCs
4	8.b	Develop and operationalize a global strategy for youth employment
5	9.a	Facilitate sustainable and resilient infrastructure development in developing countries through enhanced financial, technological and technical support to African countries, LDCs, landlocked developing countries and small island developing states
6	9.b	Support domestic technology development, research and innovation for industrial diversification and value addition to commodities
7	10.a	Implement the principle of special and differential treatment for developing countries, in particular LDCs, in accordance with World Trade Organization agreements
8	11.c	Support LDCs, including through financial and technical assistance, in building sustainable and resilient buildings utilizing local materials

continued

Table 5.a.4 Continued

Sl No.	SDG Targets	
9	12.1	Implement the 10-Year Framework of Programmes on Sustainable Consumption and Production Patterns
10	13.b	Promote mechanisms for raising capacity for effective climate change-related planning and management in LDCs and small island developing states
11	14.7	Increase the economic benefits to small island developing states and LDCs from the sustainable use of marine resources, including through sustainable management of fisheries, aquaculture and tourism
12	14.a	Increase scientific knowledge, develop research capacity and transfer marine technology, taking into account the Intergovernmental Oceanographic Commission Criteria and Guidelines on the Transfer of Marine Technology, in order to improve ocean health and to enhance the contribution of marine biodiversity to the development of developing countries, in particular small island developing states and LDCs
13	15.b	Mobilize significant resources from all sources and at all levels to finance sustainable forest management and provide adequate incentives to developing countries to advance such management, including for conservation and reforestation
14	16.8	Broaden and strengthen the participation of developing countries in the institutions of global governance
15	17.2	Developed countries to implement fully their official development assistance commitments
16	17.4	Assist developing countries in attaining long-term debt sustainability through coordinated policies
17	17.5	Adopt and implement investment promotion regimes for LDCs
18	17.6	Enhance North-South, South-South and triangular regional and international cooperation on science, technology and innovation
19	17.7	Promote development, transfer, dissemination and diffusion of environmentally sound technologies to developing countries
20	17.8	Fully operationalize the technology bank and science, technology and innovation capacity-building mechanism for LDCs by 2017
21	17.9	Enhance international support for implementing effective and targeted capacity-building in developing countries to implement the SDGs
22	17.10	Promote a universal, rules-based, open, non-discriminatory and equitable multilateral trading system under the World Trade Organization
23	17.12	Realize timely implementation of duty-free and quota-free market access on a lasting basis for all LDCs
24	17.15	Respect each country's policy space and leadership to establish and implement policies for poverty eradication and sustainable development
25	17.16	Enhance the Global Partnership for Sustainable Development, complemented by multi-stakeholder partnerships that mobilize and share knowledge, expertise, technology and financial resources, to support the achievement of the SDGs
26	17.19	Build on existing initiatives to develop measurements of progress on sustainable development that complement GDP, and support statistical capacity-building in developing countries

Sources: authors' compilation based on United Nations (2015), UNCTAD (2016), UN DESA (n.d.) and UN-OHRLLS (2016a).

Table 5.a.5 Aligning the 21 SDG targets indicated as 'no target in 7FYP' with other national and sectoral policies of Bangladesh

SDG target	Policy of Bangladesh	Alignment
1.4	National Women Development Policy (2011)	Overlapping in essence
2.5	–	No target
5.4	National Women Development Policy (2011)	Overlapping in essence
8.2	National Skills Development Policy (2011)	Overlapping in essence
8.4	National Industrial Policy (2016)	Overlapping in essence
8.10	Perspective Plan of Bangladesh (2010–21)	Overlapping in essence
9.1	National Industrial Policy (2016)	Overlapping in essence
9.4	National Sustainable Development Strategy (2010–21) National Industrial Policy (2016)	Overlapping in essence
10.7	–	No target
11.a	–	No target
11.b	–	No target
12.8	National Sustainable Development Strategy (2010–21)	Overlapping in essence
14.6	National Sustainable Development Strategy (2010–21)	Overlapping in essence
14.b	National Sustainable Development Strategy (2010–21)	Overlapping in essence
15.a	National Sustainable Development Strategy (2010–21)	Overlapping in essence
16.1	–	No target
16.4	–	No target
16.7	–	No target
16.a	–	No target
16.b	–	No target
17.14	National Sustainable Development Strategy (2010–21)	Overlapping in essence

Source: authors' compilation.

Table 5.a.6 Variable, data and stationarity of empirical analysis

Variable (SDG indicator)	ADF with trend	ADF with drift	ADF with no constant	Phillips–Perron $Z(t)$	Result of stationarity test
	Level				
GNI per capita	2.171	8.682***	11.058***	7.783***	Level: Stationary
Disbursement of project aid to agriculture sector in US$ million (2.a.2)	0.272	0.357	1.176*	0.363	First difference: Stationary
Annual growth rate of real GDP per employed person in BDT (8.2.1)	-2.198	-1.730**	8.008***	-1.314	Second difference: Stationary
Total airports passenger movement in '000 number (9.1.2)	-4.251**	-0.695	0.969	0.151	First difference: Stationary
Industry value added as per cent of GDP (9.2.1)	-2.374*	-1.150	2.377*	-1.186	First difference: Stationary
Manufacturing employment as a proportion of total employment (9.2.2)	2.950	4.631***	3.310***	2.902*	Second difference: Stationary
Total revenue as per cent of GDP (17.1.1)	-3.129	-2.718***	1.123	-2.719*	First difference: Stationary
Proportion of domestic budget funded by domestic taxes (17.1.2)	-3.223	-4.291***	0.953	-4.748***	Level: Stationary
Personal remittances received as per cent of GDP (17.3.2)	-0.903	-0.903	0.956	-0.988	First difference: Stationary

Source: authors' estimations.

Note
Levels of significance: *** 1%; ** 5%; * 10%.

Table 5.a.7 List of variables for empirical analysis

Variable as in source	Short name of variable (SDG indicator)	Data available
GNI per capita, Atlas method in current US$	GNI per capita	1990–2015
GDP per capita growth as annual per cent	GDP per capita growth (8.1.1)	1990–2015
Disbursement of project aid to agriculture sector in US$ million	Disbursement of project aid to agriculture sector in US$ million (2.a.2)	1990–2015
Annual growth rate of real GDP per employed person in BDT	Per employee real GDP growth (8.2.1)	Seven periodic years
Total airports passenger movement number in thousands	Air passenger number in thousands (9.1.2)	1999–2015
Industry value added as per cent of GDP	Industry value added as per cent of GDP (9.2.1)	1990–2015
Manufacturing employment as a proportion of total employment	Manufacturing employment as per cent of total (9.2.2)	Six periodic years
Total government revenue as a proportion of GDP, by source	Total revenue as per cent of GDP (17.1.1)	1994–2016
Proportion of domestic budget funded by domestic taxes	Tax revenue as per cent of budget (17.1.2)	1994–2016
Volume of remittances in US$ as a proportion of total GDP	Personal remittances received as per cent of GDP (17.3.2)	1990–2015
Number of passengers carried by Bangladesh Railway in thousands	Number of railway passengers in thousands (9.1.2)	1995–2015
Number of passengers carried by water transport operated under Bangladesh Inland Water Transport Authority in thousands	Number of waterway passengers in thousands (9.1.2)	1996–2015
Net official development assistance (ODA) received in constant 2013 US$	Net ODA constant 2013 US$ (10.b.1)	1990–2014
Foreign direct investment (FDI), ODA and South–South cooperation as a proportion of total domestic budget	FDI net inflows as per cent of budget (17.3.1)	1994–2015
FDI, ODA and South–South cooperation as a proportion of total domestic budget	Net ODA as per cent of budget (17.3.1)	1994–2014
Debt service as a proportion of exports of goods and services	Debt service as per cent of exports (17.4.1)	1990–2015
Proportion of population with access to electricity	Population having electricity (7.1.1)	2000–14
Material footprint, material footprint per capita, and material footprint per GDP	Material footprint per capita (12.2.1)	2000–10

Source: authors' elaboration.

Notes

1 Available from: http://kh.one.un.org/content/dam/unct/cambodia/docs/RIA_Cambodia _Analysis_07Oct2016.pdf [Accessed 30 September 2017].
2 Name of the variable of SDG indicators for the analysis has been tailored according to the sources.

References

Alabi, R. A., 2014. *Impact of agricultural foreign aid on agricultural growth in Sub-Saharan Africa: A dynamic specification*. AGRODEP Working Paper 0006. Washington, DC: International Food Policy Research Institute.

Allen, C., Metternicht, G. and Wiedmann, T., 2017. *An iterative framework for national scenario modelling for the Sustainable Development Goals (SDGs)*. Sustainable Development. Available from: http://dx.doi.org/10.1002/sd.1662 [Accessed 12 September 2017].

Bangladesh Planning Commission, 2012. *Perspective plan of Bangladesh 2010–2021: Making Vision 2021 a reality*. Perspective Plan. Dhaka: General Economics Division, Planning Commission, Government of Bangladesh.

Bangladesh Planning Commission, 2013. *National sustainable development strategy (2010–2021)*. Dhaka: General Economics Division, Planning Commission, Government of Bangladesh.

Bangladesh Planning Commission, 2015. *The Millennium Development Goals: Bangladesh progress report 2015*. Dhaka: General Economics Division, Planning Commission, Government of Bangladesh.

Bangladesh Planning Commission, 2016. *Integration of Sustainable Development Goals (SDGs) into the 7th Five Year Plan*. Dhaka: General Economics Division, Planning Commission, Government of Bangladesh. Available from: www.plancomm.gov.bd/wp-content/uploads/2016/11/Integration_SDG_7FYP_Final.pdf [Accessed 27 January 2017].

Bastian, M., Heymann, S. and Jacomy, M., 2009. Gephi: An open source software for exploring and manipulating networks. *ICWSM*, 8, 361–362.

BBS, 2016. *Statistical yearbook of Bangladesh 2015*. Dhaka: Bangladesh Bureau of Statistics.

BBS, 2017. *Gross domestic product (GDP)* [online]. Dhaka: Bangladesh Bureau of Statistics. Available from: www.bbs.gov.bd/site/page/dc2bc6ce-7080-48b3-9a04-73cec782d0df/Gross-Domestic-Product-(GDP) [Accessed 8 June 2017].

Bhattacharya, D., Khan, T. I. and Sabbih, M. A., 2016. *Delivering on the promise: Ensuring the successful implementation of the 2030 Agenda in Bangladesh*. Dhaka: Save the Children in Bangladesh.

Bose, N., Haque, M. E. and Osborn, D. R., 2007. Public expenditure and economic growth: A disaggregated analysis for developing countries. *Manchester School*, 75 (5), 533–556.

Economic Relations Division, 2016. *Flow of external resources into Bangladesh 2015–2016*. Dhaka: Ministry of Finance, Government of Bangladesh. Available from: www.erd.gov.bd/site/page/84648784-9e8a-4760-8e47-6d20ad3013a8/Flow-of-External-Resources-2016 [Accessed 8 June 2017].

FERDI, 2016. *Human assets index* [online]. Clermont-Ferrand: Fondation pour les études et recherches sur le développement international. Available from: www.ferdi.fr/en/node/883 [Accessed 15 December 2016].

Gupta, A. S., 2007. *Determinants of tax revenue efforts in developing countries*. IMF Working Paper 184. Washington, DC: International Monetary Fund.

Kaya, O., Kaya, I. and Gunter, L., 2012. Development aid to agriculture and economic growth. *Review of Development Economics*, 16 (2), 230–242.

Keane, J. and te Velde, D. W., 2008. *The role of textile and clothing industries in growth and development strategies*. London: Overseas Development Institute.

Kritikos, A. S., 2014. Entrepreneurs and their impact on jobs and economic growth. *IZA World of Labor*, 8, 1–10.

Lalarukh, F. and Chowdhury, M. S., 2013. Contribution of VAT to the GDP of Bangladesh: A trend study. *Journal of Business Studies*, 34 (2), 131–141.

Le Blanc, D., 2015. Towards integration at last? The Sustainable Development Goals as a network of targets. *Sustainable Development*, 23 (3), 176–187.

MoF, 2017. *Bangladesh economic review 2017* [online]. Dhaka: Ministry of Finance, Government of Bangladesh. Available from: www.mof.gov.bd/site/page/44e399b3-d378-41aa-86ff-8c4277eb0990/BangladeshEconomicReview [Accessed 8 June 2017].

Norton, G. W., Ortiz, J. and Pardey, P. G., 1992. The impact of foreign assistance on agricultural growth. *Economic Development and Cultural Change*, 40 (4), 775–786.

Otte, E. and Rousseau, R., 2002. Social network analysis: A powerful strategy, also for the information sciences. *Journal of Information Science*, 28 (6), 441–453.

Rahman, M., Khan, T. I. and Sadique, M. Z., 2016. Implication of the 2030 Agenda for the Istanbul programme of action. In: LDC IV Monitor, *Tracking progress, accelerating transformations: Achieving the IPoA by 2020*. London: Commonwealth Secretariat, 19–28.

Siddique, A., Selvanathan, E. A. and Selvanathan, S., 2012. Remittances and economic growth: Empirical evidence from Bangladesh, India and Sri Lanka. *Journal of Development Studies*, 48 (8), 1045–1062.

Su, D. and Yao, Y., 2016. *Manufacturing as the key engine of economic growth for middle-income economies*. ADBI Working Paper 573. Tokyo: Asian Development Bank Institute.

Uddin, G. S. and Sjö, B., 2013. Remittances, financial development and economic growth in Bangladesh. *South Asia Economic Journal*, 14 (2), 261–273.

UN DESA, n.d. *LDC criteria* [online]. New York: United Nations Department of Economic and Social Affairs. Available from: www.un.org/development/desa/dpad/least-developed-country-category/ldc-criteria.html [Accessed 8 June 2017].

UNCTAD, 2016. *The Least Developed Countries Report 2016: The path to graduation and beyond making the most of the process*. New York: United Nations Conference on Trade and Development.

United Nations, 2011. *Programme of action for the least developed countries for the decade 2011–2020*. A/CONF.219/3/Rev.1. New York: United Nations.

United Nations, 2015. *Transforming our world: The 2030 Agenda for sustainable development*. A/RES/70/1. New York: United Nations.

UN-OHRLLS, 2016a. *State of the least developed countries 2016*. New York: United Nations Office of the High Representative for the Least Developed Countries, Landlocked Developing Countries and Small Island Developing States.

UN-OHRLLS, 2016b. *Priorities of LDCs in the context of the SDGs and the post-2015 development agenda*. New York: United Nations Office of the High Representative for the Least Developed Countries, Landlocked Developing Countries and Small Island Developing States.

UNSD, 2017. *SDG indicators: Global database* [online]. New York: United Nations Statistics Division. Available from: http://unstats.un.org/sdgs/indicators/database [Accessed 8 June 2017].

Van Stel, A., Carree, M. and Thurik, R., 2005. The effect of entrepreneurial activity on national economic growth. *Small Business Economics*, 24 (30), 311–321.

World Bank, 2016. *New country classification by income level* [online]. The Data Blog. Washington, DC: World Bank. Available from: https://blogs.worldbank.org/opendata/new-country-classifications-2016 [Accessed 25 March 2018].

World Bank, 2017. *World development indicators* [online]. Washington, DC: World Bank. Available from: http://data.worldbank.org/data-catalog/world-development-indicators [Accessed 8 June 2017].

6 Pursuing a graduation strategy within the global and regional environment

What are the pitfalls for Bangladesh?

Towfiqul Islam Khan and Muntaseer Kamal

Introduction

It may not be an oversimplification to state that the global and regional environment will be less conducive for the least developed countries (LDCs) in upcoming years. Maintaining the momentum of development is likely to be challenging for many LDCs in view of a rather inhospitable global environment. Already plagued with low income levels, structural weaknesses, inefficient technologies and few growth prospects, LDCs are now subject to a new set of, and often interrelated, global and regional challenges and potential shocks. These challenges include climate change, stagnant official development assistance (ODA), protectionist measures of advanced economies, illicit financial flows (IFFs) and tepid economic recovery after the global financial crisis of 2007–08. Indeed, United Nations General Assembly (UNGA 2016) also identified similar emerging challenges namely, climate change, proliferation of natural disasters, conflicts and rising capital outflow to be exacerbating the long-standing structural challenges faced by the LDCs. Associated costs emergent from external shocks may fall disproportionately on LDCs. Hence, such external challenges may affect graduation and smooth transition, unless concerted actions are taken both domestically as well as by the international development community (Dahlman and Mealy 2016).

Over time, Bangladesh has encountered a number of external shocks and suffers from a multitude of systemic deficiencies. Bangladesh was mostly unscathed from the global financial crisis during 2007–08 as its financial and capital markets are largely insulated from the global market. However, as the crisis protracted, Bangladesh experienced an export earnings slowdown, lower outward migration, declined revenue earnings and a loss of competitiveness as stimulus packages were put in place by other countries (Rahman *et al.* 2010). The natural disasters in 2007–08 and consequent food grain scarcity alongside international restrictive measures resulted in a food price spike. This ultimately led to loss of welfare, decline in real gross domestic product (GDP), reduction in international trade and rise in inflation (Raihan and Khan 2013). Absence of good governance and a liable and transparent policy environment has also restrained Bangladesh from the realisation of its full socio-economic potential

(Rahman *et al.* 2014). Limited capacity of domestic institutions has also been a root cause behind this.

The United Nations Conference on Trade and Development (UNCTAD 2016) rightly pointed out that, for an LDC, graduation is only the 'first milestone' in the development path, it is certainly not the 'winning post'. In view of the above, it has become essential to analyse the implications of said challenges as Bangladesh prepares for LDC graduation and subsequent smooth transition. However, instead of looking at the traditional domestic features associated with LDC graduation and ensuing transition, this chapter will attempt to highlight the relevant pitfalls originating from the global and regional arena.

Following this introduction, the next four sections of the chapter identify various persistent and emerging global and regional challenges affecting prospects for LDC graduation and smooth transition. These sections also attempt to assess the potential impacts of the identified challenges, particularly during Bangladesh's period of LDC graduation to be followed by smooth transition. The penultimate section investigates the readiness of national development plans and policies to address these challenges as part of Bangladesh's smooth transition strategy. The final section concludes by outlining a way towards formulating a national plan informed by the identified global and regional challenges.

The global economy is undergoing multiple transitions in terms of economic and geopolitical rebalancing, ongoing technological change and emerging social and political risks. These transitions will have far-reaching impacts on Bangladesh's economy, which is becoming increasingly integrated with the global and regional economies. As Bangladesh prepares for LDC graduation and beyond, its strategies will need to be contextualised in this new global order. From this perspective, this chapter aims to answer four key questions:

- What will be the key global and regional challenges for Bangladesh during the period of smooth transition (2024–27) after LDC graduation and are there any interrelations among them?
- What impacts could these challenges have on Bangladesh's graduation and smooth transition?
- With Bangladesh's graduation and ensuing transition in mind, are there any gaps regarding these challenges in the existing policy regime?
- What more could be done to address the gaps in the policy regime?

With a view to assess the implications of the aforementioned challenges for Bangladesh as the country formulates its graduation and smooth transition strategies, this chapter applies the following analytical framework. Identified global and regional challenges are categorised under four broad clusters: economic, technological, environmental, and governance and security. The impacts of these challenges on Bangladesh's LDC graduation and smooth transition are assessed along with global trends. Moreover, a perception survey was also conducted among relevant stakeholders in Bangladesh's development – including policymakers, academics and development partners – to validate the relevance of said challenges. The readiness of national and international development plans and policies to tackle these challenges is investigated according to six broad categories: external resources, other financial flows, trade and connectivity, technology, peace and conflict, and national and international governance. To this end, a mapping exercise is conducted to identify responsible institutions and existing national plans, policies and strategies to address the identified challenges.

The chapter reviews a wide range of national and international literature and policy documents. Secondary data from both national and international sources are analysed. Secondary data sources include several Bangladesh government agencies including the Ministry of Finance, its Economic Relations Division (ERD) and the Bangladesh Bureau of Statistics. Several international databases, including those of the Organisation for Economic Co-operation and Development (OECD) and World Bank, were used.

Economic pitfalls

Plateauing of ODA

One of the major challenges faced by LDCs in recent decades is the declining availability of ODA from developed countries and the international community. The majority of developed countries have not kept their commitments to provide 0.7 per cent of gross national income (GNI) as development assistance to developing countries in general and 0.15–0.20 per cent of GNI to LDCs as per the Istanbul Programme of Action (IPoA). Additionally, LDCs generally lack the resources to tackle external shocks, such as the global financial crisis and climate change, and thus often rely upon assistance from developed countries. Hence, fluctuations and reductions in ODA disbursements may further impede LDCs' development processes. Moreover, there has been a shift in ODA allocation to LDCs from productive sectors, such as infrastructure, to social sectors such as health and education (UNCTAD 2016). As a result, LDCs have to increasingly opt for more expensive and tied sources of finance for infrastructure.

Only six major development partners – Norway, Luxembourg, Sweden, Denmark, Germany and the United Kingdom (UK) – fulfilled their commitments to provide 0.7 per cent of GNI as development assistance in 2016 (Figure 6.1). The average donor disbursement was only 0.4 per cent of GNI, while the disbursement of the OECD's Development Assistance Committee (DAC) member countries as a group was even lower at 0.3 per cent of GNI. Nevertheless, ODA has been on a rising trend since 2012. Compared to 2015, net ODA flows from DAC countries increased by 8.9 per cent in real terms during 2016. Part of the expansion in 2016 was due to higher in-donor refugee costs. Between 2015 and 2016, in-donor refugee costs' share of total net ODA increased from 9.2 per cent to 10.8 per cent. If such costs are excluded, net ODA increased by 7.1 per cent in real terms in 2016 (OECD 2017a).

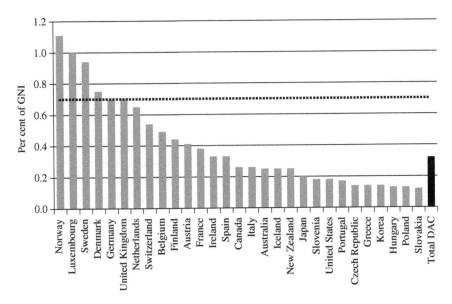

Figure 6.1 Net ODA disbursement as per cent of GNI by DAC donors in 2016.
Source: OECD (2017a).

At the Third International Conference on Financing for Development in 2015, donors committed to reversing the declining trend in ODA to LDCs. Although, bilateral aid to LDCs rose by 4 per cent in real terms during 2015 compared to the previous year, this upward trend could not be sustained during 2016 as bilateral aid to LDCs fell by 3.9 per cent in real terms from 2015 (United Nations 2017a). On average over 2013–15, ODA to LDCs accounted for 0.09 per cent of DAC countries' GNI, which is well below the target of 0.15–0.20 per cent.[1] Over a longer term, net ODA as a share of LDCs' GDP declined from around 10 per cent in 1990 to 4 per cent in 2015 (UN-OHRLLS 2017). One striking issue is that LDCs have not been receiving their fair share of aid. The unequal distribution of ODA has emerged as an area of concern at a time when future flows of ODA have become uncertain. The preferences of developed countries have led to the emergence of 'aid darlings' and 'aid orphans' among LDCs (Bhattacharya and Khan 2014).[2] Guinea, Madagascar and Nepal were identified as aid orphans during the 2006–12 period (Ericsson and Steensen 2014).

Bangladesh attained lower middle-income country (LMIC) status in 2015. In the past, Bangladesh was highly reliant on aid as a share of GDP. The country was heavily dependent on food and commodity aid in the years following its independence in 1971. Economic Relations Division (2016a) shows that, from fiscal year[3] (FY) 1972 to FY1981, share of food and commodity aid rose from 51.2 per cent to 98.7 per cent in total ODA received by Bangladesh. Matching this trend in ODA, bilateral assistance accounted for 63.3 per cent to 85.7 per cent of total ODA received during the same period, with the rest being multilateral assistance. Almost the entirety of ODA received now falls into the category of project aid, mostly to finance investment. In FY2016, the share of project aid in total ODA received was 99 per cent. Commensurate with this changing pattern of ODA, the share of multilateral assistance rose to about 67 per cent in FY2016, while bilateral assistance fell to 33 per cent. During the post-independence decade, the share of ODA in GDP ranged between 3.7 per cent and 7.9 per cent. In FY2009, this share fell to 1.8 per cent and followed a downward trajectory to reach 1.6 per cent in FY2016 (Figure 6.2). These trends indicate that Bangladesh's dependence on ODA is declining. At the same time, they point to the growing significance of domestic resource mobilisation.

ODA commitments to Bangladesh can be considered in two ways. First, simple allocations to sectors can be examined based on key macro areas (using OECD Creditor Reporting System three-digit purpose codes). If necessary, relevant sub-areas could also be considered. Second, a simple index of relative specialisations can be constructed for the aforementioned sectors (Keane *et al.* 2010). The index is defined as the ratio between share of country *i* in total ODA for a specific sector *s* and the share of country *i* in total ODA:

$$S_{is} = \frac{\dfrac{ODA_{is}}{\sum_{j=1}^{n} ODA_{js}}}{\dfrac{ODA_{i}}{\sum_{j=1}^{n} ODA_{j}}}$$

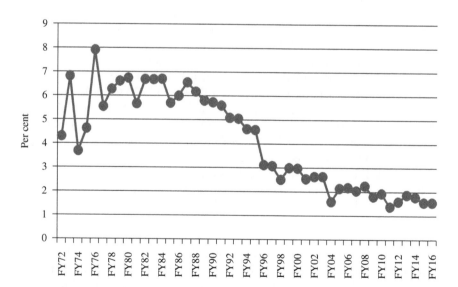

Figure 6.2 ODA received by Bangladesh as share of GDP.

Sources: authors' calculations based on World Bank (2017a) and Economic Relations Division (2016a).

Here, ODA_{is} and ODA_i are ODA in sector s and total ODA for country i, respectively (both in United States dollar (US$) million), n is the total number of recipients, with j denoting each recipient. In this case, only developing countries were considered as beneficiaries. A value of the index greater than 1 means that country i is receiving more ODA in a particular sector compared to other developing countries.

Analysis of data suggests that social infrastructure and services, and economic infrastructure and services are the major sectors to which ODA has been allocated in Bangladesh. The specialisation index presented in Table 6.1 shows which sectors are relatively overfunded or underfunded in the country compared to other developing countries. Bangladesh is only marginally overfunded in the social infrastructure and services sector during the recent years. The sector's index value fell below 1 in 2012 and 2015. Compared to other developing countries, Bangladesh generally receives more aid for education, particularly basic education. In recent years, on average, the transport and storage, and energy sectors received greater attention with respect to ODA allocations. Conversely, the production sectors, on average, were underfunded compared to other developing countries.

A key policy concern for Bangladesh is the low level of ODA disbursements as a share of commitments, which was 94.2 per cent in FY2005 but fell to 49.3 per cent in FY2016 – exhibiting a generally declining trend (Economic Relations Division 2016a). This situation has created some uncertainty in the Government of Bangladesh's (GoB) implementation process for its Annual Development Programme. Also, there is generally a gap between targeted and actual expenditure from project aid when implementing the Annual Development Programme. However, the issue cannot be fully comprehended through a simple analysis of current commitment and disbursement trends. According to Bjornestad *et al.* (2016), disbursement as a share of actual allocation is about 90 per cent per year. The challenge, then, might be the prolonged time gap between donors making commitments and ministries using disbursements. As per Rahman *et al.* (2010), disbursement will rely more on Bangladesh's absorptive capacity than the availability of aid. Economic Relations Division (2016b) mentioned timely project implementation to be the key determinant to accelerate the pace of aid disbursement. Hence, there is scope for the GoB to streamline relevant processes and reduce the large aid pipeline that stood at US$22.2 billion at the end of FY2016 (Economic Relations Division 2016a).

The trend of ODA commitments in Bangladesh against their trend from FY1995 to FY2016 are presented in Figure 6.3. The trend was calculated using the Hodrick-Prescott filter (H-P filter).[4] The volatility of ODA commitments seems to be declining gradually over time as the trend line comes closer to commitments.

Another lens through which ODA can be looked at is concessionality. The ODA received by Bangladesh can be divided into grants and loans. There is no need for the country to repay the grants that it receives, but loans must be repaid with interest after a certain period of time. The share of loans in total ODA has increased over time and gradually overtaken the share of grants (Figure 6.4). In FY2016, the share of loans in total ODA was 84.2 per cent, with

Table 6.1 Allocations of ODA commitments across sectors in Bangladesh (specialisation index)

Sector	2005	2006	2007	2008	2009	2010	2011	2012	2013	2014	2015	Average
1 Social infrastructure and services	1.68	1.32	0.92	0.79	0.78	1.03	1.41	0.99	1.07	1.12	0.83	1.09
1.1 Education	2.80	1.43	0.89	1.07	1.21	1.23	2.11	1.76	1.93	1.55	1.78	1.61
1.1.1 Basic education	1.97	0.89	1.58	1.35	1.71	2.70	5.42	3.95	1.46	3.49	1.73	2.39
1.2 Health	3.56	2.03	0.48	0.89	0.78	0.59	1.74	1.32	0.68	1.06	1.15	1.30
2 Economic infrastructure and services	1.56	1.17	1.70	1.46	1.57	1.74	1.65	1.40	1.21	1.24	2.03	1.52
2.1 Transport and storage	1.39	0.80	1.54	0.20	0.76	1.28	2.97	1.23	1.29	0.19	1.57	1.20
2.2 Communications	3.21	7.53	0.18	5.94	0.18	0.22	0.06	8.60	0.11	1.29	1.87	2.65
2.3 Energy	2.07	0.56	2.12	3.54	3.69	1.85	0.92	0.77	1.72	2.72	2.39	2.03
3 Production sectors	0.42	1.16	0.30	0.98	0.73	1.19	0.35	0.97	0.55	0.60	1.05	0.75
4 Multi-sector/ cross-cutting	1.15	1.62	2.40	2.13	2.20	0.73	0.70	1.24	1.45	1.44	1.02	1.46
5 Commodity aid/ General programme assistance	1.83	1.85	1.66	0.32	1.24	0.65	0.33	1.99	1.45	1.35	1.30	1.27
5.1 General budget support	1.38	1.64	0.89	0.00	1.05	0.00	0.00	1.91	1.60	1.64	1.44	1.05
6 Action relating to debt	0.08	0.49	0.06	0.05	0.02	0.01	0.00	0.01	0.00	0.02	0.02	0.07

Source: authors' calculations from OECD (2017b).

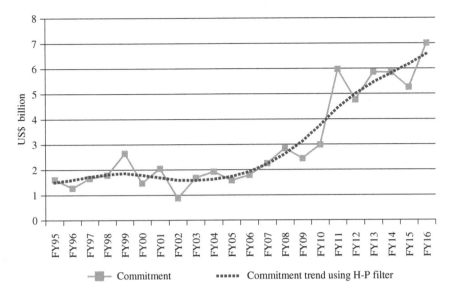

Figure 6.3 ODA commitments against their trend in Bangladesh.
Source: authors' calculations from Economic Relations Division (2016a).

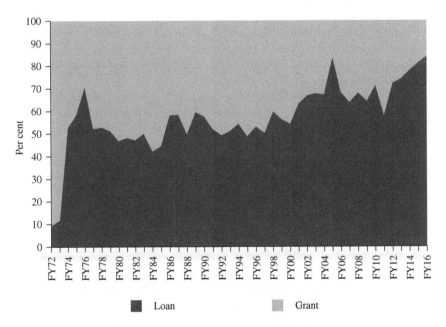

Figure 6.4 Changes in the share of aid disbursement by concessional status.
Source: authors' calculations from Economic Relations Division (2016a).

the remaining share being grants. LDC graduation would increase the costs of external financing rather than reducing its availability (UNCTAD 2016). Hence, the issues of debt sustainability and debt management might pose challenges for Bangladesh in the medium- to long-term.

Bangladesh has had a mixed experience with foreign aid. The key reasons could be attributed to both the government and donors. The donors' current approach towards the aid delivery mechanism has various inadequacies including disconnect between financial contribution and policy influence, limited domestic policy autonomy brought forth by conditionalities, lack of ownership in proposed policy packages and resultant unenthusiastic implementation, cookie cutter approach towards policy suggestions without recognising complex country-specific context. Another aspect often overlooked is the cumbersome policies, procedures and practices of donor agencies – each of which have plentiful reporting requirements and insist on specific ways of doing things – thus putting enormous pressure on the limited administrative capacity of the recipient countries (Easterly 2002). Addressing such issues require changes in the existing donor approach such as allowing for greater flexibility in the delivery of aid, providing recipients with ample policy space and emphasising results. However, these changes will not be sufficient by themselves unless complemented by governmental measures to ensure good governance, conducive economic atmosphere, and enhancement of domestic absorption and implementation capacities (Quibria and Islam 2015). Khan (2014) observed that aid can influence economic and political outcomes by altering the rent seeking behaviour of the relevant entities. The impact of ODA may vacillate depending on the interaction between aid and already established economic and political underpinnings. In this context, structure of economic and political forces must be taken into cognisance while designing foreign assistance policies of Bangladesh in future.

As mentioned earlier, although the dependence on ODA in Bangladesh is decreasing, the significance of domestic resource mobilisation is increasing. Though the volatility of ODA commitments is declining, various process lags are impeding Bangladesh from reaping the full benefits. The gradual decline of concessional ODA might pose some challenges in the coming years with respect to debt management.

Tepid economic recovery and protectionist measures by developed countries

The global financial crisis led to a worldwide economic slowdown, which affected not only developed countries but also LDCs and other developing countries. This notion is also supported by UNGA (2016). The fall in food and oil prices further restrained supply-side productivity opportunities in developed countries, which trickled down to LDCs in the forms of reduced aid, restricted trade and increased migration (CDP 2012, Fic 2014). In LDCs, the ratio of foreign reserves to external debt stocks rose from 55 per cent in 2010 to 60 per cent during the 2011–13 period (UN-OHRLLS 2016a). The global decline in oil demand and prices translated into unsustainable subsidies and public infrastructure investments in oil-importing countries. The reduction of available fiscal space might adversely affect social protection and export promotion initiatives in many LDCs (UN-OHRLLS 2016a). There was an increase in inflation during 2007–08, which coincided with the global financial crisis (World Bank 2017a). Inflation rose far higher in LDCs than high-income countries, implying that low-income countries (LICs) are more vulnerable to price fluctuations. Although GDP growth in high-income countries had recovered after the crisis, LDCs have experienced declining GDP growth. Nevertheless, the impact of the crisis on unemployment in LDCs appears to be limited when compared to developed countries.

According to the United Nations (2017b), the global economy is projected to grow by 2.7 per cent in 2017 and 2.9 per cent in 2018, which are rates lower than the average growth rate of 3.4 per cent seen in the decade prior to the global financial crisis. Notably, the estimate for global GDP growth in 2016 was revised downward by 0.7 percentage points compared to the previous year. The revision was due to weaker-than-expected GDP growth in the United States (US), Japan and many commodity-exporting countries in Africa, the Commonwealth of Independent States, and Latin America and the Caribbean. LDCs, on the other hand, are projected to grow by 5.2 per cent in 2017 and 5.5 per cent in 2018. These rates are well below the annual target of at least 7 per cent articulated as part of the Sustainable Development Goals (SDGs). Not attaining this target may pose a threat to both sufficient private financing and critical public expenditure on health, education, social protection and climate change adaptation. Also, growth in global trade declined by 1.2 per cent in 2016, which is the slowest pace since the global financial crisis. This decline implies that LDCs' prospects for growth by relying on foreign markets are limited.

Developing countries already face a number of trade barriers when exporting goods and services to developed countries, including applied tariffs, quotas, intellectual property rights, distribution restrictions, restriction on post-sales services and border procedures. Moreover, the pace of the removal of trade barriers is very slow. For instance, only 25 per cent of the 2,835 trade-restrictive measures applied to World Trade Organization (WTO) members since 2008 had been eliminated by mid-May 2016 (WTO 2016b). Since LICs will lose access to trade preferences upon graduation from the LDC category, any proliferation of trade barriers might have negative consequences for graduated countries and their smooth transition processes. Additionally, applied tariff rates applied to LICs and middle-income countries (MICs) declined steadily overall over the 2000–12 period, but curiously they were on average higher for LICs than LMICs (Figure 6.5).

With the loss of trade preferences from the European Union's (EU) 'Everything But Arms' (EBA) arrangement, which provides duty-free and quota-free access to all products except arms and ammunition from LDCs, graduated countries are at risk in terms of economic growth prospects. Furthermore, the EU

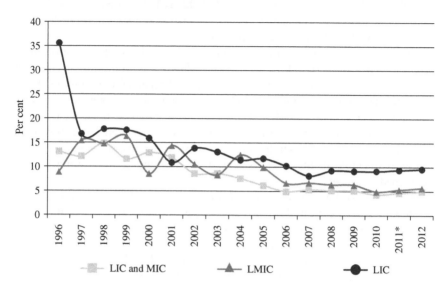

Figure 6.5 Applied tariff rates (weighted mean, all products).

Source: World Bank (2017a).

Note
* Refers to the value for 2011 being unavailable and thus estimated by the authors.

initiated a series of free trade agreement negotiations with developing countries including India which may undermine the trade preferences for LDCs. Another challenge for LDCs' smooth transition is the depreciation of the British pound (GBP) following the UK's decision in June 2016 to leave the EU, widely known as Brexit, which affects LICs by way of the declining real value of remittances, export earnings and development assistance (Sieler and Raschen 2016). For instance, LDCs' exports to the UK would likely decline by 0.6 per cent or US$500 million due to Brexit and the countries most affected in such a scenario include Bangladesh, Kenya, Mauritius and Fiji (Mendez-Parra *et al.* 2016).

Brexit has emerged as an unanticipated impediment to Bangladesh's future market access to the UK, which is the country's third largest export destination after the US and Germany. However, the EU, as a whole, is the largest export market for Bangladesh (as per EPB (2017), 54.6 per cent of total exports from Bangladesh went to the EU in FY2016). Bangladesh enjoys a 12 per cent preference margin for its apparel industry under the EU's EBA arrangement, which provides considerable price advantages. Moreover, the EU agreed to relax its rules of origin provision for LDCs from two-stage to one-stage transformation as of 1 January 2011, while other developing countries remain subject to the two-stage requirement.

Bangladesh might lose the aforementioned benefits in the UK market after Brexit is completed in March 2019. Based on 2014 data, Mendez-Parra *et al.*

(2016) estimated that Bangladesh's total exports will decline by 1.2 per cent as a consequence of Brexit. The key factors considered in this estimation were depreciation of the GBP coupled with lower GDP in the UK. The estimation does not consider the price and income effect from the rest of the EU, which the authors note makes their analysis a conservative estimation of short-term trade effects. The magnitude of Brexit's long-term adverse impacts will hinge on the outcome of negotiations between the UK and EU (World Bank 2017b). Jensen and Snaith (2016) asserted that regardless of the considerable economic costs associated with Brexit, party political factors have become more influential in setting up the Brexit negotiations than demands from vested interest groups. Hobolt (2016) argued that the anti-immigration and anti-establishment sentiments that brought forth Brexit are gaining momentum in other parts of Europe.

Since 20 January 2017, US President Donald Trump has held the reins of the American executive branch with a unified Republican Congress rallying behind him. The Trump administration has been criticised for scrapping the Trans-Pacific Partnership, attacking the North American Free Trade Agreement, threatening to impose high tariffs on imports from China and other trading partners, deserting the Paris Agreement on climate change and discrediting climate change as a 'Chinese hoax'. Policy initiatives for the US economy could have substantial ripple effects – through the economy's sheer size and degree of integration with the global economy – around the world. A robust US economy is essential for the dynamism of the global economy. Increasing trade barriers and policy uncertainty could, through feedback loops, adversely impact economic growth in the US as well as across the global economy (World Bank 2017b).

There have been significant disputes between developed and developing countries including LDCs regarding market access for agricultural and manufactured goods, services and other issues. The difficulty of reaching a consensus during the WTO's Doha Development Round negotiations in 2001 may have caused the recent shift towards mega-regional trade agreements (RTAs) (Putzhammer *et al.* 2016). Countries appear to have slowly shifted from preferring global agreements within the WTO to bilateral trade agreements and RTAs. The emergence of four mega-RTAs – the signed but unratified Trans-Pacific Partnership agreement among 12 countries, the Transatlantic Trade and Investment Partnership being negotiated between the US and EU, and the Regional Comprehensive Economic Partnership and Free Trade Agreement of the Asia-Pacific being pursued by China – raises a host of short- and long-term questions for the multilateral trading system and WTO. The countries involved in mega-RTAs seek to deepen market access gains by going beyond the WTO's multilateral tariff levels to harmonise policies and regulations that influence the cross-border movement of services, capital and labour (Palit 2015, Putzhammer *et al.* 2016).

Mega-RTAs could significantly reduce market access for LDCs' exports in RTA-participating countries (Palit 2015). Reduced access would be mainly due to the elimination of import tariffs on a wide range of items between participating countries, which would cause significant preference erosion[5] for LDCs. Indeed, new preferential market access always leads to some degree of trade diversion for non-participating countries (Elliott 2016). The actual impacts on LDCs will depend on the specifics of mega-RTAs, which are yet to be concluded. They will also depend on whether WTO member countries continue to advance the 'post-Bali agenda' (referring to the agenda following the Ninth Ministerial Conference of the WTO in 2013) with a view to consolidate the WTO's centrality as a multilateral trade negotiation platform (WEF 2014). The withdrawal of the US from the Trans-Pacific Partnership on 23 January 2017, which means that the agreement cannot be ratified, is expected to have positive impacts on LDCs for the time being.

In this changing global environment, the biggest challenges for Bangladesh will be linked to market access. Since the US is a major export destination for the country, developments there may affect Bangladesh in the coming years. Although the withdrawal of the US from the Trans-Pacific Partnership might come as a relief, Bangladesh will have to remain cautious because there is a possibility that the US will sign bilateral trade agreements with other countries in order to import goods at lower rates. Moreover, Bangladesh's absence from mega-RTA negotiations may impact its future trade potential. Bangladesh should therefore evaluate its economic eligibility and political scope for applying to the EU's Generalised System of Preferences plus scheme and assess opportunities for bilateral and multilateral negotiations on market access, including the Regional Comprehensive Economic Partnership and Free Trade Agreement of the Asia-Pacific.

Rise of new technologies

Rising automation and robotics

The world is on the brink of a 'fourth industrial revolution', which has its roots in the third – the digital revolution that began in the mid-twentieth century. A characteristic feature of the fourth industrial revolution is crisscrossing of physical, digital and biological domains brought forth by a blending of technologies. New technologies enable supply-side changes through creating novel ways of serving existing needs and disrupting industrial value chain norms. Major demand-side shifts are also taking place against the backdrop of changing company practices as a result of increasing transparency, consumer engagement and new forms of consumer behaviour (Schwab 2016). While the fourth industrial revolution is expected to have many benefits (e.g. a more connected world, further scope for cooperation, machine-assisted and complex tasks, long-term gains in productivity and efficiency, more effective logistics and global value chain processes, and lower trade costs), it is also likely to cause severe disruptions in the labour market. Degryse (2016) categorised the diverse impacts of the fourth industrial revolution into four broad headings:

- Job creation: the origination of new sectors, products and services.
- Job change: new human–machine interactions, new forms of jobs and digital management.
- Job destruction: jobs are at risk due to computerisation, automation and robotisation.
- Job shift: new digital platforms, crowdsourcing and relocation of services.

According to the World Bank (2016), the repercussions for developing countries hinge on the pace of technological disruption. The jobs that will likely be adversely affected by automation, which are concentrated in the agriculture and manufacturing sectors, are largely in developing countries. Labour markets in developed countries have already shifted towards the services sector. Acemoglu and Restrepo (2016) also acknowledged the concerns regarding automation and new technologies and resultant inequality. In this setting, they find that both automation and creation of new tasks may raise inequality in the short-term by reducing the employability of low-skill workers and directly favouring the high-skill workers. Nevertheless, the medium-term outlook can be very different as complex tasks are later standardised and taken up by low-skill workers.

Given looming changes in the structures of labour markets in developing countries, the LDCs with vast numbers of unskilled workers are most at risk, while skilled workers in developed countries have a comparative advantage in the automated job market. The number of robots around the world has more than doubled recently from 99,000 in 2000 to 254,000 in 2015 (IFR 2016). The majority of the aforementioned robots are employed in the automotive industry and electronics industry with recent surges in metal and machinery industry, and rubber and plastic industry. According to Qureshi and Syed (2014), the robotics industry generates 170,000–190,000 jobs worldwide, most of which are in Brazil, China, Germany, South Korea and the US. Hence, the LDCs with relatively less-skilled workers have been experiencing low per-capita income growth, which will affect their graduation and smooth transition prospects.

Since automation is becoming cheaper, LDCs are losing their low labour cost advantage, which is adversely affecting trade, remittances and foreign direct investment (FDI) into LICs. The costs of three key technological innovations – drones, DNA sequencing and solar energy – have fallen significantly in recent years (Table 6.2). On average, the costs are falling at the rates of 56 per cent per year for drones, 65 per cent per year for DNA sequencing and 16 per cent per year for solar energy.

The fourth industrial revolution is poised to transform ways of life and livelihoods. It will likely take longer for LICs to feel its impacts, however. The majority of jobs in LDCs are mostly low-tech with limited application of information and communication technology (ICT) in urban job sectors. Additionally, lower wage rates with larger shares of jobs involving manual non-routine labour makes investment in technology costlier for firms. Hence, even though two-thirds of all jobs in developing countries can technically be automated, technological advancements are somewhat restrained by lower wages

Table 6.2 Falling costs of key technological innovations

Technology	Year	Cost (US$)
Drones (cost per unit)	2007	100,000
	2013	700
DNA sequencing (cost per unit)	2000	2.7 billion
	2007	10 million
	2014	1,000
Solar energy (cost per kilowatt hour)	1984	30
	2014	0.16

Source: WEF (2017).

and sluggish technology adoption. Adjusting for technological feasibility and adoption time lag, approximately 47 per cent of all jobs in Bangladesh are susceptible to automation (Figure 6.6).

Job displacement and job loss due to technological advancements are fundamental parts of economic development (WEF 2017). Technological advancements substitute some human labour, but they also increase the skills of the remaining labour force and new entrants into the labour market. The increase in skills leads to rising productivity, which engenders economic growth and releases human as well as financial resources to be used in sectors with higher returns (World Bank 2016). Essentially, advancement in technology goes hand in hand with structural transformation.

An alarming trend associated with structural transformation is the incidence of 'premature deindustrialisation'.[6] According to Dasgupta and Singh (2007), premature deindustrialisation refers to the fall in the share of employment in the manufacturing sector or an absolute decline in such employment at a much lower level of GNI per capita compared to the historical trends of developed countries. Similarly, Rodrik (2016) mentioned that, compared to the early industrialisers, countries are exhausting their industrialisation prospects faster and at much lower levels of GNI. The economic consequences of this trend are the reduction of growth potential of an economy, implausibility of income convergence with developed countries and removal of rapid growth channels. Furthermore, he proclaimed premature deindustrialisation to be an impediment to democratisation via its disrupting effect on the bargains between the elite and non-elite (Rodrik 2015).

According to Rodrik (2015), mass political parties are often a by-product of industrialisation. In case of premature deindustrialisation, industrial setting loses its usual form and is based mostly around informality, a diffused set of small enterprises and petty services. Consequently, mutual interest among the non-elite becomes divergent, political organisation gets impeded and class solidarity starts attenuating. In the resultant absence of an organised labour force, non-elites do not possess a proper representation in collective bargaining. Thus, premature deindustrialisation might make democratisation less likely and more fragile.

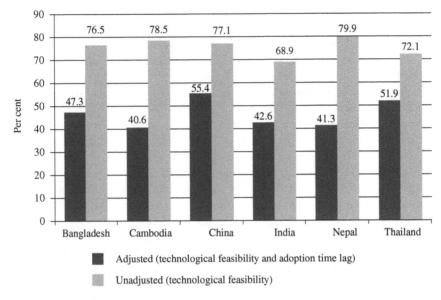

Figure 6.6 Estimated shares of jobs that are susceptible to automation.
Source: World Bank (2016).

Rising automation and robotics is expected to cause major labour market disruption in the future. Although its adverse impact may affect Bangladesh at a later stage, relevant labour market strategies need to be put in place so that it does not come as a shock in the form of severe socio-economic implications.

Barriers to technology transfer

Technology has made it possible to use new products and services that contribute to increasing income levels globally and improving quality of life for those who are able to afford and access ICT facilities. Since the main beneficiaries of technological advancements are developed countries, a 'digital divide' between developed and developing countries is evident. In fact, Krugman (1979) attributed technological innovation to be the root cause of wage differentials between developed and developing countries. The major sources of cross-border technology transfer are the flows of trade and FDI from developed to developing countries. Given the draw of automation, many developed country firms are moving their production processes from LDCs to their home countries. For instance, Japan has withdrawn its electronics, assembly parts and textile firms from the Asia-Pacific region due to the expansion of automation on its own territory (Sagasti 1994, cited in Kenaroğlu 2003). With the loss of trade and FDI, along with the expiration of the Agreement on Trade-Related Aspects of Intellectual Property Rights (TRIPS) and related ICT features, the transfer of technology to LDCs is at a minimum, which adversely affects capacity building processes and efficiency gains.

LDCs' investments in science, technology and innovation remain weak. As a result, the gap between LDCs and the rest of the world regarding capacity to explore scientific and technological knowledge has been widening. For instance, while OECD countries spent about 2.4 per cent of their GDP on research and development in 2013, the amount spent by LDCs was negligible. Although the Technology Bank recently established by the UN to facilitate technology transfer to LDCs aims to increase their capacities for scientific and technological innovation as well as help them overcome structural barriers and integrate into the global knowledge economy, resource constraints and insufficient scientific literacy have resulted in little generation, diffusion and application of scientific knowledge in LDCs. Thus, the 'digital divide' between LDCs and other developing and developed countries may deepen, which could be detrimental for their graduation and subsequent smooth transition.

The gaps in the numbers of trademark and patent applications between high-income countries, LICs and MICs have been closing, however. While the numbers of trademark applications in high-income countries were higher before 2003, the trend reversed in the following years. Convergence occurred much later – during 2013–14 – in the case of patent applications (World Bank 2017a). Much of the convergence can be explained by the growing participation of emerging economies such as China and India.

Technological adjustments have been often linked to rising inequality and a related trend is polarisation within the labour market. This 'hollowing out' phenomenon occurs when the share of the labour force in high-skilled occupations alongside the share of labour in low-skilled professions increase, but the share of labour in middle-skilled employment decreases (World Bank 2016). Given this possibility, the GoB needs to tactfully devise strategies to realise the full potential of Bangladesh's demographic dividend in the coming years.

Climate change and finance

With increasing globalisation and use of fossil fuels, there has been a surge in greenhouse gas emissions alongside a rise in average surface temperatures and significant climate change in recent years. Rapidly growing populations are further degrading the world's natural environment. The UN Environment Programme projected that annual global emissions will rise to 53 gigatonnes of carbon dioxide equivalent by 2020 and 60 gigatonnes by 2030. Furthermore, the world's average temperature could increase by 4.8 degrees Celsius in the highest emissions scenario. Such an increase is expected to have adverse effects on agricultural production and the functioning of ecosystems as well as cause the extinction of flora and fauna. Moreover, incidences of groundwater scarcity and flooding are expected to rise in upcoming years (IPCC 2015).

LDCs in general and small island LDCs in particular are most vulnerable to climate change impacts because of their geographical locations as well as lack of economic, institutional, technical and scientific capabilities to adapt to and manage climate-related shocks. Moreover, the high level of poverty in LDCs increases their vulnerability to climate change. The increase in climate-related natural disasters such as floods, cyclones and droughts come with huge human and economic costs for LDCs. For instance, flash floods in the Solomon Islands in 2014 destroyed houses, infrastructure and water and sanitation facilities, with economic losses amounting to 4.7 per cent of the country's GDP (UN-OHRLLS 2016a). Economic Relations Division (2016b) mentioned that, on average, Bangladesh loses 1.8 per cent of GDP annually due to its geographical location and proliferation of natural disasters. Additionally, climate change severely threatens agricultural production and food security in LDCs since these countries do not have effective climate change adaptation and mitigation measures. Inefficient institutions, regulations and legal frameworks in developing countries along with the lack of carbon pricing, inadequate financial support and significant fossil fuel subsidies are major barriers to achieving climate change adaptation and mitigation goals (IPCC 2015).

Financing has always been a critical issue when it comes to climate change adaptation and mitigation initiatives. In this context, the Least Developed Countries Fund was established under the UN Framework Convention on Climate Change in November 2001 to address the climate change adaptation needs of LDCs. Among developed countries, Germany has led in terms of the amounts being pledged and deposited (Figure 6.7). Although the US falls behind the UK in terms of pledges, the country is second in terms of deposits. Given the new administration in the US, the prospects of increased financing by the country over the medium term are low. Indeed, political considerations may have greater influence on climate finance in the future at the global level. McCright and Dunlap (2011) analysed the impact of political orientation on the perspective of citizens of the US regarding climate change. They found that the Liberal and Democratic perspective concerning climate change is more congruous with scientific consensus. Furthermore, the impacts of educational attainment and self-reported understanding on global warming issues are positive for Liberals and Democrats, but are weaker or negative for Conservatives and Republicans. Indeed, McCright and Dunlap (2011) found considerable ideological and partisan divergence on the issue of climate change.

The Least Developed Countries Fund has various shortcomings. Its project-driven approach often fails to integrate itself into national development processes of LDCs. Financing remains insufficient and unstable as it depends on voluntary contributions from developed countries. Available data indicate that 86 per cent of an already low pledged amount has been actually deposited (Climate Funds Update 2017). Limited resources narrow the scope of national adaptation programmes of action from a wide set of actions to specific projects (UNCTAD 2010, cited in UNCTAD 2016). Although the amounts deposited in the fund totalled approximately US$962 million from 25 countries up to 2015, that level of financing was estimated to be less than one-fifth of the cost of implementing national adaptation programmes of action across all LDCs

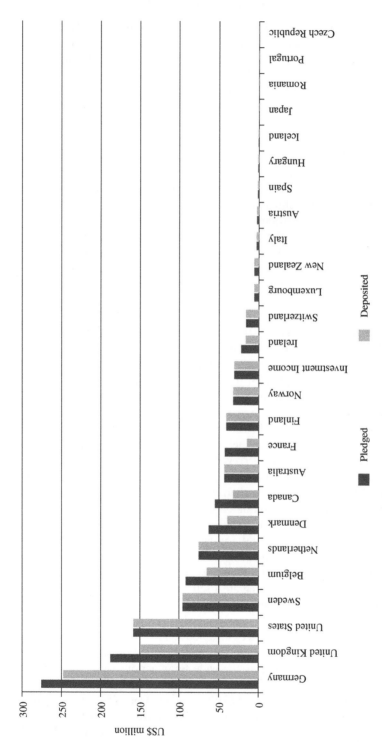

Figure 6.7 Contributions to the Least Developed Countries Fund by major donors from 2001.

Source: Climate Funds Update (2017).

Note

Data up to January 2017.

(Tenzing *et al.* 2015, cited in UNCTAD 2016). The 2015 UN Climate Change Conference in Paris pledged a further US$1.5 billion to address climate change impacts, but the extent to which this commitment will be fulfilled is uncertain (UNCTAD 2016).

The Special Climate Change Fund – also established in 2001 under the UN Framework Convention on Climate Change – focuses on adaptation, technology transfer, mitigation and economic diversification. Like in the case of the Least Developed Countries Fund, the contributions received by the Special Climate Change Fund are far from adequate. Finance allocated to climate change initiatives is very much concentrated. For example, none of the ten countries that received half of the US$7.6 billion in climate finance available in 2014 was an LDC. However, 69 per cent of the approximately US$1.3 billion in adaptation finance was allocated to LDCs, though not all LDCs obtained such finance (UNCTAD 2016). The scale, availability and accessibility of climate finance remain considerable constraints for LDCs.

Bangladesh's efforts tend to be inclined towards developing resilience against climate change impacts. Hence, climate finance in Bangladesh's context is mostly in the forms of flows from domestic and external sources geared towards adaptation measures. From the available statistics on external financial flows to Bangladesh, the multi-donor Bangladesh Climate Change Resilience Fund does not appear to be too encouraging with a very low level of funding, while other sources such as the Climate Investment Funds, Green Climate Fund and Global Environment Facility, are also relatively insignificant. Climate finance opportunities presented by domestic and bilateral sources should thus be pursued (Bjornestad *et al.* 2016).

However, lack of coordination between funding entities working in Bangladesh may hinder the efficient utilisation of the available opportunities. Khan *et al.* (2013) found that there was no harmonised effort regarding the selection of projects or allocation of funds. The authors also found instances of political interference to take up non-eligible projects. They also highlighted systemic weaknesses in the oversight and corruption control process. Questions were raised regarding the capacity and independence of the Anti-Corruption Commission to challenge cases of corruption and fraud in climate finance delivery. The authors also found lack of a complaint reporting mechanism.

LDC graduation has a direct impact on climate finance since graduated countries lose their access to LDC-specific funding, particularly through the Least Developed Countries Fund. While other sources may remain available, these countries will need to compete for finance against other developing countries. This situation could impose an additional constraint given the limited institutional and human capabilities of recently graduated countries (UNCTAD 2009). According to Uprety (2015), the long, complex process of accessing climate finance might be challenging even for other developing countries. The high level of fragmentation prevalent in the field of climate finance may exacerbate this process. The immensely complex global architecture of climate finance currently comprises 29 implementing agencies, 21 multilateral funds and seven bilateral funds and initiatives (UNCTAD 2016). Better coordination among the many relevant stakeholders in Bangladesh has become an exigency. More transparency in project cycles and robust integrated data systems are mandatory for oversight and control of corruption in the field (Khan *et al.* 2013).

Given the limited scale and scope of the current opportunities, Bangladesh must venture to newer avenues for adequate climate finance prospects. The bureaucratic process behind international climate finance must be streamlined while accountability and transparency in implementation of climate change-related projects at the national level must be ensured.

Governance and international security challenges

Conflict and the refugee crisis

Insecurity and the global refugee crisis go hand in hand. Every year, multitudes of people are subject to forced migration due to war, conflict, persecution and natural disasters. In 2015, the number of international migrants and refugees reached 244 million, which is 41 per cent higher than in 2000 (UN DESA 2016). Political unrest across the Middle East and particularly the ongoing civil war in Syria, which began in March 2011, have caused millions of refugees to risk crossing into neighbouring countries and further away in Europe, with the share of refugees in global migration rising to 50 per cent in 2014–15 (IMF 2016). Men, women and children seeking safety and shelter internationally are extremely vulnerable, as many people go missing, drown at sea or fall prey to criminal groups in their attempts to escape violence and ill treatment.

The number of refugees originating from LDCs has been increasing steadily since 2008 and noticeably accelerated in 2014–15. In fact, this number was 5.7 million in 2008 which jumped to 7.4 million in 2014, and then further increased to 8.1 million in 2015. The share of refugees originating from LDCs to total refugees has also been rising since 2008 (World Bank 2017a). This trend may indicate that there are growing socio-economic concerns in LDCs.

The flipside of the coin is the considerable stress experienced by the countries receiving massive influxes of refugees. The LDCs, which are least able to fulfil the development needs of their own populations, let alone the humanitarian needs often linked with refugee crises, took in a larger number of refugees in 2015 than in 2008 (Figure 6.8). Moreover, the share of refugees hosted by LDCs to total refugees has been increasing since 2010, which has put immense pressure on these LDCs' economies. For instance, Mayer (2014) showed that Lebanon lacks the capacity to host such a large number of Syrian refugees and integrate them into Lebanese society in an appropriate manner. At the same time, host developing and developed countries might divert their development assistance from other priorities to help refugees, which could in turn exacerbate situations in LDCs.

A recent influx of Rohingya community from Myanmar has created an unprecedented scenario in Bangladesh. A frightening number of members from

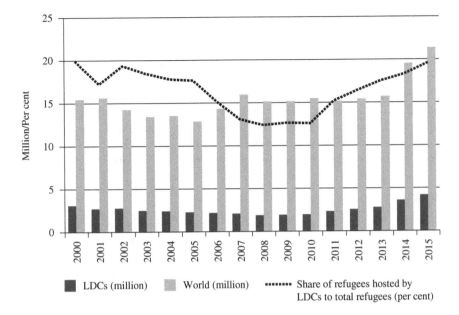

Figure 6.8 Trends in refugees seeking asylum.
Source: World Bank (2017a).

the persecuted community have taken shelter in neighbouring Bangladesh since a violent crackdown started in late August 2017.[7] There is an acute necessity for food, shelter, health care and child protection amongst the refugees. With limited resources, Bangladesh had no alternative but to provide basic support. Nevertheless, larger contributions from the global community will be required to maintain such support. More importantly, if this crisis continues, which may happen, Bangladesh is likely to face a number of challenges in socio-economic, environmental, political and peace and security context.

Cross-border and inter-state terrorism

Terrorism has emerged as one of the key threats to democracy, economic development and lasting peace. According to IEP (2016), terrorist activity around the world decreased by 10 per cent in 2015 compared to 2014. Deaths from terrorist activities also decreased from 32,685 in 2014 to 29,376 in 2015. However, 2015 is still the second deadliest year since 2000. Indeed, the number of deaths from terrorist activities increased almost ninefold since 2000. Terrorism can impact countries by raising the costs of economic activity. The World Bank (2017b) asserted that terrorism and conflict can adversely affect a country's development trajectory through increased uncertainty, slow investment and increased cost of doing business. Moreover, insecurity and geopolitical tensions can derail efforts towards regional cooperation and integration, while increased expenditure on security can aggravate fiscal vulnerabilities. Countries with wealthier and diversified economies can better cope with the effects of terrorism than LDCs that have smaller or poorer economies (Bandyopadhyay *et al.* 2015). Terrorism may disrupt productive activities in a certain sector of a diversified economy, but resources can easily be shifted to an unaffected sector. For LDCs, terrorist incidents might result in shifts of resources towards less productive activities or to another country entirely. Developed countries have sophisticated resources that can be devoted to counter-terrorism, which may not always be the case in developing countries. Hence, a terrorist attack in an LDC is likely to have relatively greater and protracted macroeconomic costs.

IFFs

IFFs have become too common in developing and developed countries alike. Alongside illegal movements of people and goods out of LDCs, there is also illegal transfer of funds, including both money and capital. Blankenburg and Khan (2012) argued that a primary reason behind capital flight by political actors in developing countries is the possibility of asset expropriation if their opponents come into power. On the other hand, Baker (2005) has found illicit financial outflow through multinational businesses as the largest component of overall IFF, which is followed by proceeds originated from criminal activities, and public-sector corruption. Indeed, IFFs incorporate all forms of finance that are illegally earned, transferred or used, such as through tax evasion, corruption, trade misinvoicing, money laundering, smuggling or terrorist financing by individuals or firms (Khan 2016). Herkenrath (2014) mentioned that apart from having an investment and growth impeding impact, IFFs indirectly inhibit advancement in human development and delivery of basic human rights. Every year, significant outflows from LDCs could be otherwise used to provide public services that improve development trajectories. Given their resource constraints and inadequate market access, LDCs experience severe social and economic impacts due to IFFs, specifically the curtailment of public and private domestic investment and expenditure. According to the OECD (2014), IFFs out of developing countries including LDCs are estimated to exceed FDI and aid flows into LDCs. Outflows adversely affect LDCs' growth prospects, which ultimately hinder LDC graduation and smooth transition.

IFFs from LDCs increased significantly during the 2004–13 period – from US$14.1 billion in 2004 to US$40.2 billion in 2013 (Kar and Spanjers 2015). Money laundering, which is the process of transforming the proceeds of crime and corruption into legitimate assets, is a possibility in this case. Money laundering undermines the financial sector, which in turn impairs the long-term economic growth and welfare of LDCs. Although anti-money laundering efforts and international cooperation are in place to fight corruption in and IFFs from LDCs, weak public policies, duplication of structures within bureaucracies and lack of coordination mechanisms for anti-money laundering and anti-corruption agendas remain problems (Pereira and Fontana 2012).

Bangladesh is no exception in this regard. According to estimates by Kar and Spanjers (2015), IFFs from the country were on an increasing trend over the 2004–13 period, totalling almost US$9.7 billion in 2013 (Figure 6.9). In every year, IFFs far exceeded ODA received by the country. The majority of IFFs were likely due to trade misinvoicing, which was responsible for 86.4 per cent of IFFs in 2013. Trade misinvoicing is the primary measurable means for illicitly shifting funds out of developing countries (Kar and Spanjers 2015). Based on a 100-country scale ranking IFFs as a percentage of GDP, Bangladesh's rank worsened over time as it stood in sixty-ninth position in 2004 and fortieth position in 2013 (Figure 6.10).

Kar and Schjelderup (2015) mentioned that unrecorded capital flight – IFFs and other types of capital flight – on a substantial and persistent scale may diminish a developing country's growth potential to a greater extent than any recorded outflows. Growth potential decreases when relevant institutions in that country redirect resources away from productive activities, and initiatives designed to improve living standards and reduce inequality among citizens. According to Khan (2016), IFFs from Bangladesh were about 3.6 times the size of the GoB's education budget and 8.2 times the size of its health budget in 2013. If 25 per cent – the highest income tax rate in Bangladesh – of these outflows could be retained as tax revenue, the health budget could be tripled or the education budget could be doubled.

According to Khan and Akbar (2015), IFFs from developing countries adversely affect their investment regimes. On a similar note, Kar (2011) asserted

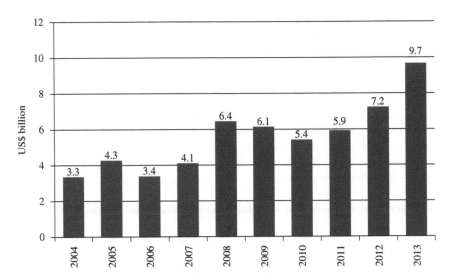

Figure 6.9 Trend of IFFs from Bangladesh, 2004–13.

Source: Kar and Spanjers (2015).

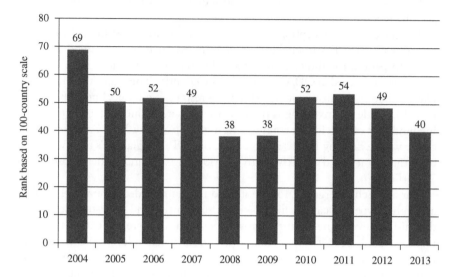

Figure 6.10 Bangladesh's ranking by IFFs as per cent of GDP (based on 100-country scale).

Sources: authors' calculations from Kar and Spanjers (2015) and World Bank (2017a).

that developing countries are missing out on opportunities to invest in their domestic economies due to the increasing incidence of IFFs. As per Herkenrath (2014), IFFs deny countries the opportunity to invest substantial amounts that could catalyse economic growth and usefully supplement foreign loans and aid in funding the public sector. Moreover, IFFs incentivise organised crime, corruption and rent-seeking, which can subsequently increase IFFs. The World Bank (2013) explained that curbing IFFs can help finance development by mobilising more domestic resources through tax collection and by saving foreign exchange reserves. Considering the growing significance of domestic resource mobilisation for Bangladesh, curtailing IFFs should be a top priority.

In terms of refugee issues, cross-border and inter-state terrorism and IFFs, concerted global and domestic effort is a must. Considering recent refugee and terrorism issues, Bangladesh must devise cogent policies as early as possible. Given the substantial opportunity cost of IFFs, adequate enforcement from the relevant part of government is mandatory.

Review of national efforts in view of emerging external challenges

In reviewing Bangladesh's existing national policies towards addressing the challenges identified above, it is important to also ascertain the relevance of these challenges in the country's context. A survey was conducted by the authors to estimate the degree of relevance and possible impact of the identified challenges. The sample for the survey consisted of senior officials from various government institutions as well as members of a variety of Bangladesh's development partners. A total of 32 responses was received. The respondents were asked to rate the identified challenges on a scale of 1 to 7 (lowest to highest) on two dimensions: relevance and impact. Summary statistics from the survey show the average rating that each challenge received (Figure 6.11). All challenges were rated 'high relevance' and 'high impact', which corroborates the notion that the identified challenges are of foremost importance in Bangladesh's context. Against this backdrop, it is well advised to take all of these challenges into policy cognisance.

The GoB's policy towards graduation from the LDC category is only implicit in the Perspective Plan of Bangladesh for the 2010–21 period, which envisions Bangladesh as an MIC by 2021 (Bangladesh Planning Commission 2012). However, the Seventh Five Year Plan (7FYP) for the 2016–20 period, which is the second phase of the Perspective Plan, does not include LDC graduation as a

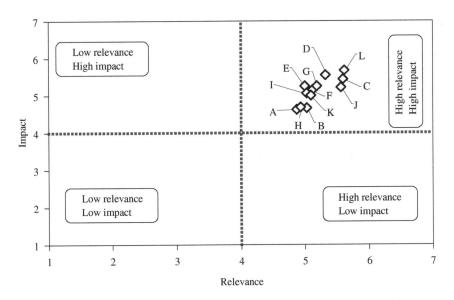

Figure 6.11 Results of perception survey on identified challenges.

Source: authors' calculations from survey data.

Notes
(A) declining ODA; (B) tepid recovery of the global economy; (C) possible protectionist trade policies by developed countries; (D) increasing trade-restrictive measures; (E) failure to take advantage of regional cooperation; (F) declining available finance for preparation in the face of increasing climate-related natural disasters; (G) declining available finance for ensuring agricultural production and food security through climate change adaptation; (H) addressing conflict and the refugee crisis; (I) tackling cross-border and inter-state terrorism; (J) growing IFFs; (K) rising automation and robotics; (L) expiration of TRIPS facilities and related ICT features resulting in barriers to technology transfer.

Table 6.3 Existing policies, plans, acts, strategies or initiatives to address Bangladesh's smooth transition challenges

Cluster	Challenge	Policy, plan, act, strategy or initiative	Institution
External resources	ODA	National Policy on Development Cooperation (draft finalised but unapproved), Strengthening finance for 7FYP and SDGs in Bangladesh (2016), Bangladesh Joint Cooperation Strategy (2010)	ERD
	Climate finance	Bangladesh Climate Change Strategy and Action Plan (2009), Climate Change Trust Act (2010), Climate Fiscal Framework (2014)	ERD, Ministry of Environment and Forests, Finance Division
	South–South cooperation	National Policy on Development Cooperation (draft finalised but yet unapproved), Strengthening finance for 7FYP and SDGs in Bangladesh (2016)	ERD
Other financial flows	Domestic resource mobilisation	National Board of Revenue Modernisation Plan (2011–2016), Value Added Tax and Supplementary Duty Act (2012), Customs Act (2014)	Internal Resources Division
	Investment	National Industrial Policy (2016), Bangladesh Economic Zones Act (2010)	Ministry of Finance, Ministry of Industries
	IFFs	National Strategy for Preventing Money Laundering and Combating Financing of Terrorism (2015–17), Money Laundering Prevention Act (2012)	Bank and Financial Institutions Division, Anti-Corruption Commission, Internal Resources Division, Ministry of Home Affairs
Trade and connectivity	Tariff and non-tariff barriers	Export Policy (2015–18), Import Policy Order (2015–18)	Ministry of Commerce, Ministry of Foreign Affairs
	Trade facilitation	Export Policy (2015–18), Toward New Sources of Competitiveness in Bangladesh: Key Findings of the Diagnostic Trade Integration Study (2015)	Ministry of Commerce, Ministry of Foreign Affairs
	Connectivity	Bangladesh-Bhutan-India-Nepal Motor Vehicles Agreement (2015), Bay of Bengal Initiative for Multi-Sectoral Technical and Economic Cooperation, Bangladesh-China-India-Myanmar Economic Corridor	Road Transport and Highways Division

Technology	TRIPS	National Information and Communications Technology (ICT) Policy (2015)	Ministry of Science and Technology
	Productivity	National Information and Communications Technology (ICT) Policy (2015), National Industrial Policy (2011), National Skills Development Policy (2011), Skills Development: A Priority Agenda for Accelerated Growth (2016)	ICT Division, Ministry of Education, Ministry of Industries
Peace and conflict	Conflict, violence and terrorism	Anti-Terrorism Act (2009), Mutual Legal Assistance in Criminal Matters Act (2012)	Ministry of Home Affairs, Ministry of Law, Justice and Parliamentary Affairs
	Cross-border and inter-state terrorism	India-Bangladesh Coordinated Border Management Plan (2011)	Ministry of Home Affairs, Border Guard Bangladesh
National and international governance	–	Commitment for Golden Bengal: National Integrity Strategy of Bangladesh (2012), Annual Performance Agreements	Ministry of Home Affairs, Ministry of Law, Justice and Parliamentary Affairs, Ministry of Foreign Affairs

Source: authors' compilation.

key milestone (Bangladesh Planning Commission 2015). Additionally, it does not outline an explicit smooth transition strategy. The only mention of Bangladesh's graduation from the LDCs comes in the context of increased attention on relatively high tariff and para-tariff levels, faced by exporters to the country, subsequent to Bangladesh's graduation from the LDC category or crossing the middle-income threshold (Bangladesh Planning Commission 2015).

In view of the above, a mapping exercise was conducted to identify existing national policies, plans, acts, strategies and initiatives to tackle the emerging global and regional challenges that may hamper Bangladesh's smooth transition after graduation. The challenges identified above were grouped into six broad clusters – each cluster comprises a number of challenges – according to their implications for Bangladesh's graduation and smooth transition and their relevance to national policies. Existing national policies, plans, acts, strategies and initiatives as well as the institutions responsible for formulating and implementing them are presented in Table 6.3.

Policies towards coping with declining external resources

In development cooperation, external resources include ODA (grants and concessional loans), climate finance, Aid for Trade, non-concessional loans, vertical funds and funds from international foundations, commercial borrowings and other types of cooperation such as South–South and triangular cooperation (Bjornestad et al. 2016). Three key external resources for Bangladesh are ODA, climate finance and South–South cooperation.

ODA

Given declining ODA and other foreign aid, the GoB prepared a draft National Policy on Development Cooperation that, when finalised, will act as a consolidated framework for mobilising and managing international development cooperation. The policy aims to provide a coherent, integrated institutional and policy approach to development cooperation that ensures it is needs based and results oriented and does not pose challenges or significant risks to Bangladesh's debt sustainability. The ERD will be responsible for implementing this policy. In addition, an Independent Development Finance Assessment was recently prepared by Bjornestad et al. (2016) – the ERD provided leadership – with a view to strengthen finance for implementation of 7FYP and the SDGs in Bangladesh. Considering both domestic and external resources, the assessment provides a mapping of past and current sources of development finance. The GoB established the Bangladesh Joint Cooperation Strategy in 2010 as a formal mechanism for partnership with development partners to facilitate implementation of international commitments on aid effectiveness.

Climate finance

The GoB defines climate finance as the flow of resources towards activities that reduce greenhouse gas emissions or develop resilience to climate change impacts (MoEF 2009). Acknowledging the importance of the issue of climate change, it formulated the Bangladesh Climate Change Strategy and Action Plan in 2009. Subsequently, it created the Bangladesh Climate Change Trust Fund and uses its own development and non-development budget resources to finance projects as part of the implementation of the strategy and action plan. The aim of these projects is to reduce climate-related vulnerabilities. The Climate Change Trust Act, 2010 was enacted to set up institutional arrangements for management of the Bangladesh Climate Change Trust Fund (MoEF 2016). Following the recommendation of the Climate Public Expenditure and Institutional Review carried out in 2012 under the auspices of the Bangladesh Planning Commission's Poverty-Environment-Climate Mainstreaming project, the Finance Division of the Ministry of Finance established a Climate Fiscal Framework in 2014 to ensure the effective use of domestic and international climate finance within the national budget process (MoF 2014). The framework identifies the demand for and supply of national climate finance as well as forecasts Bangladesh's future climate finance needs.

South–South cooperation

Bangladesh maintains strong development cooperation with many non-traditional donors such as China, India, Iran, Kuwait, Malaysia, Saudi Arabia, Turkey and the United Arab Emirates. South–South cooperation is an emerging source of finance that has great potential for the country. Still, there are issues that should be addressed to better align this type of cooperation with country priorities and subsequently achieve its full potential. The ERD has been working on South–South and triangular cooperation, but much work remains since there is no separate unit yet for either of these types of cooperation. Further, quality data and information about South–South cooperation are scarce, a situation that is similar to those in many other countries (Bjornestad *et al.* 2016).

Recent institutional changes at the ERD, which is responsible for ODA management, will allow it to step up the mobilisation of other, less traditional flows of development finance in the coming days. It will be able to build on lessons learned from ODA management and the effectiveness of traditional aid. The GoB recently approved a new wing for development effectiveness at the ERD that will initially focus on achieving better coordination and use of South–South cooperation and climate finance. To ensure maximum development impact of emerging financial flows, the GoB will also explore other types of development finance.

Policies towards harnessing resources from other official flows

Domestic resource mobilisation

Domestic resource mobilisation is key in financing development. To this end, reforms will be critical in harnessing potential revenue in a country. It may be noted that Liberia increased its domestic revenue three to five times by simplifying the property value assessment process. Besides, after automation of the collection system and consequent reduction in error and fraud opportunities, Rwanda's annual tax revenue jumped by 6.5 times (UN-OHRLLS 2016b). The National Board of Revenue's (NBR) Modernisation Plan (2011–16), the Value Added Tax and Supplementary Duty Act, 2012 and the Customs Act, 2014 are a few key efforts by the GoB to increase tax revenue. Regrettably none of the envisaged legal reforms could be enforced. The NBR expected that the implementation of the Modernisation Plan would enable it to achieve a tax–GDP ratio of 13 per cent, improve service for taxpayers through web-enabled tax administration and reduce tax pendency in the courts by 80 per cent by 2016. In reality, implementation has been rather slow. The Value Added Tax and Supplementary Duty Act, 2012 proposes a unified online system for the purpose of value added tax registration, return submission, tax payments and refunds. The Act's main idea is a uniform value added tax rate of 15 per cent. However, concerns of small- and medium-sized enterprises could not be fully addressed and an agreed framework for implementing the law could not be reached by the GoB and the business community of the country. Requirements for successful implementation of the Act include infrastructure development, human resource and skills development, adequate training of relevant officials and compliance preparation for relevant stakeholders (CPD 2017).

Investment

The GoB has adopted the National Industrial Policy, 2016, which replaced the National Industrial Policy, 2010, to boost overall investment in the country. The new policy, which will be in effect for five years, labels certain industries as 'high-priority industry' (MoI 2016). These industries will be aided by the GoB through financial incentives as well as policy support for quick development. As stated in the new policy, high-priority industries are those that provide large-scale employment through rapid expansion and earn high revenues. The GoB targets seven sectors: agricultural products and food processing, garments, ICT and software, pharmaceuticals, leather and leather products, light engineering, and jute and jute products.

Special economic zones (SEZs) have helped many developing countries to boost private investment including FDI. In this context, Lao PDR can be mentioned as an example. The country was able to attract considerable private investments through – *inter alia* – implementation of SEZs. A total of 206 factories were operating in said zones during 2012–13. Within the capital city of

Vientiane, more than 60 per cent of SEZ development was completed, resulting in a total investment of above US$40.6 million. From 2011 to 2015, Lao PDR's GDP grew by nearly 7 per cent per annum (UN-OHRLLS 2016b). The Bangladesh Economic Zones Act, 2010 was formulated with the objective to establish 100 economic zones by 2030 in areas with potential to increase investment and address issues related to inadequate revenue from export processing zones (EPZs). Selected areas include both underdeveloped and backward regions to encourage rapid economic development (MoLJPA 2012a). For industries working within EPZs, there are several incentives offered by the GoB to facilitate FDI. For example, the NBR offers complete tax exemption on a company's dividend income and capital gains resulting from transfer of shares as well as technical assistance for a period of ten years of commercial operation. In addition, a ten-year tax holiday for investors and 12-year tax holiday for developers of economic zones and high-tech parks are offered. Implementation of the Act is crucial to enhance Bangladesh's investment prospects.

IFFs

In order to prevent vast IFFs, the GoB introduced the Money Laundering Prevention Act, 2012 and National Strategy for Preventing Money Laundering and Combat Financing of Terrorism 2015–17. The latter includes a set of 11 strategies aimed at minimising the damaging effects of capital flight (Bangladesh Bank 2015). There are specific mentions of curbing trade-based money laundering, regularly updating and maintaining a national money laundering and terrorist financing risk assessment report, and introducing a risk-based approach to monitoring and supervision of all reporting organisations (banks, financial institutions, money changers, etc.). Moreover, the strategy calls for preventing corruption as it poses high risks of increased money laundering. Tackling IFFs resulting from criminal activities as well as domestic and cross-border tax evasion is also outlined in the strategy.

In the context of the Money Laundering Prevention Act, 2012, a number of agencies gained powers that were previously only held by the Anti-Corruption Commission. Law enforcement agencies under the Ministry of Home Affairs and any agency nominated by Bangladesh Bank's Bangladesh Financial Intelligence Unit, such as the Ministry of Finance's Internal Resources Division and Bank and Financial Institutions Division, may now conduct investigations related to money laundering. Further, the definition of human trafficking was altered – now receiving money by providing a fraudulent promise to send someone abroad is considered a crime. In addition, the fine for money laundering was raised by 50 per cent to Bangladeshi taka two million.

Policies towards addressing trade and connectivity challenges

Tariffs and non-tariff barriers

Bangladesh's exports became a major source of revenue after the country opted for a more open market-based economy. Since FY2000–01, Bangladesh has applied most-favoured-nation tariff rates to facilitate smooth implementation of the GoB's import policy (MoF 2016a). Bangladesh Planning Commission (2015), and Kathuria and Malouche (2015) both called for restructuring the country's tariff regime by reducing effective protection levels and eliminating the consequent anti-export bias, which directly affects domestic consumer welfare. Bangladesh introduced several policies such as Export Policy 2015–18 and Import Policy Order 2015–18 to facilitate trade induced development. Import policy emphasises easing the process of importing raw materials for export-oriented industries, while its export policy prioritises 12 sectors labelled as having 'most potential' and 14 other sectors labelled as 'special development' (MoC 2015, 2016). The GoB provides both financial and technical assistance to develop these sectors. Notably, Bangladesh's exporters face several non-tariff barriers when trading with neighbouring India (Rahman 2012). A Joint Group of Customs Officials meeting is held annually to discuss issues such as removal of non-tariff barriers, upgradation of infrastructure, certification by the Bangladesh Standards and Testing Institution and reduction of customs complexities (Rahman 2015).

Trade facilitation

Trade facilitation can be defined as reducing both complexity and the costs of trade transaction processes. It aims to ensure that trade takes place in an efficient, transparent and predictable manner (SWEPRO n.d.). Many LDCs have found trade facilitation measures beneficial for enhancing trade. UN-OHRLLS (2016b) mentioned the examples of introduction of an automated system for customs data and investment in one-stop border posts in Zambia and improvement of customs procedures and advanced container handling machinery in Tanzania towards curtailing time in trade. Indeed, for Bangladesh, it is critical to reduce lead-time significantly to boost trade.

In September 2016, Bangladesh ratified the WTO's Trade Facilitation Agreement, which will likely accelerate the movement, release and clearance of goods including goods that are in transit (WTO 2016a). Two other major efforts are Export Policy 2015–18 and the World Bank's Diagnostic Trade Integration Study. The latter analyses the internal and external limitations to further integration with the global economy and keeps in view the long-term goals of employment creation, mitigation of poverty as well as enhancement of citizen welfare (Kathuria and Malouche 2015). The GoB's key actions towards improving trade facilitation include the launch of a national logistics strategy, establishment of the rail inland container depot on the outskirts of Dhaka at Tongi, development of the inland water transport sector, improvement in the efficiency of Dhaka–Chattogram road connectivity, and working closely with India to improve the efficiency of common land border posts. Trade facilitation may also arise through reduction of trade finance costs, which can be achieved by leaving title documents open and not assigning them to a local bank as well as making hindrance-free current account transactions through payments for samples and consultants (Kathuria and Malouche 2015). Duty-free, quota-free market access offered by India for all but 25 products, simplification of rules of origin and selective cooperation through a general trade cooperation agreement with China may be the GoB's preferred solutions in order to facilitate exports to China and India as they remain important trading partners for Bangladesh (Bangladesh Planning Commission 2015).

Connectivity

Bangladesh will need to fully utilise the potential of its suitable geographical location by enhancing regional connectivity. Among the LDCs, in recent years, Lao PDR exhibited an average 12 per cent annual export growth during the 2011–15 period of which a key contributing factor was participation in free trade areas like the Association of Southeast Asian Nations (UN-OHRLLS 2016b). At present, Bangladesh is actively involved in various regional connectivity initiatives, namely the Bangladesh-China-India-Myanmar Economic Corridor, Bay of Bengal Initiative for Multi-Sectoral Technical and Economic Cooperation, South Asian Association for Regional Cooperation Highway Corridor and Bangladesh-Bhutan-India-Nepal Motor Vehicles Agreement. The Bangladesh-China-India-Myanmar Economic Corridor is a sub-regional initiative that explores prospects for cooperation, specifically among landlocked and relatively backward regions of these four countries. The Centre for Policy Dialogue in Bangladesh, Yunnan Academy of Social Sciences in China, Centre for Policy Research in India and Ministry of Border Trade of Myanmar were the pioneering institutions that agreed to launch the initiative in 1999. In 2013, the countries organised a 12-day, 3,000-kilometre car rally from Kolkata, India through Bangladesh, India and Myanmar to Kunming, China, which played a catalytic role in stimulating concerned stakeholders' interest (MoRTB 2016).

The Bay of Bengal Initiative for Multi-Sectoral Technical and Economic Cooperation is a sub-regional initiative involving countries in South Asia and Southeast Asia including Bangladesh, Bhutan, India, Myanmar, Nepal, Sri Lanka and Thailand. In December 2005, the countries formally requested technical assistance from the Asian Development Bank to undertake a transport infrastructure and logistics study (ADB 2008). Completed in 2008, it was endorsed in 2009 and forms the core of transport planning in the two sub-regions. The main objective of the policy framework and strategies included in the study is to help formulate sub-regional policies and strategies in relation to specific transport and logistical issues that constrain trade or raise transport costs.

A sub-regional meeting of the secretaries of transport of Bangladesh, Bhutan, India and Nepal on road transport connectivity was held in February 2015, where the objective was to reach consensus on a draft framework agreement to facilitate trade and investment in the sub-region through transport connectivity. The Bangladesh-Bhutan-India-Nepal Motor Vehicles Agreement was signed during a successive transport ministers meeting in June 2015. Notably, the agreement does not explicitly mention transit, particularly between northeast India and the rest of the country through Bangladesh.

Policies towards enhancing the role of technology

TRIPS

The GoB formulated the National Information and Communication Technology Policy, 2015 with the aim of developing and promoting the ICT sector. This has huge potential which is mentioned in several acts and policies enacted in recent years, ensuring its effective use to achieve development goals. Further, the policy seeks to help make the GoB more transparent and accountable through expansion and development of the ICT sector. It outlines how to ensure skill and human development and provide public services through public–private partnership. It also acts like a guideline for the ICT sector to realise the GoB's vision to turn Bangladesh into an MIC by 2021 and developed country by 2041. The policy includes ten specific objectives, 56 strategic themes and 306 programmes that are to be implemented through short-, medium- and long-term action plans. The timeframes were set at 2016, 2018 and 2021, respectively (MoPTIT 2015). The policy, which is more promotional and developmental than regulatory, does not cover issues related to intellectual property rights. Therefore, it is difficult to foresee the realisation of the stated objectives and vision of a 'Digital Bangladesh' once TRIPS cease to be in effect.

Productivity

The growth of labour productivity is key to increasing GNI per capita. The GoB has adopted various policies and plans to address the issue of productivity. These include the National Information and Communication Technology Policy, 2015, National Industrial Policy, 2016 and National Skills Development Policy, 2011. In 2016, the Ministry of Finance published a report entitled *Skills Development: A Priority Agenda for Accelerated Growth* (MoF 2016b). In addition to the national ICT and industrial policies, the main aims of which are outlined above, the National Skills Development Policy, 2011 aims to improve the quality and relevance of skills development in Bangladesh, establish more flexible and responsive delivery mechanisms that better service the needs of labour markets, individuals and communities, improve access to skills development for various groups of citizens including women and people with disabilities, encourage participation for development of skills by industry-related organisations, employers and workers and improvement of skills acquisition in communities, and enable more effective planning, coordination and monitoring of skills development activities by different ministries, donors, industries, and public and private providers (MoE 2011). Currently, 23 ministries and divisions are involved in skills training to address skills needs in the country's labour market (MoF 2016b). Private training providers also provide skills training with financial assistance from the GoB and development partners.

Policies towards maintenance of peace and conflict resolution

Conflict, violence and terrorism

With a view to mitigate conflict, violence and terrorism, the GoB introduced two specific acts, namely the Anti-Terrorism Act, 2009, which was later amended to Anti-Terrorism Rules, 2013, and Mutual Legal Assistance in Criminal Matters Act, 2012. According to the Anti-Terrorism Act, 2009, courts are unable to charge accused individuals without the final say from the Ministry of Home Affairs. However, according to the Anti-Terrorism Rules, 2013, courts can now accept videos, photographs and audio clips found on social media platforms, such as Facebook, Twitter and Skype, as evidence during trials. The Anti-Terrorism Rules, 2013 also prohibit the use of Bangladesh's land for the purpose of any activity related to terrorism inside the country or against any other countries, the use of all types of illegal arms and explosives and the creation of 'panic' among the public through any terrorist activity. Also, Bangladesh Bank was vested certain powers to take necessary steps to identify and prevent any transactions carried out by any reporting agency with intent to commit an offence under the amended Act. All offences charged under the amended Act are non-bailable and capital punishment was introduced in a case where someone is proven to have financed terrorism. One of the main challenges that remain is the potential of abuse of power when charged under this law. The Mutual Legal Assistance in Criminal Matters Act, 2012 was passed to facilitate international cooperation and allows the GoB to seek assistance from foreign governments in relation to criminal proceedings (MoLJPA 2012b).

Cross-border criminal activity

The India-Bangladesh Coordinated Border Management Plan was signed in 2011 to reduce the number of killings and crime and maintain peace and harmony along Bangladesh and India's common border. The border guards of both countries agreed to take counter-measures to prevent any sort of trans-border crimes such as smuggling of drugs, fake currency, gold and cattle as well as human trafficking. Together, they planned to increase vigilance by visiting areas that are susceptible to these sorts of criminal activities. Close coordination and adequate approaches by both countries' border guards are important to curb cross-border criminal activities. Efforts have been made to raise the level of trust through coordinated patrols and exchange of information between the two border guards. The plan identified certain officers from both countries whose responsibilities are to ensure peaceful solutions to issues that have arisen alongside discussing problems with counterparts and promoting confidence-building measures.

Policies towards strong institutions and good governance

Strong institutions and good governance are essential for a country's development. According to Betts and Wedgwood (2011), countries can achieve proper development through effective and accountable institutions and systems. The GoB has two initiatives to strengthen institutions and improve governance – the National Integrity Strategy of Bangladesh and Annual Performance Agreements. The former is a comprehensive good governance strategy that was released to prevent corruption, specifically identifying ten government institutions and six non-government institutions, as well as improve national integrity within government and society (Cabinet Division 2012). Its implementation should be a priority for the GoB since there are crucial links between corruption, violation of human rights, poverty, exclusion, environmental degradation, vulnerability and conflict. Corruption is often responsible for the diversion of public resources away from economic development initiatives.

The GoB introduced Annual Performance Agreements during FY2015 to monitor the performance of ministries and divisions and raise the efficacy of results-oriented budgetary allocations. All ministries and divisions are required to sign agreements with their respective subordinate departments to improve public services, transparency and accountability. Such agreements identify the major strategic objectives of a ministry or division for a particular year, the activities proposed to achieve them and the progress in implementation of those activities at the end of the year. The success of the initiative is yet to be assessed.

Policy guidelines for an LDC graduation strategy for Bangladesh

Bangladesh is expected to graduate from the LDC category in 2024 while the LDC-specific international support measures are likely to expire by 2027. As has been argued in this chapter, graduation alone should not be considered a success; rather, graduation with momentum should be considered the overarching objective. Gaining such momentum requires shifting towards the production of higher-value goods and services by increasing investment in the ICT sector, diversifying exports and exporting higher-end products. For Bangladesh, there is a need for a concrete LDC graduation strategy to facilitate the graduation process in the context of infrastructure gaps, high trade barriers and lack of adequate investment including FDI. These issues must be highlighted and discussed during the mid-term review of the 7FYP in 2018.

The 7FYP anticipates and identifies various critical issues, but others have emerged in recent years. Certain issues have always been a hindrance to Bangladesh's development. Domestic resource mobilisation as a share of GDP is lower in Bangladesh than most developing countries. The share of income tax in the NBR's total revenue collection had been rising in recent years, but FY2016 witnessed that share decline for the second consecutive year. The country's future economic growth prospects may depend on labour productivity. Adequate measures have not been taken to enhance human and skills development in the context of a changing demographic dividend. With climate change impacts being an increasingly critical issue, Bangladesh needs adequate financial assistance as it is particularly vulnerable.

In order to increase private investment in the country, the GoB needs to change the investment composition by focusing on infrastructure and the manufacturing sector through the establishment of SEZs and EPZs to attain the targeted US$9.6 billion (Bangladesh Planning Commission 2015) in FDI inflows. As mentioned in 7FYP, there may be potential for a substantial rise in productivity through infusion of FDI in Bangladesh's readymade garment (RMG) industry outside EPZs. Increased productivity could effectively push garment exports up the value chain, thus benefiting Bangladesh by raising export earnings. Improving the investment environment through financial sector reforms, tax and legal reforms, better governance and business regulations that attract investors is compulsory. The GoB anticipated the majority of these issues and responded with strategies, policies or laws to advance development.

One of the issues that has intensified is the current ODA scenario. In addition to declining ODA, the quality of aid and attached terms and conditions must be considered as they may have developmental impacts on Bangladesh. The GoB will need to enhance the quality of governance along with declining inflow of ODA. Trade-related obstacles, such as tariffs and non-tariff barriers, are also causes for concern – removing non-tariff barriers will be particularly beneficial for Bangladesh, though the country's high transport costs may act as a bigger barrier than non-tariff barriers. If proper measures are undertaken by the GoB, the country will experience increasing export competitiveness and further deepening and broadening of economic cooperation in South Asia at bilateral, sub-regional and regional levels. Further, trade liberalisation needs to be strategised to support industrialisation including reforming the tariff regime to restructure an effective protection level. It is also advisable for Bangladesh to prioritise industrialisation in view of its growing domestic market together with export promotion. Industrial policy support also needs to go beyond the RMG-centric incentives by re-examining the policy support measures in favour of non-RMG industries in order to diversify the country's product and market base.

Remittance inflows to Bangladesh are crucial as they enable socio-economic development at both national and household levels. Recently, remittances have been declining owing to a shift of remittances to informal channels alongside the economic slowdown in Gulf Cooperation Council countries and Europe. The GoB plans to extend incentives to Bangladeshi migrant workers to encourage them to remit earnings through official channels instead of unofficial channels. Moreover, ILO (2014) has shown that migrants originating from Bangladesh pay the most for migrating overseas. Effectively resolving this situation will require specific planning and effective implementation. Also, IFFs are responsible for draining vital resources from developing countries that could be used for much-needed public services including security, justice and basic social services such as health and education. In order to counter this problem, the GoB formulated certain strategies and enacted laws related to money laundering. However, more emphasis should be on trade misinvoicing through strict and effective measures by the NBR's transfer pricing cell.

The GoB is actively involved in increasing regional connectivity and South–South cooperation through various projects that are improving prospects for regional cooperation and integration, but more effective communication and implementation by relevant ministries are needed and should be strictly monitored. Bangladesh's ICT sector is considered to be a 'thrust sector' as it has greater employment opportunities, is a source of export earnings and helps make the GoB more transparent and accountable. To realise the vision of a 'Digital Bangladesh', adequate fiscal policy support is required. Investment in essential network infrastructure will be a challenge. Rapid development of the sector will imply a rise in skilled labour and thus boost economic growth prospects.

Among emerging issues, the first priority must be addressing terrorism. Never in its history did Bangladesh face any major terrorism-related activity until the 2016 Holey Artisan incident. Twenty-two civilians, five terrorists and two police officers died during this incident. Nine Italian and seven Japanese citizens were among the victims. The GoB has acknowledged the issue. The GoB is constantly vigilant in terms of counter-measures, but terrorism at the grassroots level must be better addressed to ensure peace and thus enhance the country's economic growth prospects.

The GoB's existing policy regime only partially addresses emerging external challenges. As it prepares for graduation and smooth transition, the GoB needs to put adequate emphasis not only on reviewing the existing policy regime, but on accelerating implementation of policies, plans, acts, strategies and initiatives. Indeed, the country must prepare a development plan in view of the prospective LDC graduation process which needs to take cognisance of the aforesaid external challenges. It is also true that Bangladesh will not be able to fully address these challenges by only using domestically oriented efforts. Necessary global support to this end will be critical. Indeed, many of the challenges will require global solutions. In the past, Bangladesh was one of the leaders pursuing LDCs' interests at the global level. Going forward, the country must continue to play such a role in various global platforms and push for integrating the UN platforms to find solutions to the global developmental challenges. With the country set to graduate from the group, it is also time for the country to build new alliances at the regional and global level particularly with the non-LDC LMIC group. As international support measures remain inadequate, it is critical for the country to exploit the available opportunities. This will also test the institutional capacity of the country along with ensuring good governance at all levels. Hence, the success of the country's navigation during its transformational journey of LDC graduation over the next decade amid the inhospitable external environment will hinge on its strategic planning and its capacity to implement the required actions in a timely manner.

Notes

1 However, seven countries – Denmark, Finland, Ireland, Luxembourg, Norway, Sweden and the UK – met the target during 2015 (UN-OHRLLS 2017).
2 Similarly, foreign direct investment (FDI) is being increasingly concentrated in a few resource-rich countries, such as Mozambique and Tanzania (Moazzem and Raz 2014).
3 In Bangladesh, the fiscal year is from 1 July to 30 June the following year.
4 The H-P filter was introduced by Hodrick and Prescott (1997). It enables decomposing any flow variable into a cyclical component and trend component. It decomposes a series x_t (where x_t is the logarithmic form of the actual series X_t) into a cycle x_t^c and a trend x_t^g by minimising the following function:

$$\sum_t \left(x_t - x_t^g \right)^2 + \lambda \sum_t \left[\left(x_{t+1}^g - x_t^g \right) - \left(x_t^g - x_{t-1}^g \right) \right]^2$$

Here, the cyclical component is defined as $x_t^c = x_t - x_t^g$. The parameter λ is a positive number that penalises variability in the trend component. For this analysis, λ was considered to be 6.25 following Ravn and Uhlig (2002) and de Jong and Sakarya (2016).
5 Preference erosion happens when one country's preferential access to another's market is eroded through a new trade arrangement agreed by the destination country.
6 According to Rodrik (2016), the term was introduced by Dasgupta and Singh (2007), although Kaldor (1966) referred to deindustrialisation much earlier in the British context.
7 It may also be mentioned that another 300,000 Rohingya from Myanmar had already taken shelter in Bangladesh before the recent surge (UNHCR 2017).

References

Acemoglu, D. and Restrepo, P., 2016. *The race between machine and man: Implications of technology for growth, factor shares and employment.* NBER Working Paper 22252. Cambridge: National Bureau of Economic Research.

ADB, 2008. *Bay of Bengal initiative for multi-sectoral technical and economic cooperation (BIMSTEC) transport infrastructure and logistics study (BTILS).* Technical Assistance Consultant's Report TA 6335-REG. Manila: Asian Development Bank.

Baker, R., 2005. *Capitalism's Achilles heel: Dirty money and how to renew the free-market system.* Hoboken, NJ: John Wiley & Sons.

Bandyopadhyay, S., Sandler, T. and Younas, J., 2015. The toll of terrorism. *Finance and Development,* 52 (2), 26–28.

Bangladesh Bank, 2015. *National strategy for preventing money laundering and combating financing of terrorism 2015–2017.* Strategic Paper. Dhaka: Bangladesh Bank.

Bangladesh Planning Commission, 2012. *Perspective plan of Bangladesh 2010–2021: Making Vision 2021 a reality.* Perspective Plan. Dhaka: General Economics Division, Planning Commission, Government of Bangladesh.

Bangladesh Planning Commission, 2015. *Seventh Five Year Plan FY2016 – FY2020: Accelerating growth, empowering citizens*. Five Year Plan. Dhaka: General Economics Division, Planning Commission, Government of Bangladesh.

Betts, J. and Wedgwood, H., 2011. *Effective institutions and good governance for development: Evidence on progress and the role of aid*. Evaluation Insights 4. Paris: Network on Development Evaluation of the OECD Development Assistance Committee.

Bhattacharya, D. and Khan, T. I., 2014. The challenges of structural transformation and progress towards the MDGs in LDCs. *In*: LDC IV Monitor, *Istanbul programme of action for the LDCs (2011–2020): Monitoring deliverables, tracking progress – analytical perspectives*. London: Commonwealth Secretariat, 1–32.

Bjornestad, L., et al., 2016. *Strengthening finance for the 7th Five Year Plan and SDGs in Bangladesh: Findings from an independent development finance assessment*. Dhaka: Government of Bangladesh.

Blankenburg, S. and Khan, M., 2012. Governance and illicit flows. *In*: P. Reuter, ed. *Draining development? Controlling flows of illicit funds from developing countries*. Washington, DC: World Bank, 21–68.

Cabinet Division, 2012. *Commitment for golden Bengal: National integrity strategy of Bangladesh*. Dhaka: Government of Bangladesh.

CDP, 2012. *The United Nations development strategy beyond 2015*. New York: Committee for Development Policy.

Climate Funds Update, 2017. *Data dashboard* [online]. Available from: https://drive.google.com/file/d/0B9Z56hbbQZAPU3N1eUtndGFuUE0/view [Accessed 20 March 2017].

CPD, 2017. *State of the Bangladesh economy in FY2016–17: First reading*. Dhaka: Centre for Policy Dialogue.

Dahlman, C. and Mealy, S., 2016. Obstacles to achieving the Sustainable Development Goals: Emerging global challenges and the performance of the least developed countries. *In*: LDC IV Monitor, *Tracking progress, accelerating transformations: Achieving the IPoA by 2020*. London: Commonwealth Secretariat, 49–61.

Dasgupta, S. and Singh, A., 2007. Manufacturing, services and premature deindustrialization in developing countries: A Kaldorian analysis. *In*: G. Mavrotas and A. Shorrocks, eds. *Advancing development: Core themes in global economics*. Basingstoke: Palgrave Macmillan, 435–456.

de Jong, R. M. and Sakarya, N., 2016. The econometrics of the Hodrick-Prescott filter. *Review of Economics and Statistics*, 98 (2), 310–317.

Degryse, C., 2016. *Digitalisation of the economy and its impact on labour markets*. ETUI Working Paper 2016.02. Brussels: European Trade Union Institute.

Easterly, W., 2002. The cartel of good intentions: The problem of bureaucracy in foreign aid. *Journal of Policy Reform*, 5 (4), 223–250.

Economic Relations Division, 2016a. *Flow of external resources into Bangladesh 2015–2016*. Dhaka: Ministry of Finance, Government of Bangladesh.

Economic Relations Division, 2016b. *Mid-term review of the implementation of the Istanbul programme of action for the LDCs for the decade 2011–2020*. Dhaka: Ministry of Finance, Government of Bangladesh.

Elliott, K., 2016. *How much 'Mega' in the mega-regional TPP and TTIP: Implications for developing countries*. CGD Policy Paper 079. Washington, DC: Center for Global Development.

EPB, 2017. *Statistic data* [online]. Dhaka: Export Promotion Bureau, Ministry of Commerce, Government of Bangladesh. Available from: http://epb.portal.gov.bd/site/files/9efa4995-2501-4c9e-8ca6-8b8f7208c3a0/Statistic [Accessed 20 March 2017].

Ericsson, F. and Steensen, S., 2014. *OECD-DAC development brief: Where do we stand on the aid orphans?* Paris: Organisation for Economic Co-operation and Development.

Fic, T., 2014. *Global economic policies and developing countries: NiGEM scenarios for the post-2015 agenda.* London: National Institute of Economic and Social Research.

Herkenrath, M., 2014. Illicit financial flows and their developmental impacts: An overview. *International Development Policy/Revue internationale de politique de développement,* 5 (3), 1–15.

Hobolt, S. B., 2016. The Brexit vote: A divided nation, a divided continent. *Journal of European Public Policy,* 23 (9), 1259–1277.

Hodrick, R. J. and Prescott, E. C., 1997. Postwar US business cycles: An empirical investigation. *Journal of Money, Credit, and Banking,* 29 (1), 1–16.

IEP, 2016. *Global terrorism index 2016: Measuring and understanding the impact of terrorism.* Sydney: Institute for Economics and Peace.

IFR, 2016. *World robotics 2016.* Frankfurt: International Federation of Robotics.

ILO, 2014. *Promoting cooperation for safe migration and decent work.* Dhaka: ILO Country Office in Bangladesh, International Labour Organization.

IMF, 2016. *World economic outlook: Subdued demand – symptoms and remedies.* Washington, DC: International Monetary Fund.

IPCC, 2015. *Climate change 2014: Synthesis report.* Geneva: Intergovernmental Panel on Climate Change.

Jensen, M. D. and Snaith, H., 2016. When politics prevails: The political economy of a Brexit. *Journal of European Public Policy,* 23 (9), 1302–1310.

Kaldor, N., 1966. *Causes of the slow rate of economic growth of the United Kingdom: An inaugural lecture.* Cambridge: Cambridge University Press.

Kar, D., 2011. *Illicit financial flows from the least developed countries: 1990–2008.* Discussion Paper. New York: United Nations Development Programme.

Kar, D. and Schjelderup, G., 2015. *Financial flows and tax havens: Combining to limit the lives of billions of people.* Washington, DC: Global Financial Integrity.

Kar, D. and Spanjers, J., 2015. *Illicit financial flows from developing countries: 2004–2013.* Washington, DC: Global Financial Integrity.

Kathuria, S. and Malouche, M. M., 2015. *Toward new sources of competitiveness in Bangladesh: Key findings of the diagnostic trade integration study.* Directions in Development. Washington, DC: World Bank.

Keane, J., *et al.,* 2010. *Bangladesh: Case study for the MDG gap task force report.* Research Reports and Studies. London: Overseas Development Institute.

Kenaroğlu, B., 2003. *Implications of information technology in developing countries and its impact in organizational change.* STPS Working Paper 0302. Ankara: Science and Technology Policy Studies Center, Middle East Technical University.

Khan, M. H., 2014. Aid and governance in vulnerable states: Bangladesh and Pakistan since 1971. *Annals of the American Academy of Political and Social Science,* 656 (1), 59–78.

Khan, M. Z. H., Haque, M. and Rouf, M., 2013. *An assessment of climate finance governance: Bangladesh.* Dhaka: Transparency International Bangladesh.

Khan, T. I., 2016. *Illicit financial flows in the context of Bangladesh* [online]. Dhaka: Centre for Policy Dialogue. Available from: http://cpd.org.bd/wp-content/uploads/2016/06/Illicit-Financial-Flows-in-the-Context-of-Bangladesh.pdf [Accessed 20 March 2017].

Khan, T. I. and Akbar, M. I., 2015. *Illicit financial flow in view of financing the post-2015 development agenda.* Southern Voice Occasional Paper 25. Dhaka: Southern Voice on Post-MDG International Development Goals.

Krugman, P., 1979. A model of innovation, technology transfer, and the world distribution of income. *Journal of Political Economy*, 87 (2), 253–266.

McCright, A. M. and Dunlap, R. E., 2011. The politicization of climate change and polarization in the American public's views of global warming, 2001–2010. *Sociological Quarterly*, 52 (2), 155–194.

Mayer, R., 2014. *The Syrian refugee crisis: The tensions between refugee rights and host country capacity*. Unpublished.

Mendez-Parra, M., Papadavid, P. and te Velde, D. W., 2016. *Brexit and development: How will developing countries be affected?* ODI Briefing. London: Overseas Development Institute.

Moazzem, K. G. and Raz, S., 2014. Foreign direct investment for development and productive capacity building in LDCs. In: LDC IV Monitor, *Istanbul programme of action for the LDCs (2011–2020): Monitoring deliverables, tracking progress – analytical perspectives*. London: Commonwealth Secretariat, 355–392.

MoC, 2015. *Export policy 2015–2018*. Dhaka: Ministry of Commerce, Government of Bangladesh.

MoC, 2016. *Import policy order 2015–2018*. Dhaka: Ministry of Commerce, Government of Bangladesh.

MoE, 2011. *National skills development policy – 2011*. Dhaka: Ministry of Education, Government of Bangladesh.

MoEF, 2009. *Bangladesh climate change strategy and action plan 2009*. Dhaka: Ministry of Environment and Forests, Government of Bangladesh.

MoEF, 2016. *The climate change trust act, 2010*. Dhaka: Ministry of Environment and Forests, Government of Bangladesh.

MoF, 2014. *Climate fiscal framework*. Dhaka: Ministry of Finance, Government of Bangladesh.

MoF, 2016a. *Bangladesh economic review 2016*. Dhaka: Ministry of Finance, Government of Bangladesh.

MoF, 2016b. *Skills development: A priority agenda for accelerated growth*. Dhaka: Ministry of Finance, Government of Bangladesh.

MoI, 2016. *National industrial policy-2016*. Dhaka: Ministry of Industries, Government of Bangladesh.

MoLJPA, 2012a. *The Bangladesh economic zones act, 2010*. Dhaka: Ministry of Law, Justice and Parliamentary Affairs, Government of Bangladesh.

MoLJPA, 2012b. *Mutual legal assistance in criminal matters act, 2012*. Dhaka: Ministry of Law, Justice and Parliamentary Affairs, Government of Bangladesh.

MoPTIT, 2015. *The national information and communication technology (ICT) policy-2015*. Dhaka: Ministry of Posts, Telecommunications and Information Technology, Government of Bangladesh.

MoRTB, 2016. *Regional road connectivity: Bangladesh perspective*. Dhaka: Ministry of Road Transport and Bridges, Government of Bangladesh.

OECD, 2014. *Illicit financial flows from developing countries: Measuring OECD responses*. Paris: Organisation for Economic Co-operation and Development.

OECD, 2017a. *Development aid rises again in 2016*. Paris: Organisation for Economic Co-operation and Development.

OECD, 2017b. *Development* [online]. Paris: Organisation for Economic Co-operation and Development. Available from: http://stats.oecd.org/ [Accessed 15 March 2017].

Palit, A., 2015. *Regionalism and mega-trading blocs: A policy-maker's handbook*. London: Commonwealth Secretariat.

Pereira, P. G. and Fontana, A., 2012. *Using money laundering investigations to fight corruption in developing countries: Domestic obstacles and strategies to overcome them.* Working Paper 14. Basel: Basel Institute on Governance.

Putzhammer, F., Felbermayr, G. and Aichele, R., 2016. *The forgotten continent: The effects of mega-regional free trade agreements on Africa.* Global Economic Dynamics Study Series: Effects of Mega-Regional Trade Agreements (Part-3). Gütersloh: Bertelsmann Stiftung.

Quibria, M. G. and Islam, A., 2015. The case study of aid effectiveness in Bangladesh: Development with governance challenges. *In:* B. M. Arvin and B. Lew, eds. *Handbook on the economics of foreign aid.* Cheltenham: Edward Elgar Publishing. Available from: https://papers.ssrn.com/sol3/papers.cfm?abstract_id=2589930 [Accessed 21 September 2017].

Qureshi, M. O. and Syed, R. S., 2014. The impact of robotics on employment and motivation of employees in the service sector, with special reference to health care. *Safety and Health at Work,* 5 (4), 198–202.

Rahman, M., 2012. *Trade-related issues in the Bangladesh-India joint communiqué: Maximising Bangladesh's benefits and strategies for the future.* SABER Governance Working Paper 23145. Canberra: South Asian Bureau of Economic Research.

Rahman, M., ed., 2015. *Towards regional integration in South Asia: Promoting trade facilitation and connectivity.* Dhaka: Centre for Policy Dialogue.

Rahman, M., et al., 2010. *Global financial crisis discussion series.* Bangladesh phase 2: Paper 12. London: Overseas Development Institute.

Rahman, M., Khan, T. I. and Amin, M. A., 2014. *The economy of tomorrow: How to produce socially just, sustainable and green dynamic growth for a good society case study of Bangladesh.* Bonn: Friedrich-Ebert-Stiftung.

Raihan, S. and Khan, T. I., 2013. *Impact of Indian policies on rice price in Bangladesh.* CPD-CMI Working Paper 4. Bergen and Dhaka: Chr. Michelsen Institute and Centre for Policy Dialogue.

Ravn, M. O. and Uhlig, H., 2002. On adjusting the Hodrick-Prescott filter for the frequency of observations. *Review of Economics and Statistics,* 84 (2), 371–376.

Rodrik, D., 2015. *Premature deindustrialization in the developing world* [online]. Dani Rodrik's Weblog. Available from: http://rodrik.typepad.com/dani_rodriks_weblog/2015/02 [Accessed 17 June 2017].

Rodrik, D., 2016. Premature deindustrialization. *Journal of Economic Growth,* 21 (1), 1–33.

Schwab, K., 2016. *The fourth Industrial revolution: What it means, how to respond* [online]. Geneva: World Economic Forum. Available from: www.weforum.org/agenda/2016/01/the-fourth-industrial-revolution-what-it-means-and-how-to-respond [Accessed 17 June 2017].

Sieler, S. and Raschen, M., 2016. *What does Brexit mean for developing countries?* KfW Development Research 28. Frankfurt: KfW Development Bank.

SWEPRO, n.d. *General aspects of trade facilitation* [online]. Stockholm: SWEPRO – Swedish Trade Procedures Council. Available from: www.kommers.se/SWEPRO/In-English/What-is-trade-facilitation [Accessed 17 June 2017].

UN DESA, 2016. *International migration report 2015.* New York: United Nations Department of Economic and Social Affairs.

UNCTAD, 2009. *The state and development governance.* The Least Developed Countries Report 2016. New York: United Nations Conference on Trade and Development.

UNCTAD, 2016. *The path to graduation and beyond: Making the most of the process.* The Least Developed Countries Report 2016. New York: United Nations Conference on Trade and Development.

UNGA, 2016. *Report on the comprehensive high-level midterm review of the implementation of the Istanbul programme of action for the least developed countries for the decade 2011–2020.* New York: United Nations General Assembly.

UNHCR, 2017. *Bangladesh operational update.* Geneva: United Nations High Commissioner for Refugees. Available from: https://data2.unhcr.org/en/documents/download/61455#_ga=2.202578198.607351093.1521119538-1576529122.1521119538 [Accessed 15 February 2018].

United Nations, 2017a. *The sustainable development goals report 2017.* New York: United Nations.

United Nations, 2017b. *World economic situation and prospects 2017.* New York: United Nations.

UN-OHRLLS, 2016a. *State of the least developed countries 2016.* New York: United Nations Office of the High Representative for the Least Developed Countries, Landlocked Developing Countries and Small Island Developing States.

UN-OHRLLS, 2016b. *Lessons learned from five years of implementing the Istanbul programme of action for the least developed countries.* New York: United Nations Office of the High Representative for the Least Developed Countries, Landlocked Developing Countries and Small Island Developing States.

UN-OHRLLS, 2017. *State of the least developed countries 2017.* New York: United Nations Office of the High Representative for the Least Developed Countries, Landlocked Developing Countries and Small Island Developing States.

Uprety, B., 2015. *Financing climate change adaptation in LDCs* [online]. Available from: www.iied.org/financing-climate-change-adaptation-ldcs [Accessed 17 June 2017].

WEF, 2014. *Mega-regional trade agreements: Game-changers or costly distractions for the world trading system?* Geneva: World Economic Forum.

WEF, 2017. *Digital transformation initiative: Unlocking $100 trillion for business and society from digital transformation.* Geneva: World Economic Forum.

World Bank, 2013. *Financing for development post-2015.* Washington, DC: World Bank.

World Bank, 2016. *World development report 2016: Digital dividends.* Washington, DC: World Bank.

World Bank, 2017a. *World development indicators* [online]. Washington, DC: World Bank. Available from: http://data.worldbank.org/data-catalog/world-development-indicators [Accessed 16 March 2017].

World Bank, 2017b. *Global economic prospects, January 2017: Weak investment in uncertain times.* Washington, DC: World Bank.

WTO, 2016a. *Bangladesh ratifies trade facilitation agreement* [online]. Geneva: World Trade Organization. Available from: www.wto.org/english/news_e/news16_e/fac_27sep16_e.htm [Accessed 17 June 2017].

WTO, 2016b. *World trade statistical review 2016.* Geneva: World Trade Organization.

Index

Page numbers in **bold** denote tables, those in *italics* denote figures.